A WALKER'S GUIDE TO THE ISLE OF WIGHT

The wonderful view north-west from St Catherine's Point to Tennyson Down and The Needles

A walker's guide to the

ISLE OF WIGHT

by

Martin Collins & Norman Birch

CICERONE PRESS
MILNTHORPE, CUMBRIA

Reprinted 2000, 2004, 2009
ISBN-13: 978 1 85284 221 5
ISBN-10: 1 85284 221 0

A catalogue record for this book is available from the British Library
Printed by KHL Printing, Singapore

DEDICATION

This book is dedicated to the memory of Norman James, walker and Step by Step guide who loved the Island well.

ACKNOWLEDGEMENTS

Martin Collins would like to thank Jane Jones and her staff at Isle of Wight Tourism for hospitality and 'fixing it' on numerous occasions during my visits to the Island; Mike Archbold of Acadia Communications and Red Funnel Ferries; Andy Newman of Wightlink Ltd; Nikki Gallop of Hovertravel; Malcolm Peplow; Bob and June Ennis; the proprietors of visitor attractions, too many to mention individually, who generously gave their time to show me round and provide background information; Europa Sports of Kendal and Lowe Alpine walking gear; The Brasher Boot Co; and last but by no means least, Diana for her encouragement throughout the research and writing of this guidebook.

Norman Birch would like to thank walk leaders Jill Green and John Hague; Wiltax Coaches for ever-reliable support and transport.

This book has been compiiled in accordance with the Guidelines for Writers of Path Guides produced by the Outdoor Writers' Guild.

Martin Collins is one of the country's leading authors of guidebooks for walkers and a frequent contributor to the outdoor press.

Norman Birch, who lives on the island, has walked some 10,000 miles (16,000km) guiding and researching on the Island's trails.

Front Cover: Looking back to the chalk cliffs of Tennyson Down on the west coast of the island.

CONTENTS

All maps and illustrations by Martin Collins

ADVICE TO READERS

Readers are advised that, while every effort is made by our authors to ensure the accuracy of guidebooks as they go to print, changes can occur during the lifetime of an edition. Please check the Cicerone website (**www.cicerone.co.uk**) for any updates before planning your trip. It is also advisable to check information on such things as transport, accommodation and shops locally. Even rights of way can be altered over time. We are always grateful for information about any discrepancies between a guidebook and the facts on the ground, sent by email to info@cicerone.co.uk or by post to Cicerone, 2 Police Square, Milnthorpe LA7 7PY.

INTRODUCTION

Natives of the Isle of Wight and its long-term residents are proud of their independence from mainland Britain and the opportunity this provides to live life at a more leisurely pace. Even though ferries carry prodigious numbers of passengers, The Solent effectively cushions the Island against rapid change: any talk of a bridge link is pure blasphemy! As a result, arrival on the Island is like entering a time-warp, peeling back the years to England as it might have been 30 or 40 years ago.

Many first-time visitors are astonished at the variety of landscapes and scenery. It's as if all the richest attributes of southern England were distilled and brought together in this one place, encapsulating everyone's childhood dream of a rural idyll. Over half the Island is designated as Areas of Outstanding Natural Beauty, while innumerable habitats and 'remote zones' are protected as Sites of Special Scientific Interest.

Without doubt the Isle of Wight contains some of the finest countryside walking in the whole of the UK, with much to offer whatever your ability. There may be an absence of moors and mountains but nonetheless it is possible to find solitude if that is what you seek. Equally, welcoming pubs and tea-rooms in villages right across the Island lend conviviality to refreshment stops along the trail.

The Island's concentration of diverse landscapes, historical sites, Victorian seaside resorts and sleepy villages in an area measuring only 13 miles (21km) by 23 miles (37km) at its widest points means that although distances are large enough to provide a challenge, even short routes never lack variety. This manageable scale combined with a well maintained infrastructure of footpaths and bridleways make it a rambler's paradise. With an enviable sunshine record and fresh air that Alfred Lord Tennyson declared to be "worth sixpence a pint", this delightful, idiosyncratic corner of England beckons all lovers of unspoiled countryside and bracing coastline.

A POTTED HISTORY

During its earliest period of prehistory, the Isle of Wight was joined to the land mass we now call Britain and simply lay south of the River Solent. When the Ice Age ended some 6-8000 years ago and the great ice sheets melted, sea levels began to rise, flooding the valley of the River Solent. Eventually a channel was formed and Wight became an island. Other river estuaries - notably those of the Newtown, Medina and Yar - were also inundated. As temperatures increased, a dense blanket of deciduous woodland spread across the island.

As in many other parts of Britain, however, this tree cover was drastically reduced by early man's husbandry of domestic livestock and his cultivation of cereal crops, both of which entailed clearing the land. Despite pollen evidence that this occurred, the only extant legacy from the New Stone Age today are the Longstone megalith near Mottistone and the Afton Down long barrow.

Much more prolific are remains from Bronze Age man's occupation. Over 240 burial mounds have been identified, mostly on the chalk downs which he continued to clear and along which his trade routes ran - the ancient ridgeways we walk today. Interestingly, Iron Age hillforts which are such a feature of neighbouring mainland 'Wessex' are almost entirely absent from the Isle of Wight.

AD43 saw the arrival of Emperor Claudius whose successor, Vespasian, named the island Vectis and brought it under Roman rule. Villas - essentially farmsteads run on traditional lines - were built at Newport and Brading (both still well preserved) and elsewhere, encouraging the growth of coastal trade from local harbours.

Following the Roman withdrawal, Vectis regained its independence from mainland Britain. Throughout the Dark Ages its fertile soil and mild climate attracted the attentions of various ethnic and cultural migrants, not all benevolent: the Jutes, Christian Saxons and then, far more consequentially, the Normans.

Quick to appreciate the Island's strategic importance, William the Conqueror imposed his new order and initiated the building of Carisbrooke Castle. Norman families colonised the countryside, putting up manors and constructing churches. Many present-day villages contain the recognisable nucleus of communities that developed organically in suitable locations: a church surrounded by stone and thatch cottages near the former mill, bakehouse and possibly brewery.

During the 14th century several disastrous French raids were mounted against both the southern mainland and the Island, including a siege of Carisbrooke Castle which, however, failed. Continuing French threats prompted the hasty building of more coastal defences by the Tudor government, funded by the spoils of monastic dissolution. Confidence thus restored, the island enjoyed an increasing sense of security, bolstered by non-involvement in the English Civil War.

Elizabethan and Jacobean descendants of the original Norman settlers - families such as the Oglanders of Nunwell and the Worsleys of Appuldurcombe - put up splendid manor houses in favoured spots beneath the downs; several are now open to the public while others have become farms. In fact the 17th and 18th centuries saw a general improvement in prosperity with the victualling of ships from the Island's rich harvests of crops and meat a rapidly growing industry. But whilst such wealth brought gentility and ease to some, life for the farm labourer or fisherman remained harsh and many were not averse to the odd bit of smuggling or shipwreck plundering.

At last in the early 19th century came the Highways Act and the replacement of old rutted tracks with proper roads. France's aggressive foreign policy led to yet more coastal fortifications being built in the mid-1800s but the feared invasion never materialised and they were not used, consigned to the ranks of other 'Palmerston follies' (after the prime minister of the day).

Finally the railways arrived and with them the advent of tourism as we know it. Ferry services responded to the new demand for Solent crossings and the industrious Victorians built their fashionable seaside resorts complete with elegant piers and promenades here on the 'English Riviera'. Eminent visitors from the arts, sciences and aristocracy boosted the Island's reputation and it rapidly grew as a still somewhat exclusive holiday retreat. Notably falling under its spell was Queen Victoria herself who, with Prince Albert and their children, built and occupied Osborne House near Cowes for over half a century until her death in 1901.

In modern times the Island has established itself firmly as a wholesome family holiday destination and as a precious enclave of unspoiled rural England. As well as its AONBs, there are some 27 miles (43km) of Heritage Coast, with organisations such as The National Trust and English Heritage protecting many of the Island's greatest natural and historical treasures.

LANDSCAPES, HABITATS AND TOWNS

The Island's geology and hence its landscapes are dominated by a spine of chalk which runs west to east from The Needles to Culver Cliff. Smaller outcrops occur in the south where you can find the Island's highest summit at 787ft (240m) on St Boniface Down. Before Wight became an island, these thick beds of limestone continued west into Dorset whose downs and dramatic white cliffs echo those of Wight. Except west of Newport where it broadens out into gently rolling downland, the chalk ridge is steep and narrow. Where it is not under cultivation or afforested the thin, lime-rich soil supports springy turf and a variety of lime loving plants and flowers - in short, marvellous walking country!

Away from the sea and salt-laden winds, orchids, viper's bugloss and other gems of nature thrive. Downland plants attract many insect species, notably butterflies, while rabbits and hares can be seen bounding across the turf in many locations. Nesting on the high chalk cliffs at West High Down and Culver are found seabirds such as guillemots, razor-bills and even puffins.

Along the Island's southern coast between Chale and Shanklin some of Europe's most extensive landslips, both from historical and more recent times, have created a sheltered, lushly vegetated Undercliff. Ventnor's famous botanical gardens contain many sub-tropical plants and trees. The landslips are caused by a top layer of porous chalk and sandstone slipping seawards over underlying Gault clay, known appropriately as 'blue slipper'. The exposed west coast too is unstable, its cliffs highly susceptible to marine erosion. Here 'chines', or coastal ravines scoured out by the elements where streams flow into the sea, interrupt progress on the coastal path. In the strata of sandstones and mudstones, more fossilised dinosaur bones and footprints have been unearthed than anywhere else in the UK.

Much of northern Wight consists of low hills sloping gently

down to the shores of The Solent. The tidal estuaries and saltmarsh of rivers such as the Medina, Newtown and Yar support abundant birdlife; creeks meander inland through woods and meadows. Southern Wight, by contrast, tends to have lighter, well-drained soils whose prodigious fertility bears a variety of 'greenhouse' and arable crops.

There are no large areas of woodland by mainland standards but several modest forests exist, such as Brighstone in the west and Parkhurst in the north, all managed by the Forestry Commission. At the foot of the downs, along stretches of the north, east and south coasts and right across the rolling countryside inland, small woods and copses provide wonderful displays of wildflowers, ferns, mosses and lichens. Red squirrels can be seen in most woods, foxes and badgers are common and there are good populations of most small native mammals such as stoats, weasels, voles, mice and shrews. Discerning birdwatchers may spot long-eared owls and nightjars at dusk in early June.

Of the Island's towns, Newport, situated almost in the geographical centre, is the administrative hub. Roads radiate from it like spokes in a wheel and from early times it has been a focus for trade and commerce, echoed today by its busy shopping centre.

On the sheltered and sunny south-eastern coast lie the Island's main seaside resorts of Ventnor, Shanklin and Sandown, all boasting fine beaches, family accommodation and holiday entertainments.

The four ferry terminals linking with the mainland are Yarmouth, Cowes (east and west), Fishbourne and Ryde. Yarmouth, a small, historic town with a marina-harbour, stands on the Yar estuary at the gateway to the holiday and residential settlements of West Wight. Cowes, a bustling, world-renowned yachting mecca complete with boatyards and maritime industry, is split into two parts by the River Medina, crossed by the 'Floating Bridge' chain ferry. Fishbourne, little more than a village with a ferry terminal, lies at the mouth of Wootton Creek not far from the busy harbour and popular holiday resort of Ryde which dominates the north-eastern shoreline.

Wight's long and exposed south-west coast and its less accessible north-west shore between Yarmouth and Cowes are both sparsely populated. Elsewhere, coastal settlement is consistently quite dense. Much of the interior away from obvious beauty spots and visitor attractions feels surprisingly remote: now that machines have largely superseded people, farmland is managed by relatively few workers. And with over 600 miles (965km) of footpath and bridleway to choose from, walkers are likely to be thin on the ground! There is, however, a liberal scattering of villages and hamlets, most of which possess at least a post office / stores and a pub.

WALKING GEAR

Because the Isle of Wight lies to the south of mainland Britain, it receives considerable protection from cold northerly and easterly winds. Sunshine hours are long and being surrounded by sea there is little in the way of serious frost or snow so the climate is a very pleasant one. Moist and sometimes windy Atlantic weather brings gales and sea mists from time to time but sheltered locations can usually be found in the east of the Island. Late spring and early summer tend to be driest, July and August warmest, though weather statistics countrywide have been turned upside down by conditions experienced over recent years.

You are unlikely to need gear suitable for serious hill or mountain walking. The Island's highest point is less than 800ft (244m) above sea level so the cooling effect of altitude (around 3 degrees Centigrade per 1000ft (300m) of height gained) barely comes into play. However wind combined with rain or moisture-laden air of the kind often encountered near the sea can lead to rapid loss of body heat. While your life may not be threatened on Island rambles, your comfort certainly may be unless appropriate clothing is worn.

From late autumn to early spring, warm trousers, tracksters or breeches (preferably not jeans which become cold and clammy when wet), along with a shirt and sweater, or fleece jacket will keep you cosy. Extremities can be be protected by a woolly or fleece hat, scarf and gloves if conditions are particularly chilly. To deal with wind and rain always carry a waterproof jacket (cagoule, anorak or parka); overtrousers and gaiters will be useful too in heavy rain. These outer 'shell' garments can be made from breathable fabrics such as Gortex, though cheaper proofed nylon is usually adequate when clothing damp from condensation can be readily dried out at the end of the day. During the colder winter months it is better to carry extra dry, spare clothing than risk becoming unexpectedly chilled.

Needless to say, a daysack containing a first-aid kit, map, compass and guidebook, along with some emergency food such as chocolate or mintcake, will also allow you to carry useful items such as camera, binoculars, a 'sitmat' and picnic.

Lightweight boots have become the norm for lowland rambling but bear in mind that fabric is generally less waterproof than leather. Stout shoes with a deep tread pattern may be suitable too, though less so in mud and wet grass. After rain paths do become muddy, even waterlogged in places: walking with soggy feet is a miserable affair! Your boots' grip is crucial for confidence when tackling steeper gradients so ensure the tread is adequate before starting a walking holiday.

Foot comfort is of paramount importance. Some people advocate wearing two pairs of socks, others just one. Whatever your preference, always take expert advice when purchasing footwear and test it out well before embarking on more demanding hikes.

During the summer Island weather is at its finest. However, brilliant sunshine and heat can be as debilitating, and ultimately as dangerous, as cold. Shorts and a T-shirt may be suitable for shopping or the beach but unless you are aware of the risk, serious sunburn is likely out on the trail. Uncovered skin should be liberally protected by a high-factor suncream, your head shaded by a wide-brimmed hat and your eyes by good quality sunglasses. Recent research suggests that prolonged exposure to the sun's ultra-violet rays can cause skin cancer: this risk is heightened by proximity to the sea which itself reflects large amounts of UV radiation.

In dry warm weather, ordinary trainers or even activity sandals can replace boots, though not everyone is happy losing the ankle support and impact resisting properties of the latter. Remember to carry a drink and, if the forecast is changeable, those 'shell' garments and a spare sweater.

MAPS AND WAYMARKING

Unique to the Isle of Wight is its comprehensive trail waymarking system for footpaths and bridleways. Every right of way on the Island has been allocated a number, prefixed by the initial letters of the parish, district or borough through which it passes. Thus, for example, GL63 signifies path 63 in the parish of Godshill. Of course, unless these numbers appear on maps (which they once did but no longer do) they won't actually substitute for navigation with map (and when in doubt) compass. However, path numbers can be usefully quoted in a guidebook such as this to help you find your way or determine exactly where you are.

The signs themselves also bear the names of places to which the paths lead. These old familiar dark green signposts with their white lettering which the elements have gradually eroded are slowly being replaced by more durable timber ones. Occasional red paint flashes on stile posts, gates and trees etc., along with their individual logo waymarks, denote the passage of officially designated trails such as the Tennyson Trail, Hamstead Trail, etc. Rights of way are also indicated by the use of yellow (footpath) and blue (bridleway) arrows.

A major commendation for walking on the Isle of Wight is the viability of all map-marked rights of way. If they exist on the map they can almost certainly be walked on the ground. Stiles, gates etc. will be in place, although there may be no visible trod if the way is only infrequently used. You should expect the occasional diversion - usually well signed - and there will inevitably be changes due to land usage, erosion, new building and so on which accrue over the period of time since a map was last revised.

If you come across a serious obstruction of a right of way (other than growing crops which should always be walked round if no path exists across the field), use common sense initially and attempt a sensible detour. If this fails or meets with objections from a farmer or landowner, report it to the County Surveyor, Isle of Wight Council, County Hall, Newport. All the walks in this guidebook have been thoroughly researched and will pose no problems if followed with normal care.

For route planning and a general overview of getting about on the Island, consult the OS Landranger 1:50,000 sheet 196. For navigation while out on the trail, especially if deviating from guidebook directions, the OS Outdoor Leisure 1:25,000 sheet 29 is more helpful. On it you will find field boundaries, many more named features and a level of detail that adds greatly to walking enjoyment. Where the way is obscure, perhaps due to rampant summer undergrowth, this detail becomes essential.

GETTING TO THE ISLAND AND PUBLIC TRANSPORT

The fastest way for foot passengers to cross The Solent is by hovercraft from Southsea to Ryde Esplanade; journey time is approximately 9 minutes. There is a bus link between the Southsea terminal and Portsmouth centre. This service operates every day except Christmas Day, Boxing Day and in exceptionally adverse weather conditions. With 28 years' experience behind them, Hovertravel is the longest-standing commercial hovercraft operator in the world. Phone (01983) 811000 for enquiries and reservations.

The Red Funnel Group, established in 1861, operates passenger and vehicle ferries between Southampton Terminal 1 and East Cowes. Journey time is around 55 minutes. There are up to 18 crossings per day in each direction during the summer, up to 12 in winter. Red Funnel have introduced new state-of-the-art 'Raptor' class vessels - Red Falcon and Red Osprey - to their fleet with another joining shortly. A high-speed, passenger-only catamaran service taking just 22 minutes runs between Southampton Terminal 2 and West Cowes, with up to 31 crossings daily in each direction all year round. Phone (01703) 330333 for enquiries and reservations.

Wightlink Ltd, third in this trio of ferry operators, runs vehicle ferries between Portsmouth and Fishbourne (approximately 35 minutes) and Lymington and Yarmouth (30 minutes), as well as high-speed, passenger-only catamaran crossings between Ryde Pier Head and Portsmouth Harbour - journey time around 15 minutes. Phone (0870) 582744 for enquiries and reservations.

Connecting mainland rail services run to Portsmouth Central, Portsmouth Harbour, Southampton and Lymington.

Public transport on the Island is of two kinds: Southern Vectis and smaller operators' bus services, and Island Line electric trains which run between Ryde Pier Head and Shanklin, calling at Ryde Esplanade, Ryde St John's Road, Brading, Sandown and Lake. Trains call additionally at Smallbrook Junction on days when the Isle of Wight Steam Railway is running.

Southern Vectis bus routes cover the Island comprehensively, though some routes are 'summer only'. Especially useful is the Island Explorer circular route. Purchase a Southern Vectis timetable from one of their travel centres or a Tourist Information office and you have at your fingertips details of all available bus services, an

Island route map, town plans as well as Island Line train times, ferry and hovercraft sailings and Cowes Floating Bridge operating times. An invaluable publication for the walker!

ACCOMMODATION

Plentiful accommodation of all kinds can be found right across the Island. There are luxury and family hotels, guesthouses, self-catering cottages and apartments, static and touring caravan sites and campsites: truly something to suit everyone's budget! Tourism is a vital component of the Island's economy and people are immensely friendly and welcoming.

Numerous deals are on offer, including combination ferry fare and accommodation packages, off-season and short breaks, and specialised 'themed' holidays such as Step by Step for walkers. Increasing numbers of our continental neighbours, particularly the Dutch, are discovering the delights of the Isle of Wight. There are youth hostels at Totland, Whitwell and Sandown.

Many (though not all) establishments are 'walker-friendly'. The 12 RAC accredited Wight Merit hotels certainly are, ranging in size from 6 to 50 bedrooms and including Hambledon Hotel, the Step by Step headquarters at Shanklin. A single phone call will answer your enquiries and needs: (01983) 868868.

There are over 25 established camping and caravan sites on the Island, rather more in the east than in the west. Examples of the high standards and value for money that they represent are not hard to find but the following are especially recommended for their interest in walkers and their ideal locations.

In the west, situated at Newbridge between Yarmouth and Newport, for camping, static and touring caravans - Malcolm Peplow's Orchards Holiday Park, tel: (01983) 531331.

In the east, situated at St Helens, for static caravans in a peaceful setting near Bembridge Harbour - June and Bob Ennis's Field Lane Holiday Park, tel: (01983) 872779.

For a free holiday guide to the Isle of Wight and for further information, phone the Tourist Office on (01983) 524343.

CHAPTER 1

Ten Of The Best Island Walks

Walk 1: Exploring South-West Wight - St Catherine's Point to Godshill via the Coast and Downs
Walk 2: Newport, Cowes and the River Medina
Walk 3: From Shorwell Village to Freshwater Bay
Walk 4: A Circular Hike around Shanklin
Walk 5: Exploring North-East Wight - from Wootton to Brading
Walk 6: Shanklin to Brading via Culver Cliff and Bembridge
Walk 7: Coast to Coast from Ryde to Shanklin
Walk 8: Cross-country from Carisbrooke to Shanklin
Walk 9: A Circuit of Wight's Westernmost Tip - the Ancient Isle of Freshwater
Walk 10: A Circular Hike from Whale Chine on the Island's West Coast

THE WALKS

Arranged in order of length from $8\frac{1}{2}$ miles (13.5km) to $15\frac{1}{2}$ miles (25km), the following 10 day walks have been specially devised to take advantage of the Island's most outstanding scenery. Some routes are circular, others linear but Norman Birch's intimate knowledge of walking on the Island ensures that use is made of the very best footpaths and tracks on offer.

Careful thought has been given to making the start and finish points easily accessible, either by private car or public transport. Many of the routes pass 'walker-friendly' pubs that provide a welcoming alternative to a picnic outdoors.

As well as exploring the Island's beautiful countryside and coast, the walks, like most others in this guidebook, also take in places of special interest along the way such as historical sites and tourist attractions. There is usually time to enjoy these in between sessions on the trail.

Other than by the local parish path numbering, these walks are not waymarked and while the route descriptions are detailed enough to steer you through from beginning to end, it is still advisable to carry a map and compass. Armed with these you can confidently explore off-route, take short-cuts or extend the walk, and identify landmarks. In any kind of emergency knowing where you are on a map (and preferably being able to give a grid reference) is essential.

WALK 1: EXPLORING SOUTH-WEST WIGHT - ST CATHERINE'S POINT TO GODSHILL VIA THE COAST AND DOWNS

Niton - St Catherine's Point and Gore Cliff - St Catherine's Hill - Hoy's Monument - Whitwell - Stenbury Down - Godshill. 8½ miles (14km).
Start Grid Ref: 505763

Snaking inland from one of the most dramatic parts of the coast to the honeypot of Godshill, this diverse and scenic route takes in modern and old lighthouses, a 19th-century monument, the Island's oldest pub and downland with extensive views. Not a long walk but quite a hilly one.

Clustered around a crossroads at a gap in the coastal downlands, Niton retains a 'villagey' atmosphere with thatch, stone and trees much in evidence. The church, restored by the Victorians who built their summer mansions lower down in the Undercliff, dates from the 1100s when its churchyard formed the original village green. Long before, the settlement was known to the ancient Greeks, for they loaded their ships with Cornish tin at nearby Puckaster Cove. Smuggling became rife in later years and the village was known for its delicious crabs; to avoid confusion with Knighton, between Newport and Sandown, it was known as Crab Niton.

Approximately 600m south from the centre of Niton down Barrack Shute, you come to a tree-lined track on the right called Boxers Lane and the walk starts here. At the top of the track cross stiles over a field to reach an onward path.

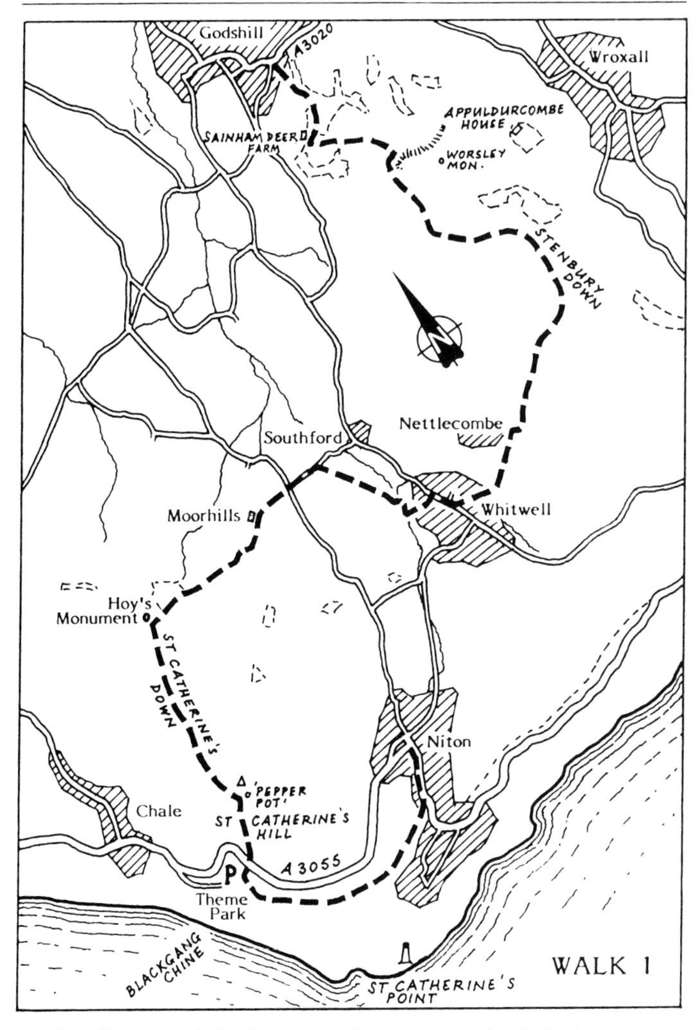

Small stumps left after council workers cut back the hedges are known as 'sodits': kick one accidentally and you'll know why!

The path follows the edge of West Cliff past Niton's 'ship to

shore' radio masts some 1/2 mile (800m) inland from the sea.

Over many thousands of years, soft sandstones and mudstones along this stretch of coast have slumped and fallen seawards over a layer of Gault clay, graphically known as 'blue slipper'. The result is a vast Undercliff characterisd by abundant birdlife, small copses, grassy hillocks and a few tenuous roads, that from Niton to Blackgang having been finally severed by a landslip in 1928. Down to your left can be seen the remains of an old nudist camp.

As you continue along the airy path (ignore path NT36 down to the left), you round St Catherine's Point, southernmost tip of the Isle of Wight.

Below you stands gleaming white St Catherine's lighthouse. It was begun in 1838 after the wreck of the fully rigged East Indiaman *The Clarendon* under Blackgang Cliffs on October 11th, 1836; of the 27 on board, only 3 survived. When the new light at last began to shine its warning in 1840, the ages-old toll of shipwreck on Wight's treacherous south-west lee shore and the Rocken End tidal race was diminished. However, the 150ft (45m) lighthouse tower itself was so often obscured by sea mist that it was lowered in 1875 to its present 84ft (25m). The main beam - one flash every 5 seconds - is visible up to 17 miles (27km) away.

Carry on above the sometimes precipitous edge of Gore Cliff until you reach well named Windy Corner where the path turns right above Blackgang Theme Park.

Blackgang's sinister name from the days of smuggling (they were reputed rivals of Sandown's White Gang) contrasts sharply with its modern reputation for quality family entertainment. A clifftop attraction since the 1840s when the entrepeneurial Dabell family from Nottingham landscaped gardens and built steps to the beach, Blackgang Chine has suffered enormously from landslip caused by the infamous 'blue slipper'. Indeed the chine itself, a dramatic ravine 500ft (152m) deep running back 3/4 mile (1200m) from the sea, no longer exists. Over the past 50 years an average of 8-10ft (3m) per annum has slipped into the sea. Major falls in 1978 and 1994 necessitated much rebuilding and further landslips will inevitably follow. In good visibility there are spectacular views from Gore Cliff along the entire west coast to the chalk cliffs of Tennyson Down and The Needles.

Approaching Hoy's Monument on St Catherine's Down

Walk through the lay-by car park/picnic area, cross the A3055 coast road, climb steps to cross a stile then angle half-left uphill towards the old lighthouse tower on the skyline.

Looking for all the world like a stone rocket, the octagonal tower (known as the Pepper Pot) was built in 1340 by a local landowner, Walter de Godeston, as a penance for his servants looting holy wine from a ship wrecked here in Chale Bay in 1314. He also built the adjacent oratory whose priest could say masses for those lost at sea and also be responsible for lighting the lamp. Being located so high above sea level, the lighthouse often became mist-shrouded, the same problem afflicting another tower built close by in 1745 and whose remains have been christened the Salt Cellar. The oratory (by the trig pillar) was demolished by Henry VIII following the Reformation.

Now walk north from the trig pillar, passing through a gate at the bottom of the initially steep descent. Hoy's Monument beckons from the far end of St Catherine's Down, a curious, bracken flanked ridge thrusting inland and providing a wonderful panorama across the width of the Island.

Hoy's Monument (sometimes known as the Alexandrian Pillar)

is a 72ft (22m) high obelisk surmounted by a stone ball. It was erected by Michael Hoy, a merchant trading with Russia, to commemorate a visit to the Island by Alexander I, Tsar of Russia, in 1814. With a nice sense of irony, a tablet on the other face of the monument, added in 1857, recalls the Britons who fell fighting Russian soldiers during the 1854-6 Crimean War.

Some 50m before the monument, turn right down on path NT78 through a small wood. Go through a gate at the bottom, bearing left onto a broad track. Ignoring a path off to the left, go through another gate and walk downhill for about 500m. Through the bottom gate, turn left and almost immediately turn right through another gate where the path leads into a field and thence onto a track (NT113) leading to the sawmill yard at Moorhills.

From now on metalled, the lane takes you to the road opposite Redhill Farm. Turn left then right into Southford Lane and in about 300m turn right onto bridleway NT112, then NT105 between fields, eventually with a hedge on your left. After a while the way crosses a hedge stile on the left into a field, goes over a little footbridge into the next field and reaches the main road at Whitwell. Turn right to pass the White Horse pub.

The White Horse specialises in delicious home cooked food and makes an excellent midday stopping place on this walk. It claims to be Wight's oldest pub, with some of its walls dating back to the 15th century. Indeed, Whitwell takes its name from White Well, visited by pilgrims in the Middle Ages.

75m past the pub, turn left between houses on NT23 and walk through what appears to be someone's back garden! Go over the stile into a field, follow the path to the far corner and cross two further stiles as well as the old dismantled railway line. Gates lead straight ahead and soon you pass the three small fishing ponds at Nettlecombe Farm. Meeting a wide track (NT2), turn right and in 100m turn left (NT119) up a rutted, tree-lined field track; higher up there are open views to your left. Emerging into a field, follow the hedged boundary as it curves round to the right. The steep hill ahead can either be tackled direct or can be circumvented to the right. At the top go over a hedge stile into the next field and follow the hedge on your left up round to another stile in the field corner. Here on the crest of Stenbury Down, bear

left to reach the narrow, surfaced access road coming up from Wroxall.

Carry on towards the radio masts and if the visibility is good, enjoy one of the Island's best viewpoints, spanning the very extremities from west to east. Where the tarmac ends, take the left-hand path through a handgate (GL51). There ensues a delightful stretch of grassy, downland walking before the way dives quite steeply and often muddily downhill. Keep along field headlands, contouring close beneath the flanks of Appuldurcombe Down (GL49) until, in about 500m, the path swings right and dips to meet a path coming up from Sheepwash Lane. Just ahead is a high deer gate and a wood; go through, bearing left down a broad track. Two further deer gates are encountered as you cross small fields and reach Sainham Deer Farm, established to breed red deer in 1987.

Turn sharp right through a gate, passing the farmhouse and duckpond, and beyond the next gate fork left down a woodland path, over a plank bridge and into a meadow, with a hedge now to your left. Two stiles later you come out at the back of the Griffin Inn in Godshill and the end of this itinerary.

Without doubt Godshill ranks as one of the Island's most popular tourist destinations. However, this is not without good reason. Refreshments and gifts are widely available and its picturesque thatched cottages beneath the hilltop presence of All Saints Church make a perfect, 'picture postcard' scene. The nostalgic Toy Museum and the Natural History Centre are both well worth visiting but don't miss Godshill's showpiece, the famous Model Village. Set in 1½ acres of the old Vicarage Gardens and based on both Old Shanklin and Godshill itself, the attraction first opened to the public in 1952, having been considerably developed since then. Hundreds of tiny trees and shrubs, 'coaxed' into miniature size, add to the astonishing realism achieved by the one-tenth scale buildings constructed from coloured cement which appears natural and weathers well. Cleverly made figures engaged in everyday activities bring the entire model to life. As well as tea rooms, there are two good pubs in the High Street: The Griffin (once the old coaching house for nearby Appuldurcombe); and The Taverners.

WALK 2: NEWPORT, COWES AND THE RIVER MEDINA

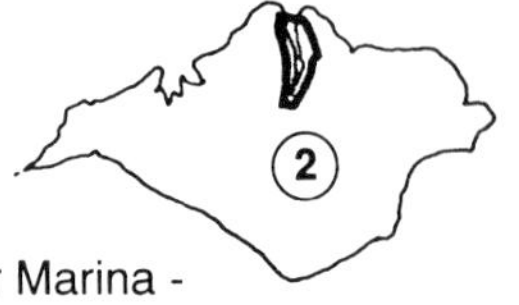

Newport Quay - Dodnor Lane - West Cowes - East Cowes - Whippingham Church - Island Harbour Marina - Newport Quay. 9 miles (15km). Start Grid Ref: 502894

A walk with gentle gradients on an old railway trackbed, riverbank paths and country lanes tracing both banks of the River Medina between Newport and Cowes. There are close-up views of dinghy sailing, a ride across the rivermouth on the Floating Bridge chain ferry, and a visit to Whippingham Church, designed during Queen Victoria's residency at nearby Osborne House. The route could of course be walked in one direction only and road transport taken back to the start.

Newport, Wight's capital and administrative centre, stands astride the highest navigable stretch of the River Medina. Roads radiate outwards to every corner of the Island and the town is usually buzzing with shoppers and holidaymakers. It was not always so important a settlement. Although Newport became capital after the decline of Newtown to the west, it was still an improvished place in the early 17th century, its houses roughly thatched and the streets unpaved. As the diarist Sir John Oglander of Nunwell House wrote: "(even) the Bailiffs themselves were but fishermen and oyster-draggers".

Newport's fortunes, however, were to change and a century later convoys of loaded grain carts would converge for the Tuesday market, some to be exported to the mainland from ships moored at the town quays. A 'beast' market also thrived. With increasing prosperity, elegant town houses were built by wealthy merchants - many fine Georgian features remain above today's shop fronts.

From St Thomas' Square in the town centre walk north-east along the Regency and Georgian terraces of Quay Street and at the bottom cross over to Town Quay.

Old wharves and warehouses have been tastefully converted into the Quay Arts Centre complex, outside which pleasure craft and commercial vessels glide by.

Bear left along Sea Street past the Arts Centre entrance with its coffee-gift shop, then turn right to pass beneath the A3020 flyover (Medina Way). Carry on along the west bank waterfront where the way leads through an industrial estate towards Blackhouse Quay and a proper riverside path on the left (N29). Beyond Newport Rowing Club's prominent boathouse and a picnic area, the path hugs the riverbank closely until at Dodnor steps on the left lead up to the now tarred trackbed of the dismantled railway. It's used by both walkers and cyclists and it's as well to keep an ear open for the latter and walk to one side of the track.

Crossing Dodnor Lane a sign (N207) declares Cowes to be 3 miles (5km) ahead - about an hour's walking. At a plank bridge over a creek, then the access road to an oil depot, you come abreast of an old paddle steamer beached on the opposite bank; this and the hilltop church at Whippingham, also in view, are passed on the walk's return leg.

The track is shady and sheltered by woodland in many places but there are good

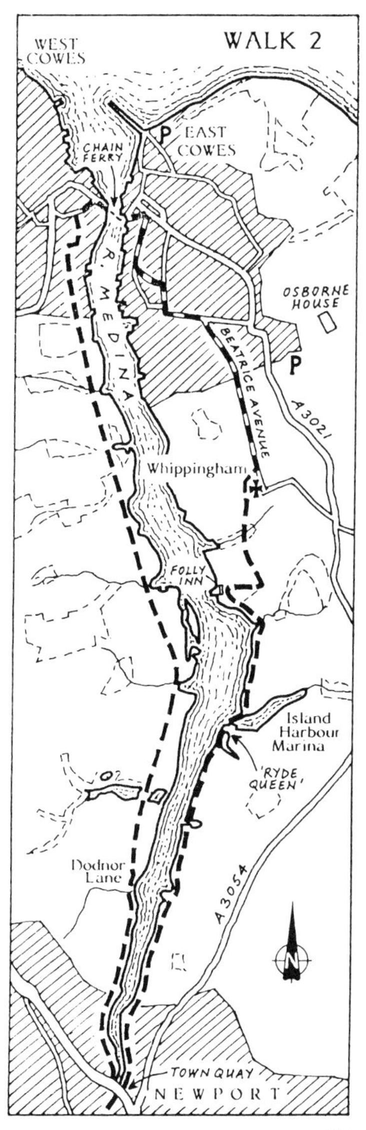

Cowes - world famous yachting mecca

river and countryside views too. Paths CS31 and 33 branch off left to Northwood then the way passes a gravel works and, over on the far bank, Cowes Power Station: somehow the Medina seems to lose its innocence in the final mile or so before it enters The Solent!

On reaching a road at the southern outskirts of West Cowes, cross over and continue a little further on the trackbed which is now reduced to a narrow pathway. You pass a small housing estate and continue into Tennyson Road. There are several onward alternatives along residential roads; one reliable route is to keep walking north and turn right down Smithards Lane then left along Arctic Road. Turn right down South Road, left along Pelham Road and right down Bridge Road. This brings you out at Medina Road, running along behind the boatyards etc. on the waterfront. Turn right to the Floating Bridge.

This vehicle and passenger chain ferry across the mouth of the River Medina operates every 10 minutes from very early to very late in the day, with a journey time of 2 minutes (dependent on weather conditions and river traffic).

Alight at East Cowes and walk ahead to York Avenue, turning

Whippingham Church

right almost immediately into Clarence Road. In about 400m fork left and after 300m turn right on Adelaide Grove. In another 300m this swings sharp left (as the B3321) onto Victoria Grove. Ignore the first right turn but take the second one - Beatrice Avenue. This soon leaves the outskirts of East Cowes behind, passes Osborne Middle School and arrives at the unusually shaped Whippingham Church.

The Royal Church of St Mildred, to give it its full name, was designed by Prince Albert. With a five-pinnacled spire more reminiscent of Balkan architecture than English, the church has become firmly established on many an Island sightseeing tour. During the reign of Queen Victoria and her long occupancy of nearby Osborne House as a country retreat, the church and scatter of estate houses that make up Whippingham village witnessed numerous royal events.

Having looked round the church, walk back north a few metres and take the footpath alongside the churchyard wall towards the river. At a stile bear half-left (almost due south) across two fields and cross a stream footbridge in the copse ahead. Walk over the next field and through trees to meet Folly Road, turning right down to the Folly Inn.

This popular riverside pub with moorings for visiting craft was originally built around an old 65ft (20m) hulk. Dinghy sailing adds colour and movement to views enjoyed over a leisurely drink or snack.

Turn left just before the inn (N122 for Newport) and walk along the riverbank, over a creek and onwards to Island Harbour Marina. Go across the lock gates and on past the hugely impressive beached paddle steamer *Ryde Queen*.

Commissioned in 1937 to carry railway passengers from Portsmouth to Ryde, she was taken over by the Admiralty during World War II but afterwards resumed her role as a ferry. At her withdrawal from service in 1960 she was the last paddle steamer on scheduled Solent crossings. Today her ironwork is rusting and her paint fading - what a shame she is not being preserved for posterity.

Walk along the rubble causeway over an arm of the Medina and continue on the riverside path.

Low-tide mudflats attract many bird species, including herons, cormorants, oyster-catchers and curlews. Further on tree foliage and bushes of hawthorn and wild rose often screen the waterway, especially in summer, but there is access to the riverbank here and there.

Three footbridges are crossed over reed filled inlets, habitats for reed buntings and sedge warblers, before you pass a recreation ground and arrive at the colourful Pirate Ship alongside Newport dock.

Straight ahead beneath the Medina Way flyover are seats from which you can watch the comings and goings of river craft before returning to the start at the town centre via Quay Street.

WALK 3: FROM SHORWELL VILLAGE TO FRESHWATER BAY

Shorwell - Limerstone Down -
The Longstone - Hulverstone -
Brook Green - Freshwater Bay.
10 miles (16km). Start Grid Ref: 457829

A walk along the flank of the downs followed by a section of coast path. Hilly in parts but with great views that many walkers often miss.

The walk starts at Shorwell (bus route 7B), a picturesque wooded village of thatched cottages set in a fold of the downs. Behind the recently refurbished Crown Inn stands many-gabled Northcourt whose gardens are sometimes open to the public. South-west from the village centre can be found mellow Westcourt Manor, connected by a footpath over the stream in Troopers Copse to Wolverton Manor, a fine, reputedly haunted Elizabethan building which is now a working farm.

From the Crown Inn, set off west along aptly named Walkers Lane and in 250m turn right onto footpath S6. A few steps ahead you pass through a gate and head half-left towards the rising flanks of Fore Down. When you reach a hedge, go through the gate

in the corner and follow the path through further gates, passing a small thicket on your left. Soon you are climbing along the top of a modest ridge and bearing right past wind-shaped trees. Go through another gate, turning left with small hills now to your right; in 400m the path starts to swing right, uphill. Ignore the gateway on your left, except to pause and admire the splendid views of the coast and English Channel. A final pull up brings you out onto the ancient ridgeway track on Limerstone Down.

The original green metal signposts for walkers are being replaced in exposed locations such as this by stout timber ones. Many walkers believe that missing numbers and letters on the old green signs are due to vandalism, but the only 'vandal' involved is the wind whose abrasive action over the years has worn away the white characters.

Turn left along the stony track (BS10) which also carries the Worsley Trail and follow it downhill alongside Brighstone Forest to the road at the National Trust's Brighstone car park. Cross over and take the small road almost opposite, colourfully called Strawberry Lane. Go down the hill past limekilns on your right and where the lane bends left, turn off right at the farm gate (BS84)

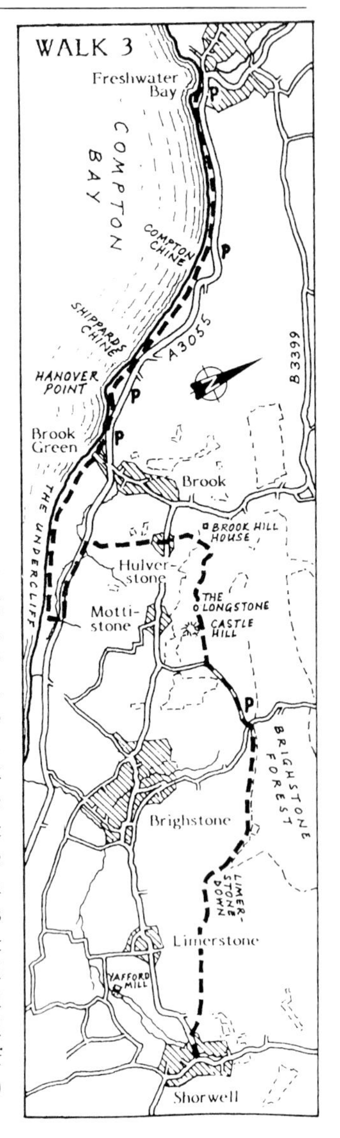

towards the famous Longstone. En route you skirt the Iron Age earthwork on Castle Hill and in a further 300m or so cross a stile to reach the Longstone.

This is one of the Island's best known archaeological monuments - a 10-ton, 13ft (4m) high megalith erected as part of a burial chamber by New Stone Age farmers some 5000 years ago. Behind the standing stone of local Greensand, and another lying prone, are the remains of the long barrow itself, though partial excavation has revealed no significant finds. An alternative name for the megalith is the 'moot stone', thought to have given nearby Mottistone its earlier name, Moteres Stan.

Leaving the stone, turn right (BS85) and follow the main forestry track, ignoring a path off to the left. On rounding some bends you will notice ahead the chimneys of Brook Hill House, a flamboyant mansion that was once the home of the celebrated author J. B. Priestley. From roughly the same vantage point, views are truly magnificent towards the chalk cliffs of West Wight.

A stile now leads into trees where, almost immediately, you

The Sun Inn, Hulverstone,
one of many country pubs that welcome walkers

turn left downhill. At first down across sloping fields, the path is soon caught between hedges and leads to the B3399 road at Hulverstone.

In front of you stands the 500-year-old Sun Inn, a stone-floored, thatched pub that heartily welcomes walkers, serves good food and real ales, and therefore makes an ideal lunch stop.

On leaving the pub, walk right (east) for about 30m then turn right, round the old school building into Hulverstone Lane (BS100). The lane starts off wide enough but eventually narrows to a path and brings you out at the main A3055 coast road.

Known as the Military Road, it provides a scenic traffic route never far from the clifftops themselves. The road was originally built to link and supply coastal fortifications against a feared French invasion during the mid-1800s.

Turn left (east) alongside the Military Road for approximately ½ mile (800m), watching for a stiled path over on the right (BS75) which leads to the cliff edge at Sud Moor. Turn right (against the usual direction for walking the coast path) and as you progress along a largely untouched corridor of grassland outside fields, look inland for a different perspective on Brook Hill House, set on its wooded hillside. Pasture fields above Roughland Cliff, part of the Mottistone Estate, take you onwards to Brook Green. Just before the chine the path veers right at some Coastguard cottages, passing the old lifeboat station on your left.

This building once housed the Island's very first lifeboat, the *Dauntless,* launched in 1860 by Mary Seely of Brook House, one from the family of well-known local benefactors. Before the station closed the *Dauntless* and her successors were to save some 263 lives.

Once over Brook Chine (small car park, emergency telephone, National Trust information board), turn left through the car park and a kissing gate to regain the cliff path. Here at Brook Bay the Military Road comes very close to the shoreline and there is a clifftop car park. Not far ahead the path rounds Hanover Point.

At low tide, although seaweed-covered, large chunks of fossilised conifers can be discerned embedded in the sandstone reef below. Rather than the site of ancient woodland (as Fossil Forest on maps implies), the fossilised trunks are more likely to have been deposited

The famous Needles from high above Scratchell's Bay

Shanklin and Culver Cliff from the flanks of St Martin's Down
The Island's entire west coast in view from Windy Corner above Blackgang Chine

as a log jam, or 'pine raft' in an ancient flooded river.

Offshore stands a conspicuous stone pillar known as The Thimble. Along with the forts and the Military Road, it belongs to the era of the French invasion scare of the 1860s and was installed as a marker for gunners at Fort Redoubt, near Freshwater.

The coast path continues north-west and quickly reaches Shippards Chine (toilets) - main access point for beachgoers in Compton Bay, where you can buy an ice-cream during the summer months. The car park, however, is succumbing to the drastic marine erosion that characterises this whole coastline. Carry straight on along the cliff path, passing the remains of a steam tug wrecked in 1947 which is visible at very low spring tides. The path is subject to cracking and slippage and has had to be re-routed at a higher level; there are steps to the beach here at the northern end of Compton Bay. Over two footbridges at shallow Compton Chine, the path then climbs towards Compton Down, crosses a stile and turns left, parallel and ever closer to the coast road.

Suddenly you are walking on markedly different terrain, for there is an abrupt geological transition from yellow-brown Wealden clays to the stunning pale greys and whites of chalk. Seawards, the downs end in steep slopes and high, precipitous cliffs; there is even concern that the coast road itself may be threatened by subsidence.

With tremendous views in both directions the way begins its descent towards Freshwater Bay on a well defined path across the grassy face of the downs. Beyond a low brush thicket you pass a small memorial to some children who died a century ago. As you approach the bay, look out for the two sea stacks below - a miniature version of The Needles; there used to be three but Arch Rock collapsed several years ago. Timber steps lead down to the east end of the little seawall promenade.

Freshwater Bay has a pebbly beach and a few fishing boats are usually moored offshore, bobbing on the swell. The sturdy sea wall was built to protect the low-lying River Yar valley after large quantities of shingle were dredged from the beach in the mid 19th century during the construction of the coastal fortifications. Cafes, shops, hotels and other amenities cater for today's holiday visitors who flock here, much as their earlier counterparts did after Alfred Lord Tennyson had established Freshwater as a mecca for artists and writers in the late 1800s.

WALK 4: A CIRCULAR HIKE AROUND SHANKLIN

Shanklin Old Village - St Martin's Down - Wroxall - Freemantle Gate - Godshill - Stenbury Down - St Boniface Down - Luccombe Landslip - Shanklin Old Village. 11½ miles (18.5km). Start Grid Ref: 583809

This is quite a hilly walk, proving to first-time visitors that the Island is not as flat as some might imagine! By way of compensation for the effort, views are outstanding.

Shanklin began as a small fishing hamlet situated at the top of its now celebrated Chine. It developed rapidly during Queen Victoria's reign in the mid-1800s when sea bathing became popular and after 1830 the Solent crossing from the mainland could be made on a regular steamer service. More instrumental still in Shanklin's success was the railway line from Ryde which opened on August 23rd, 1864. Although now uniquely run using ex London tube trains, the line remains a useful transport link between Shanklin and stations north to Ryde. Apart from the Old Village - a commercial honey-pot of tea rooms, gift shops and entertainment - Shanklin itself retains elements

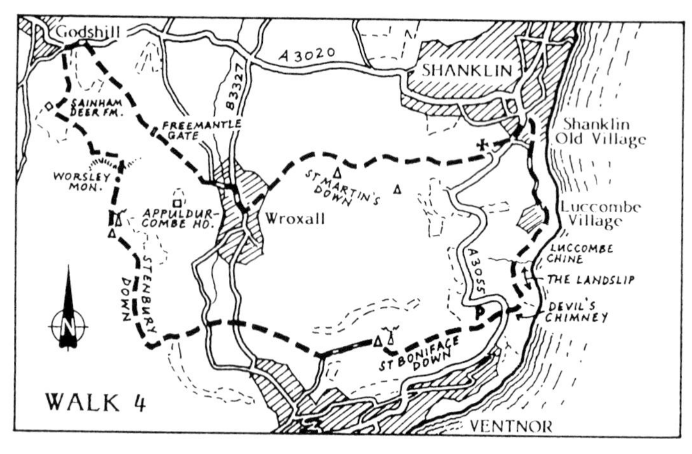

of its earlier charm, with elegant Victorian villas, beautiful public gardens and a fine bathing beach.

From Old Shanklin's famous Crab Inn walk south-west out of town in the direction of Ventnor. In 200m you will pass on your right a large grassy area known locally as The Big Mead. You soon reach St Blasius' Church and the start of our footpath (SS10) which, to begin with, is also the Worsley Trail running between Shanklin and Brighstone Forest over to the west of the Island.

Walk through the lych gate to the left of the church and cross the wall stile and the next wooden one. Emerging into a large field, continue uphill in the same general direction towards the swelling heights of St Martin's Down to your left. A couple of stiles further on there are steps to climb, a hedge now on your right, and after two more stiles you turn right to follow the hedge for about 100m. Now bear left.

Below you on the right is a small wood which still bears the scars of the hurricane that struck southern England in 1987.

Cross the gate ahead into a field and aim for the bottom left-hand corner (ignoring the stile immediately in front). The way drops a little, crosses a stile and heads down the path to join a small road, passing a cemetery on the left. In 100m bear right over the old railway bridge at Wroxall and follow Castle Road down to the B3327.

Though not especially pretty itself, Wroxall nestles in a delightful fold of the downs. Much of its history is bound up with the railway (now dismantled west of Shanklin) whose labour force was largely housed in the village while a tunnel was excavated beneath the hills.

Turn right along the road and in about 300m turn left (signposted 'Appuldurcombe House'). At the end of a long wall after a down-and-up (ignore the road on your right), you reach a small car park where the footpath continues on the right as GL44 across the field towards two tall trees. Continue up the second field and turn right along the driveway from Appuldurcombe House.

Ahead stands Freemantle Gate, the main entrance to Appuldurcombe House which, for centuries, was the seat of the Worsley family. First a convent, then the Elizabethan home of the Leigh family, the original Appuldurcombe House was demolished

Godshill Model Village

by Sir Richard Worsley and a Palladian-style mansion built in its place, the grounds landscaped by none other than Capability Brown. The house later passed to Lord Yarborough, founder and first Commodore of the Royal Yacht Squadron at Cowes, but was badly damaged during World War II. All that remain today are the magnificent pillared facade and the still beautiful grounds (open to the public).

Go through the side gate and continue straight ahead down the sandy track - the former coaching drive, passing Godshill Park House on your left. The trail soon reaches the main A3020 Shanklin to Newport road where you turn left to Godshill.

Adorned with tea-rooms and tourist attractions, Godshill reclines beneath the crowning presence of All Saints Church (hence 'God's Hill'). There is much worth visiting, including the Toy Museum, Natural History Centre and especially the famous Model Village, built to one-tenth scale and in existence since 1952 though much extended since then. There are two good pubs in the village for a lunch break: The Griffin (once the old coaching house for

Appuldurcombe) and The Taverners, also in the High Street - have a peep into the old cider bar for some unusual gifts.

To continue the walk, take the small road (Hollow Lane) at the side of The Griffin and in about 10m cross the stile on your left into path GL57. With a hedge on your right, a further two stiles lead to a small hillside wood where you take the path bearing up half-right to join a track at the top. Turn right along to Sainham Farm, passing the duckpond, and at a high metal gate turn sharp left (GL58) up the track bounded by 7ft (2m) high deer fences. (Red deer have been bred here since 1987.) Pass the Deer Shed on your left and after two more gates the way reaches woods; about 100m further on turn left through a handgate at a track junction. Follow along the top of a pasture field by the old estate wall for about 400m and watch for an unusual wall stile on the right. This path (GL63) climbs steeply through the Gat Cliff escarpment, leading you to the Worsley Monument.

This granite obelisk was built in 1774 by Sir Richard Worsley of Appuldurcombe in memory of his grandfather, Sir Robert. It was damaged by lightning strike in 1831 but was restored in 1987. The panorama from this hilltop is as extensive as any on the Island and includes a westwards glimpse of the chalk cliffs of Tennyson Down.

Carry on walking south, passing through a gate towards the stile near a wire fence. Once over it, turn left along the crest of Appuldurcombe Down and when you meet the narrow access road turn left again past the white-tipped radio mast. From hereabouts views span both ends of the Island in clear visibility.

Follow the roadway overlooking Wroxall and when it veers down left walk straight ahead through a gate and on along Stenbury Down. In about 500m turn left (V35) across the golf course towards an opening in a hedge. Beyond the next stile walk down the field, through metal gates, and head towards the bottom left-hand corner where a stile leads into Rew Lane.

Turn left then in no more than a few paces bear right through a gate. A short uphill follows, with a hedge on your left. Go through a gap round an old bottle bank to the main B3327 road. Cross over by Pit Farm Homelands (V13) and tackle the steep climb with stiles, leading into a field. At the end of the hedge on your right aim slightly right towards Wroxall Down with its radar

masts. Five hundred metres after joining the access road you reach the fenced-off radar station itself and adjacent trig pillar.

The Civil Aviation Authority radar station was one of the very first to be operational during World War II and monitored naval events in the Channel, including the D-Day landings.

Turn right (V1a) and at the far end of the perimeter fence turn left over a stile (V122). From up here on Wroxall Down, Ventnor appears like a model village far below. Go through the kissing gate and continue on path V123 along St Boniface Down, the highest land on the Isle of Wight at 787ft (240m) above sea level. There are wonderful views ahead over Sandown Bay to Culver Cliff. Continue straight over a junction by a car park and follow the path as it slopes east down Nansen Hill.

Cross the road into the car park and take the path to the left going down the steps to join the coastal path. Turn left and in 150m you will reach what many consider to be the Island's finest tea-rooms - Dunnose Cottage. With its pretty thatched roof and immaculate gardens, there is every temptation to take refreshments here; if the full works are a bit too much, you can even be served half a cream tea!

Stay on the coast path, passing above Luccombe Chine (which can be reached down a long flight of steps) and another tea-room near Luccombe Village. Eventually you will join Luccombe Road, walking downhill past the old Shanklin Hospital with continuing splendid views towards Culver Cliff. At the road junction ahead carry straight on into a sunken tree-lined path, crossing a little bridge at a ford (a good spot to wash off your boots!). All that remains is to climb the short hill back to the start at the Crab Inn in Shanklin Old Village.

WALK 5: EXPLORING NORTH-EAST WIGHT - FROM WOOTTON TO BRADING

Wootton - Havenstreet - Gallows Hill - Arreton Manor & Craft Village - Knighton - Nunwell House - Brading.
11½ miles (18.5km). Start Grid Ref: 546920

An L-shaped route from the Solent coast, up over the central chalk ridge and through deep countryside to the historic town of Brading. Not only is there varied scenery along the way - woods, downland, arable fields and picturesque hamlets - but the walk also takes in several of the Island's premier visitor attractions.

'Wootton' means 'settlement in the woods' and certainly upstream of Wootton Bridge the creek lives up to its name as it glides between the wood-fringed banks of Firestone and Briddlesford copses; these are merely remnants of the great oakwoods that once

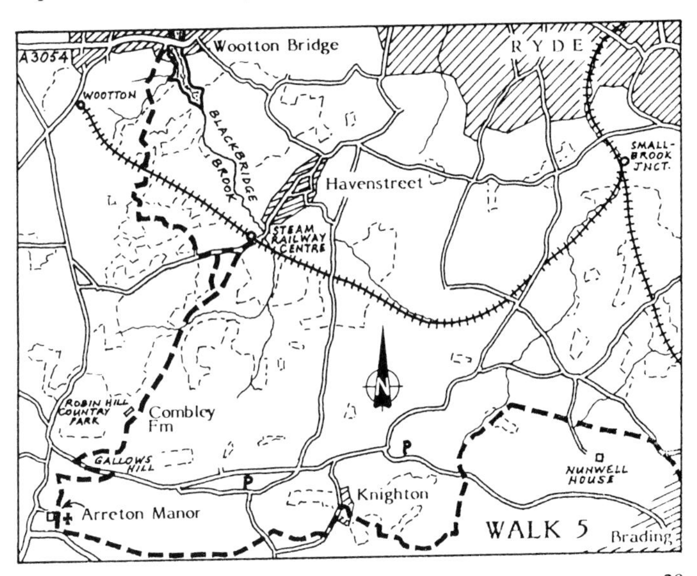

blanketed northern Wight. Downstream nearer The Solent there is much small-boat activity.

The walk starts at The Sloop Inn which used to be the miller's house when the old tide mill was operational (it stood beside the Sloop until 1962). To your left across the road causeway (originally the mill dam) can be seen part of the old mill machinery and the sluice gates. **Set off up the small road opposite (N1) leading to the boat house then follow the track. As you enter a car park bear half-right through a metal gate by a derelict house. Continue up the wide, hedged track as it curves left and right through Hurst Copse;** notice the rustic poled fence with a bricked entrance on your right by a 'Private land - No Entry' sign - it was once the entrance to an old ice house.

In 100m the track veers right (ignore a gate on the left) and as you exit the copse you are walking between a hedge and fence. Stay on the main track as it twists through Six Acre Copse and reaches the Isle of Wight Steam Railway line. Cross over, making sure to close the gates, then follow the path to the right of Woodhouse Farm towards a metal gate. Go through and in 75m join a wide track from the farm.

If you look left towards the farmyard you will see a fine example of a grain barn mounted on stones to deter mice.

Almost immediately the track bends left (past path N2 on your right) and heads towards white, stone-faced Keepers Cottage on the left. Carry on ahead and in about 400m you descend to a crosstrack. At this point the way turns sharp left (east) then swings right just before some barns at Great Briddlesford Farm. Go through a gateway and veer left past a pond surrounded by rustic fencing; bearing slightly to the right round the pond, you will confront 3 gates, the left-hand one set back. Pass through the middle gate into a track between hedge and wire fence, heading straight towards a modern house called Greenhills. Beyond the house follow the track ahead (ignore one going left behind the barn) and in 250m turn left along the Havenstreet Road. After approximately 250m, at the 'Slow' sign, turn right over a stile into path N93 'Combley Farm Lane'.

There is now a unique opportunity to visit the Isle of Wight Steam Railway's Old Branch Line whose nerve centre is just a few minutes' walk away at Havenstreet Station.

Their island location and limited financial resources have always obliged railway companies here to acquire ageing engines and rolling stock from the mainland. Such an apparent disadvantage, however, has been turned into a success story by our growing national nostalgia for the steam era. Careful restoration has brought back into service vintage locomotives and superannuated coaching stock, authentically representing the days of late 19th century and early 20th century branch line operation.

The 5 mile (8km) route through beautiful countryside is part of a rural line closed, along with innumerable others nationwide, by Dr Beeching in the mid 1960s. Tickets can be purchased for all or part of the full return journey which takes about an hour. At Havenstreet Station you can browse round the fascinating Museum Gallery and Railway Shop, enjoy a snack in the Refreshment Bar or a picnic in the gardens and soak up the sights and sounds of a working steam railway.

To regain the walk's routing from the station turn back along the road but at the first right-hand bend, turn off left on bridleway N18 (ignoring the adjacent track with a fancy post box). In 150m you pass a 'V.S.C. Private' sign then at the fork ahead keep right on the wide, tree-lined lane. About 200m further on you will meet path N93 coming in from the right, which is now described from the road.

Having crossed the stile at the 'Slow' sign into path N93, keep the wire fence on your left and cross a small field (ignore a gate to the right halfway across) to another stile by a metal water trough. Walk over a small footbridge (marked No 25) and cross the stile ahead, still keeping tight to the hedge on your right. In 150m there's another stile and little bridge leading into the bridleway from Havenstreet Station, along which turn right.

Now continue along the main track passing Guildford Heath Cottage set back in trees on your left. You soon pass Combley Lodge Cottage and arrive at Combley Farm. Turn left through a gate and walk across the farmyard in front of the farmhouse. Go through the gate, bear right onto a track between wire fences, cross the cattle grid and the path trends left towards trees on the flanks of Gallows Hill, passing a tree stump resembling a ship's

anchor. The way keeps to the main track which bends right, crosses another cattle grid and climbs to the main road (ignoring a steep track up to the left).

Hereabouts on the narrow chalk ridge downs between Newport and Brading is the site of the last public hanging on the Island. For a good pub lunch, detour 400m along to the right to the thatched Hare & Hounds; the fireplace contains a beam from the last gallows to be used for execution! Adjacent to the pub lies Robin Hill Country Park, both, incidentally, owned by the Dabell family of Blackgang Chine fame. As a kind of insurance against the eventual loss of Blackgang's Theme Park through landslip, the family company acquired the country park in 1994 and has invested heavily in its development as a prime attraction for the whole family.

Walk east beside the road along the crest of Arreton Down for about 500m, with stirring views on either side, embracing The Solent, distant mainland and Ryde to your left, and the lovely Arreton valley and south Wight to your right. Take the stile over on the right, bearing half-right again in the direction of the signpost downhill towards the corner of a wire fence; from here the Manor and church at Arreton are visible. Head towards the white house in the distance and on reaching the bottom power line pole watch for a stile about 25m in front of you in the hedge. Cross the stile and descend sharp left by a metal hand rail into a field where the clear path aims for the church. On the right is the entrance to Arreton Manor (closed Saturdays).

Much of the building dates from Elizabethan times. Over the years it has been variously owned and lived in by royalty, from Henry VIII to Charles I. Inside, spiralling stone steps lead down to 14th century rooms, a fragment of the original farmhouse built by the monks of Quarr Abbey. The Manor offers other kinds of attractions too: a Museum of Childhood, a lace collection and the National Wireless Museum. Before moving on, take a look round 12th century St George's Church, massively constructed and containing fascinating interior details.

Just beyond the Manor, keep left of the tall barn on A12 - 'Church and Main Road' - following the path round between churchyard and a large pond. Pass the Brass Rubbing Centre, Lavender House and Herb Garden at Arreton Craft Village to

reach the White Lion pub and the main A3056 road. Much of the way onwards from here follows the Bembridge Trail which starts at Chide on the outskirts of Newport.

Turn left along the pavement and in about 200m branch left on bridleway A9 past Arreton Primary School. Soon the village is left behind and you are walking on a grassy track along field headlands.

Here in the Arreton valley is some of the most fertile soil on the Island, producing a variety of crops from cereals and vegetables to garlic, glasshouse tomatoes and 'pick your own' fruit.

When you reach a long, straight crosstrack (Shepherd's Lane), consider a 500m detour to the right to visit Haseley Manor (or earmark it for another day). Raymond Young, the present owner, purchased the property in 1976 when it lay derelict, open to the elements and stripped of valuable materials. Twenty years of painstaking restoration has transformed the Manor into the wonderful complex we see today but even more astonishing was the discovery that Haseley is, indeed, one of Wight's most historic buildings - a claim verified by experts in the field. Mr Young's late wife, Krystyna, established the thriving pottery studio here which co-exists alongside a small sweet factory, gift shop and cafe, all set in beautiful gardens.

Back on the trail, continue walking east along the open field edge track until you reach a country lane just south of Mersley Farm. Turn left and in about 75m turn right by the brick wall onto path NC1 round by a house on the right. In another 75m, beyond a little stream, bear right along by a hedge (NC7), cross stiles through the ensuing fields and emerge at a road.

Throughout this stretch there are good views ahead to Ashey Down, topped by a conspicuous sea mark - a navigational aid for shipping.

Turn left on the road, passing Knighton Farm Cottage, and in 400m, at the bottom of Knighton Shute, turn right (NC45 for Kern and Alverstone). The track swings right past waterworks buildings and climbs gently to Po House where the way swings sharp right onto a rough downhill track. At the bottom keep left and walk up by a hedge through trees to cross over the sandpit access track ahead.

The onwards field track is well defined, passing through gates

and dipping before rising to Kern Farm. Just before reaching the farmhouse itself, turn right at a gate (signed 'Alverstone'), pass a bungalow then bear left to join the rutted farm track heading straight up the side of Ashey Down past old chalk pits to the ridgetop road. Cross the road into Eaglehead Copse (B58), keeping to the obvious path and passing a sign 'Nunwell B24'. Emerging into a field, stay along the left-hand edge and in 200m veer left into another copse. Follow that path for 400m, soon swinging east. Stiles lead straightforwardly across fields and over a tarmac lane near Nunwell Farm. Here you cross a stile by a large tree and continue in the same direction over fields close to New Farm on the left. Aim for trees in the middle of the next field and walk on to a stile to the left of some houses. A final stile brings you out to West Lane. Turn right to pass the main public entrance to Nunwell House.

Open on days during the summer, the manor house itself is not easy to view at a distance, being surrounded by 6 acres of landscaped gardens. Following the Norman Conquest, Richard d'Oglandre was installed as lord of the manor by William the Conqueror. Since then through the intervening centuries, the Oglanders remained one of the Island's most influential and powerful families, occupying Nunwell right up until 1980. Associations with royalty include Charles I's last night of freedom spent here, at Sir John Oglander's invitation, before his incarceration at Carisbrooke Castle which led to his execution ten months later, in September 1648.

Not far past the entrance drive, fork right along Doctors Lane beside a bungalow estate and by branching left on Cross Street you will enter Brading High Street (which unfortunately is also the busy A3055).

Standing prominently to your left at the north end of the village is 12th century St Mary's Church. Inside you'll find a wooden effigy of Sir John Oglander, the celebrated 17th century royalist and diarist - the very same Oglander who took in Charles I on that fateful November night in 1647.

Brading, a swashbuckling port known as Ye Kynge's Towne of Bradynge until it was left high and dry by the damming of the East Yar river in 1877, has become one of the Island's best known visitor attractions. Well worth seeing are the fabulous Wax Museum and

Brading's famous Wax Museum and St Mary's Church

Animal World, the Lilliput Antique Doll and Toy Museum, nearby Morton Manor vineyard and gardens, and Brading Roman Villa. On the High Street itself are a gaol, stocks and whipping post at the Old Town Hall. For delicious old-fashioned sweets, check out the toffee shop opposite the Red Lion pub.

Brading railway station, for frequent Island Line trains to Ryde or Shanklin, may be found by following the High Street south and round the sharp left bend. Fork off left (straight on) at the garage.

WALK 6: SHANKLIN TO BRADING VIA CULVER CLIFF AND BEMBRIDGE

Shanklin railway station - Sandown - Culver Cliff - Whitecliff Bay - Bembridge - Brading railway station. 12 miles (19km). Start Grid Ref: 581818

This varied route encompasses a coastal walk over Culver Cliff to the harbour town of Bembridge and a lowland ramble to historic Brading. Both ends of the walk are connected by Island Line trains.

The walk starts at Shanklin railway station, southern terminus of the Island Line. It runs to Ryde, calling at Lake, Sandown, Brading, Smallbrook Junction (for the Isle of Wight Steam Railway), Ryde St John's Road, Ryde Esplanade and Ryde Pier Head; from there frequent ferries connect with mainland trains at Portsmouth Harbour. Island Line is unique in that it uses ex-London Underground tube trains from the Piccadilly Line, equipped with simulated steam whistles! Walkers, holidaymakers and residents alike find the line extremely useful as an alternative to road transport along the busy eastern side of the Island.

On leaving the station, walk slightly left down Atherley Road and in 400m, at the traffic lights, keep straight on past the Sherwood Hotel into Hope Road. In another 400m turn left at the Channel View Hotel. (Alternatively you may choose to continue straight ahead here, turning left at the bottom of the hill and walking along the beach to Sandown, enjoying a paddle on the way!)

Climb the path at the back of the flats, passing the Hideaway Cafe on your left, and continue along the cliff path overlooking the superb sandy beaches first of Shanklin then Lake. After passing the Battery Gardens at Sandown, the way drops a little and turns right down steps,

passes some toilets then turns left along the Esplanade towards the Pier and Tourist Information Centre.

Sandown's Pavilion Theatre features many famous names in its summer season shows, boosting the town's reputation for family entertainment.

Carry on along the seafront past the War Memorial and at the far end turn left with the road up a short hill. Within about 25m bear right.

Opposite, at the corner of High Street and Victoria Road, stands Sandown Library containing a fascinating Geological and Dinosaur Museum.

Further on beyond the famous Zoo, as you pass a boating lake, notice that the land to your left is very low-lying (part of the seabed many years ago) and that you are walking on a substantial sea wall. Go through the large car park at Yaverland (toilets) and walk seaward of the Yacht Club boat park to the start of the path over grassy downland. Notices warn of cliff fall danger and indeed the edge is slipping away at Red Cliff, composed of fossil-bearing Red Sandstone. With the monument on Culver Cliff now beckoning, the path angles across open grass and climbs steadily with ever widening views over Sandown Bay. On arrival at the small road on the summit of Culver Down, aim towards the pub and tea rooms (when open displaying an astonishing variety of

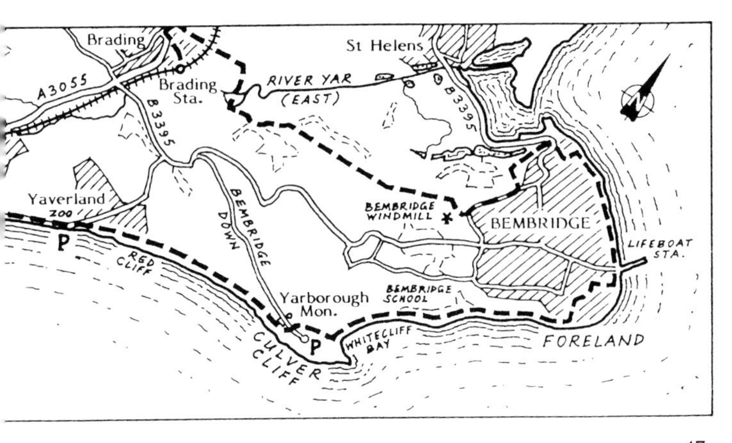

ice-cream cones!).

A great ridge of chalk stretches right across the Isle of Wight, forming The Needles and Tennyson Down in the far west, a block of downland near the Island's centre, and a steep-sided backbone which ends here at Culver Cliff. The stone monument was put up in 1849 commemorating the Earl of Yarborough, Charles Pelham, who founded the Royal Yacht Squadron at Cowes.

Go through the kissing gate towards the monument and pass it on your left. Now head half-right to pick up a well defined chalky path cutting downhill across a field. Over the stile at the bottom, waymarks guide you through bushes round past wooden chalets and a caravan park; one of the little footbridges was an old ship's gangplank. Beyond the bridge spanning Whitecliff Bay's beach slipway, the trail threads through scrubby woodland, down and up some steps and along the perimeter of Bembridge School's playing field. More landslipped terrain lies ahead, with sections of boardwalk above a tumbled undercliff and rock ledges. Eventually you reach a Coastguard lookout point and the Crab and Lobster pub, an old smugglers' haunt.

Walk left onto unsurfaced Beachfield Road and in 200m turn right, then swing left into Foreland Farm Lane. In about 100m watch for tree-lined path BB4 on the right which heads straight for the shore at Bembridge Holiday Village. Turn left along Fishermen's Walk to Bembridge lifeboat station and small car park and cafe at Lane End.

The 'Tyne' class lifeboat *Sir Max Aitken III* is housed at the seaward end of a long jetty. Bembridge village occupies the Island's easternmost tip at the mouth of the East Yar river. In common with many other Island resorts, it owes its existence largely to wealthy, leisure-and-health seeking Victorians who brought the railway here and built their villas. Despite much postwar housing development, the now extensive community remains pleasant and unspoiled. The Shipwreck Centre is well worth a visit, crammed as it is with models, pictures, diving artefacts and shipwreck treasure.

From Lane End continue along the sea wall walkway passing some beach huts and at the end carry on along the beach. In approximately 500m, just before a concrete groyne, the path heads inland towards woods. Ducking under a fallen tree, you follow

the path which becomes hedged and reaches an unmade road - Dulcie Avenue. Turn left and in 75m turn right into Pump Lane (BB3). At the end you meet the B3395 road by the Pilot Boat Inn.

It's only a short detour on the right to visit Bembridge Point for marvellous views to St Helens Fort offshore and The Duver just across the estuary mouth. Bembridge harbour is popular with dinghy sailors whose craft can be watched manoeuvring with wind and tide.

Cross the road (toilets on the right) and keep straight ahead to the Row Barge pub on your left (a good lunch stop); head directly past the old station buildings and on into trees following path BB19 - the dismantled railway trackbed. About 500m further on take path BB3 on the left up to the main road (High Street). Turn right and where the road makes a left-hand bend, go straight on (BB36 - Styne Copse) towards Bembridge Windmill.

This, the Island's only windmill in working order, still retains its wooden milling mechanism, carefully restored by the National Trust. Built of local stone in 1700, it stands 30ft (9m) and four storeys high. Explanatory displays and samples of milled grain provide a vivid insight into this once prevalent wind-driven technology.

At the windmill, the way continues (BB21 - part of the Bembridge Trail between here and Newport) over stiles across a field near Mill Farm. It then angles half-left downhill over pasture with a duckpond to your left.

At the bottom you are close to a small factory which builds the famous Islander aircraft and it will not have escaped your attention that Bembridge Airport lies ahead, with the chance of watching light aircraft taking off and landing.

Reaching level ground the path (BB20) follows a floodbank and continues straightforwardly over several more fields. At a particularly large crop field, walk across to the lone tree in the middle and keep on the same line to a stile at the far side. Now turn left, with the hedge on your right, and aim for the bottom right-hand field corner, round the stile and into trees. At the junction of several paths, bear right on BB23 to Brading.

Maps show this as Centurion Hill but there is no known association with Roman soldiers as one might expect. Instead, a small chapel dedicated to an 8th century abbot, St Urian, once stood hereabouts and his name has corrupted down the years to Centurion.

The mouth of the East Yar was finally dammed in 1877 to connect the growing settlements of Bembridge and St Helens. The tidal flow was thus blocked, creating a vast area of freshwater marsh, reed beds and meadow, but leaving the ancient seaport of Bradynge high and dry!

At the next junction in 50m turn right over two sluice gates in channels of the River Yar. Path B3 now heads along a low grassy embankment and trends left to a kissing gate at another path intersection. With a newish bungalow (The Old Brickworks) on your right, walk straight on along Quay Lane for about 1/2 mile (800m) to its junction with the main A3055 at Brading.

On your right stands 12th century St Mary's Church bearing a highly unusual little porch tower mounted on arches; inside is a chapel with fine wooden effigies of the Oglander family who lived in nearby Nunwell House from Norman times to 1980.

On your left, in some contrast, is Brading's famous Wax Museum, founded by Graham Osborn-Smith in the Island's reputedly oldest house dating from 1228. In a sequence of exquisitely detailed and imaginatively lit tableaux, the museum traces the Island's history. More gruesome but no less skilful, the Chamber of Horrors is entered off the old galleried Queen's Bower Courtyard. The adjoining Animal World is highly recommended for its taxidermy displays and exhibits - some bizarre - from the natural world.

Elsewhere in Brading will be found the fascinating Lilliput Antique Doll and Toy Museum, and the old Town Hall complete with barred gaol, stocks and whipping post. Morton Manor gardens and vineyard, as well as Brading's Roman villa, are situated just south of the village centre.

To conclude this route, turn left down the High Street to the Bullring and follow the main road round to the left; where it swings right by a garage, keep straight on to the railway station and, perhaps, a train ride back to Shanklin.

WALK 7: COAST TO COAST FROM RYDE TO SHANKLIN

Ryde - Spring Vale - Brading - Brading Down - Alverstone - Queen's Bower - Borthwood Copse - America Wood - Shanklin.
13 miles (21km). Start Grid Ref: 594929

A varied cross-country route starting with a stroll along the coast path east from the busy seaside town and ferry terminal of Ryde. Field paths and country lanes to Brading are followed by a crossing of the Island's central downland ridge. The final section passes through two lovely broadleaved woods in hills behind the popular resorts of Sandown and Shanklin. This linear walk begins and ends at railway stations on the Island Line, enabling an easy return to be made to the starting point if required.

Ryde's many hotels and guesthouses of Regency and Victorian origin recall the town's early days as a fashionable bathing resort in the 19th century. The pier's construction in 1824 allowed steamers to berth at all states of the tide so that passengers could disembark without an uncomfortable horse and carriage ride of up to 1/2 mile (800m) over bumpy low-tide sandbanks. The pier now carries the Island Line Railway out to Pier Head Station where Wightlink's high speed catamarans depart for Portsmouth. Interestingly, Island Line uses ex-London Underground tube trains of 1930s vintage on its unique service to stations between Ryde and Shanklin.

Set off east from Ryde's Esplanade railway station and cross the footbridge to the hovercraft terminal. The terminal was badly storm damaged on December 13th, 1981 and had to be re-built. Two hovercraft are in service between Ryde and Southsea (bus link to Portsmouth centre), running in all but the severest weather conditions every day of the year except Christmas Day and Boxing Day. Average crossing time is 9 minutes; parcels and Royal Mail are also carried. Since the inaugural flight on July 24th, 1965, Hovertravel have carried over 14 million passengers and can justly claim to be the world's longest standing commercial hovercraft operators.

Continue walking along the sea wall past the Ice Rink and

Canoe Lake. At Appley beach cafe stay on the sea wall prom, passing the Appley Tower.

A plaque on this Victorian Gothic folly tells of HMS *Sirius* sailing for Australia on May 13th, 1787 and arriving the following year: how travel times have changed!

Beyond Jill's Pantry at Puckpool Park, keep to the lower path along the water's edge.

A delightful fringe of trees reaches down to a good sandy beach but beachgoers should beware the fast-rising tide here at the less safe eastern end of Ryde Sands. Notice offshore the Solent forts, one of which was recently acquired by a German buyer. Spitbank Fort, nearer the mainland, can be visited by pleasure cruiser from Cowes. Squat and immensely durable, these granite structures formed part of England's defences against a perceived threat of a French invasion under Napoleon III in the mid 1860s. As history recalls, the invasion didn't materialise and such coastal fortifications became known, after the prime minister of the day, as

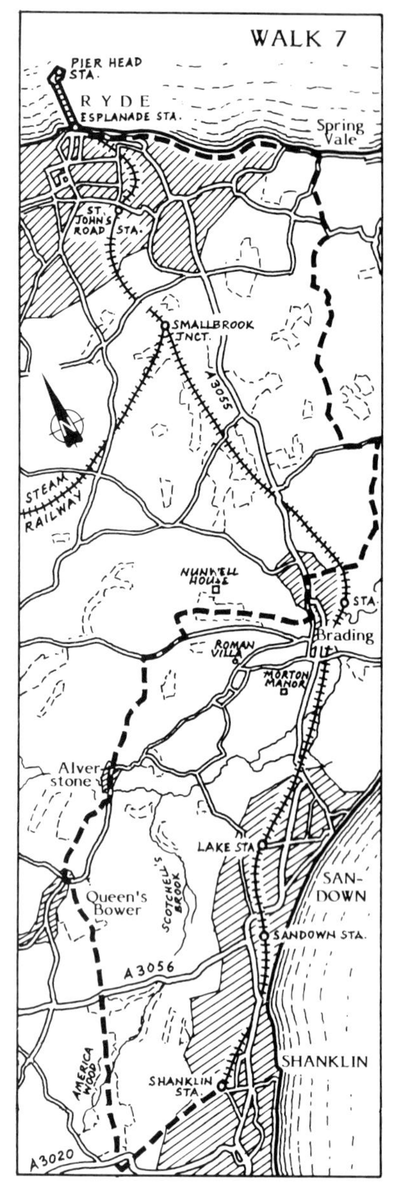

'Palmerston Follies'. On a clear day you can see the white-faced cliffs of Portsdown Hill behind Portsmouth.

The concrete wall curves round Puckpool Point (CR90), passes beach huts and meets the coast road at the Battery Inn. Continue straight on for about 500m to Spring Vale then turn right, following the brown sign for Flamingo Park.

Wandering freely on the grassy slopes of this bird sanctuary are tame peacocks, flamingos and macaws, as well as various species of duck and goose. There is a Tropical House containing more exotic birds.

Beyond the park's entrance take a path on the left (R59 Pondwell), ignoring an adjacent 'Westbrook Private' path. In 100m the way bears right past a small paddock on the left and in 150m widens into an unmade road. This in turn leads to the main B330 at the Wishing Well pub. Keep straight on and 200m ahead cross the road at a bend and take the path marked 'Private Road Westbrook Cottage', keeping to the left-hand gravel path. In a short distance where the way swings right (signed 'Westbrook Cottage private Drive'), go left. In about 30m you will cross a row of railway sleepers into a small field, heading for a gate in the right-hand corner. Go over the drainage ditch and through the gate, proceeding in the direction of a yellow waymark arrow with a fence on your left. Field gates then lead you to a track to Park Farm.

Now head towards the tall, open-sided barn in front of you and at the two metal gates go through the left-hand one, continuing along the wide track ahead. At the second metal gate, after approximately 250m, bear half-left across the field (B11 to Hill Farm). At the signpost the path goes through a hedge-gate then veers right along the farm track.

At Hill Farm turn left in front of the arch-shaped barn and on entering the field bear right and walk down to the main B3330 road (Carpenters Road). Turn left towards St Helens, passing Carpenters Farm campground, and notice the gnomes occupying the garden at the end terrace house! Within about 50m take a right turn opposite Avon View cottage and in 20m, where the track bends right to the farm buildings, keep straight on in the direction of the power line pole. When it comes into view, head towards a

gap in the tall hedge in front of you and go over the stile and slightly left, passing a short wall over the footbridge.

The water meadows and wetlands surrounding you were formed after the East Yar river was dammed at St Helens in 1877 to join that community with neighbouring Bembridge. As a consequence of that action, the navigable waters formerly extending upstream to Brading (known as Brading Haven) disappeared. The East Yar is now artificially channelled and the adjacent low-lying land with its creeks, reed beds and copses, has become a haven for birdlife.

The way continues south through a thicket and along a low embankment with the Yarborough Monument on Culver Down straight ahead in the distance. On reaching a stile (ignore one on the right), cross over and turn right along the dismantled railway trackbed of the old Brading to Bembridge branch line which closed in the mid-1950s. At the house ahead take the path to the right of a fence, passing a large telegraph pole, then at the cross-junction turn right along Quay Lane (B1 to Brading High Street) past a new bungalow called The Old Brickworks.

Once over the Island Line railway bridge, you approach some neat bungalows and at this point one option would be to take path B6 on the left to the centre of Brading. However no visit to this historic town would be complete without seeing the unusual 12th century St Mary's Church with its little porch tower mounted on arches. Inside you'll find much of interest, including wooden effigies of the Oglander family who lived at nearby Nunwell House from Norman times right up until 1980. Opposite stands the Old Town Hall, complete with stocks, barred gaol and whipping post. **To see these simply carry straight on to the top of the High Street.**

Graham Osborn-smith's famous Wax Museum and Animal World, also well worth visiting (perhaps on a separate occasion), stand at the corner of Quay Lane in what is almost certainly the Island's oldest house. Despite its rather lurid colourwash, it is an authentic Early Tudor rectory mansion dating from 1228 which at various times has been in use as an inn and a smugglers' den!

Turn left down the High Street to the Red Lion pub, a recommended lunch stop on this walk, then continue up to the Bull Ring.

It was in use as a bull baiting arena from the Middle Ages until

1820. As well as being a thriving seaport during that period, Brading has a history of settlement reaching back to the Roman occupation - witness the impressive Roman villa with its beautiful mosaic floors, situated to the south-west of the centre towards Adgestone.

Past the Bull Ring fork right up Mall Road and in about 250m turn right onto bridleway B39 towards Nunwell, passing Little Jane cottage which dates from 1547. Climb the path, ignoring left and right offshoots, until you reach the top of the incline where you join the clear track trending right into woods. Stay on this track beneath Nunwell Down for approximately 1/2 mile (800m), passing through a metal gate with trees directly ahead. In 50m, at a grey post, take the left-hand track angling uphill and curving left.

At the top, pause to admire the patchwork of fields and copses stretching north towards distant Ryde.

Now go through the gate in the left-hand field corner and head for the signpost to reach the road running along the crest of Brading Down.

You are now atop the Island's chalk 'backbone' which extends west to east from The Needles to Culver Cliff. Except to the west of Newport where it forms an upland block, the ridge is quite narrow and steep-sided, providing magnificent views and good walking. Flints found in the upper chalk layers were used to fashion weapons and tools by our neolithic ancestors. Although the seamark ahead on Ashey Down, along with another on the shore at St Helens, are old types of navigational aids, they are still occasionally helpful to shipping.

Walk west along the broad, grassy roadside verge for about 500m then cross the road onto path B43.

There are wide views over the cultivated Arreton valley to Sandown Bay. St Boniface Down, highest ground on the Isle of Wight, can be seen a little west of south.

The fenced field path drops quite steeply for about 3/4 mile (1.2km), meeting a narrow lane at the bottom which leads to the minor road at Alverstone hamlet. Go straight on, passing The Grange Country Hotel on your left and cross the little bridge over the infant East Yar river as well as the old railway trackbed. In 100m turn right (NC42) to Queen's Bower.

As the way veers sharp right, take the middle path on the left (ignoring the gate and the drive to the house). The waymark - NC42 - is in a tree. In 250m by an open picket style fence the path bears right and climbs gently through trees, crosses a lane and continues finally as a track to the road (Skinners Hill) at Queen's Bower.

Queen's Bower is thought to have been named after a 13th century Lady of the Wight, Isabella de Fortibus, who owned a hunting lodge here.

Turn left at the road and in 75m cross over and take the 'V' shaped stile into Borthwood Copse.

Now cared for by the National Trust, Borthwood Copse is a remnant of ancient hunting forest. It contains superb specimens of 400-year-old sessile oak, descendants from the great broadleaved forests that cloaked southern England following the last Ice Age.

Passing fallen trees over to your right, you soon meet the main woodland track and turn right along it. It becomes a sunken path through tree roots and tangled undergrowth; bear slightly left about 50m beyond a plank seat and a short way ahead keep straight on. Ignoring the right-hand path and several off to the left, you will reach a small clearing, pass another seat and rise to exit the southern edge of the wood.

Continue ahead on the wide track into a field and in 200m swing sharp right round the field edge, a hedge to your left (ignore the track going straight on). When you arrive at a brick and stone house near Bigbury Farm, turn left between the lower barn and the rusting tin barn where the path continues to the main A3056 Newport Road.

Cross over onto path NC37 towards America Wood. It descends and passes through a usually muddy section, crosses a small stream and a stile before reaching a narrow lane. Go up the bank opposite and over the stile and keep straight on along the field headland. In 100m go through the hedge into the next field and descend, through a wire fence and steeply down steps, crossing a little footbridge over Scotchell's Brook at the bottom. A short sharp climb out is followed by a drop over another stream footbridge. Beyond the next stile you pass an old blue gate on the left, whereafter the path meanders to the right before bearing left into trees and reaching another stile.

This Woodland Trust stile is dedicated to the memory of Francis Hanson (1932-92). With its stands of oak and sweet chestnut, America Wood is one of the most delightful spots on the Island. Originating as pasture woodland, its clearings were regularly grazed by domestic livestock and even today wildflowers such as primroses, wood anemones, celandines and bluebells brighten the glades in springtime.

Initially quite narrow, the onward path joins a wider one. Still heading south it undulates and wanders through Apsecastle Wood, crossing a footbridge (ignore the right fork just after). In 100m, at some long, low buildings on your left, turn right then in 50m turn left (not through the rustic poles). The main path now crosses a boardwalk and a timber bridge over the brook then climbs to the main A3020 road.

Cross the road to Abbottsford Lodge. The onward track starts 20m up the road to the right - NC39 to St Martin's Down and the old railway. In 50m at the metal gate, cross the stile and turn left along the dismantled trackbed of the old Shanklin to Ventnor railway. On reaching a minor road, Shanklin station lies 500m directly ahead over the main road and up steps.

Walkers wishing to return to Ryde on the Island Line can catch one of the twice-hourly trains (hourly on winter Sundays) and be there in 25 minutes.

WALK 8: CROSS-COUNTRY FROM CARISBROOKE TO SHANKLIN

Whitcombe Cross - Chillerton -
The Chequers Inn - Godshill -
America Wood - Shanklin railway station.
12 miles (19km). Start Grid Ref: 487874

A rural and at times quite remote walk south-east from the Island's heart at Carisbrooke Castle to the popular seaside resort of Shanklin. There is some intricate route-finding along the way and a good number of ups and downs but the rewards are experiencing deepest Wight countryside, wonderful views and a midway stop at the picturesque tourist 'honeypot' of Godshill.

Whitcombe Cross lies just a short distance south of the Island's only castle. Replacing an original timber fortress, the massive stone ramparts of Carisbrooke Castle remain as impressive today as they ever were. The Island governor's official residence until 1944, the castle is now in the hands of English Heritage and is well worth a visit - if not before setting out on this walk then on a separate occasion.

A narrow path between hedges leading down and up from the south-west corner of the outer moat ditch will bring you to Froglands Lane where, by turning left, you quickly reach the country road at Whitcombe Cross. With your back to the castle, follow not the road but bridleway N108 for Gatcombe which runs parallel to it at first and soon becomes a deeply sunken ancient trackway called Dark Lane. This initial section of the walk follows the officially designated Shepherds Trail, emerging into fields after about 1/2 mile (800m). Beyond a path on the left to Vayres Farm at a small dip, continue along a field headland through a gate and past a low cliff, with Gatcombe hamlet cradled in a fold of the downs below to your left. Cross straight over the track ahead and descend through trees past a house and the Isle of Wight Hunt kennels on your left to reach Newbarn Lane.

Turn right then left, following the lane (G6) and in about

400m, having passed Little Gatcombe and Newbarn farms, veer left through a hedge gap off the lane which swings sharp right. Walk up the chalky bridleway to the edge of Tolt Copse then bear slightly left. In 50m take the path on your right down a field edge and simply continue walking with a hedge on the left through gates and eventually down a sunken track to the road at Kervill Dairy, the southern end of Chillerton village.

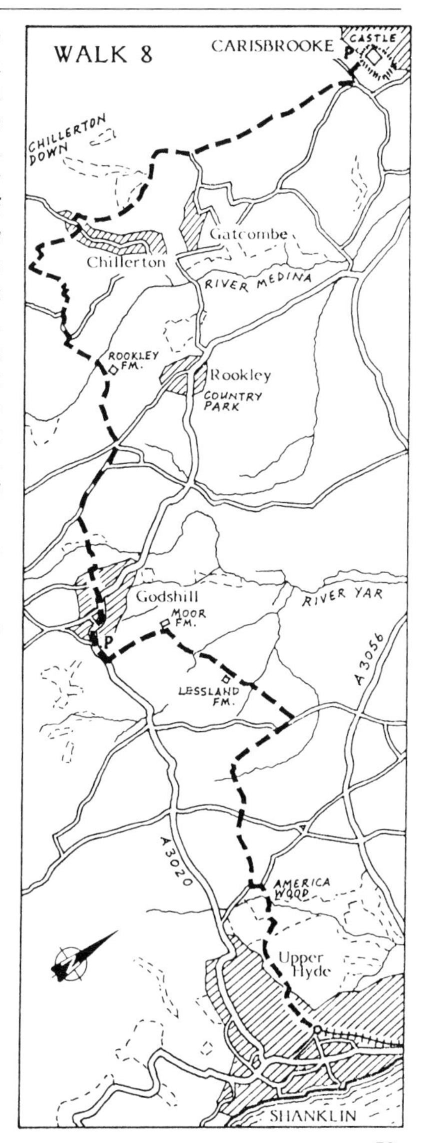

Beautiful English countryside surrounds you - a blend of cultivated fields, pasture and deep woods of oak, beech and chestnut on gently sloping hillsides. Chillerton Down's elegant sweep, topped by its TV mast, is pitted with the rounded hollows of old chalk pits.

Turn left along the Chillerton Road and in 150m turn right by a small hall into Hollow Lane (G15a). This ancient bridleway, overhung with tree roots and vegetation, climbs steadily over 200ft (60m), bearing right at the

top from a corner of open fields into a hedge-lined grassy track.

At the crosstrack ahead turn left (G15) and after about 400m watch carefully for a gate on your right. Go through and, with magnificent views, drop steeply to another gate. Turn left down the tree-lined lane towards Lower Rill Farm but about 30m before reaching it go through the gate (bearing a sign for horse-riders) and round the back of the barn, veering left to join the main farm track. Go through another gate and turn right into the narrow tarmac lane.

After winding along for some 400m or so, swing left, still on the lane, and in a further 100m turn left onto a wide track. Pass through the gate ahead and then cross a small bridge over the infant River Medina before passing a large house set back at Rookley Farm. Bear right onto the farm lane with smallholdings on your right and continue to the main road where you will find the Chequers Inn directly opposite.

This pub is 'walker-friendly' and serves excellent food.

Turn right along Bagwich Lane (or left as you come out of the pub) and in 3/4 mile (1.2km), having passed a bungalow and a caravan, turn left over a stile at the last building onto path GL22 at the side of a garden. This crosses another stile and an often waterlogged field hollow - in fact one of the tributary streams flowing into the River East Yar. Head for the kissing gate and notice the building on your right.

Before the axeing of Britain's branch line network in the 1960s, this was Godshill station and you can still make out the old platform. On a map it's possible to trace the railway line's course intermittently.

Go through the gate onto a narrow path which in a few steps jinks right round behind Scotland Farm. It joins the farm road and at a thatched cottage you reach the outskirts of Godshill. Walk straight ahead (due east) and stay in the same direction on meeting the main A3020 which runs through the village.

Note the Old School House on the left with its 'griffin' crest. This emblem of the Worsley family of Appuldurcombe House appears frequently in the locality.

In about 150m turn right onto Church Lane and climb the hill.

Here you will enjoy the most celebrated view of Godshill, one that features on thousands of postcards. It's worth taking time out to look round 15th century All Saints Church too, with its famous Christ-on-a-lily-cross mural.

Leaving the church, head downhill to the centre of Godshill and turn right along past the Model Village and all the tea rooms (perhaps treating yourself to an ice-cream en route!). The Griffin Inn, further along, was once the stables to Appuldurcombe House.

Walk east beside the main Newport to Shanklin road for about 300m and turn left (GL46) towards Moor Farm. At the farm turn right, round the back of a small brick building. Go past a barn on the left and an old caravan on the right, pass through a gate and follow the wire fence closely on your left. Don't go through the next gate but turn right, still by the fence. At the following gate go through and turn left, heading for a small stile with a white crossbar. The path now crosses a stream bridge (another Yar tributary) and goes through a hedge into a field, bearing half-left over a plank bridge and joining a broad hedged track past Lessland Farm. Keep straight on into the next field, hedge on your right, and in 200m turn right over a stile. 300m further on the way turns right onto Bathingbourne Lane, just south of extensive plant nurseries.

Where the lane veers sharp right at Green Acres Farm, keep straight ahead into a field through 2 gates. In 200m cross a stile and drop into a narrow lane, turning left and passing Bobberstone Farm buildings on your right. Turn right through a gate, then left over yet another Yar tributary stream and continue past Bachelors Farm to Canteen Road.

From here the onwards route is opposite and slightly to the right. Go through the hedge and over 2 fields, heading for Apse Manor Farm and on reaching Apse Lane turn left. Where it curves left, go over a stile on your right, down steps and half-left to follow a hedge. Keeping right will lead you over a timber bridge and 2 stiles into America Wood.

This must be one of the Island's most delectable spots, with stands of sweet chestnut and oak on ancient pasture woodland whose clearings were once grazed by domestic livestock. In their seasons the glades are brightened by primroses, wood anemones, bluebells and celandines.

In 20m turn left through 2 split fences and head towards some

long, low buildings, turning right up steps onto the wide track swinging round towards Upper Hyde Farm. Keep straight ahead along the track over a field and cross a stile, passing a house on the left and reaching a large metal gate flanked by a stile. Turn left, passing caravans and a swimming pool at Lower Hyde Holiday Village and bear right up through the main entrance to the road. Shanklin railway station now stands directly in front of you. Buses for Carisbrooke via Newport leave from the Somerfield supermarket 100m to the right.

WALK 9: A CIRCUIT OF WIGHT'S WESTERNMOST TIP - THE ANCIENT ISLE OF FRESHWATER

Yarmouth - Fort Victoria - Colwell - Alum Bay - The Needles - Tennyson Down - Freshwater Bay - the Yar estuary - Yarmouth.
13½ miles (22km). Start Grid Ref: 354896

The Island's coast is at its most dramatic in the far west where Alum Bay's famous coloured sands lead out to the chalk stacks of The Needles and the whaleback ridge of Tennyson Down. For most of the way the coast path is followed but the return leg shadows the River Yar which in former geological times would have separated the Freshwater peninsula.

As well as a busy foot passenger and vehicle ferry terminal for Wightlink's services to and from Lymington, Yarmouth, with its Tudor castle, Victorian pier and old town buildings, is also a fascinating place to browse around before or after a walk. There are shops, pubs and cafes and good transport links with the rest of the Island. Cars can be left in the large car park off the main road just south of the ferry terminal where the walk begins, a stone's throw from the town centre.

Set off west across the Yar swing bridge, opened in 1987 to allow tall-masted yachts access to the inner Yar estuary. Safest

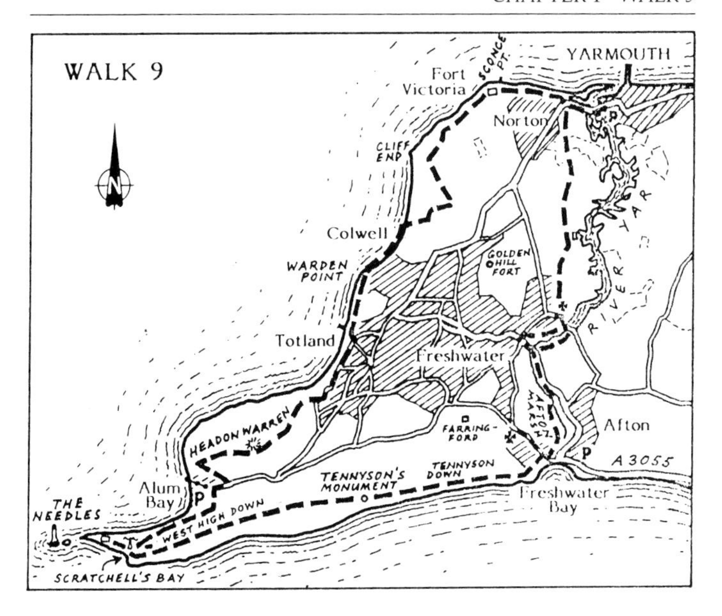

walking is on the left-hand pavement and just before the road swings left at Hallett's Shute, turn off right and continue along the sea wall from the end of Norton Spit, passing a holiday centre. (In summer, a small passenger ferry plies between the harbour and Norton Spit, providing an interesting alternative start.) In about 500m a footpath up steps into trees leads to the back of Fort Victoria, but it is usually possible to keep straight on along the shingle foreshore to the fort complex.

The sprawling, L-shaped casements, part of a once much larger site incorporating barracks, are all that remain of this mid-19th century structure. It was built to protect The Solent's very narrow channel betwen here and Hurst Spit on the mainland. Visitor attractions now include a good cafe, Planetarium, Maritime Heritage Museum and an excellent Marine Aquarium.

Pass in front of the fort to an old experimental searchlight position, and walk inland through delightful broadleaved woods, turning right along the Nature Trail here in Fort Victoria Country

Park. Further along, climbing steps provides an excellent view across to Henry VIII's Hurst Castle and the New Forest beyond.

When the path meets a minor road (Monks Lane), turn left (F6) and in 400m turn right through Brambles Chine holiday centre. Watch for the turning left (F9) along by a low wall to reach a track junction in a small clearing. Now bear right (F13) down to the shore and walk along to Colwell. (Very rarely is it impossible to walk the beach but in exceptional conditions turn left at the track junction on F10 to Yarmouth Road, Totland, via Brambles Farm. In 300m turn right to rejoin the coast path at Colwell.)

Continue along the sea wall prom past the beach huts, cafes and lifeguard lookout and walk round Warden Point with its World War II gun position.

The slumping yellow cliffs lubricated by Gault clay, locally known as 'blue slipper', create problems at various Island locations; here they threaten to engulf the sea wall in places.

Arriving at Totland's little pier, ascend the minor road to your left, under a footbridge.

Ahead stands the Sentry Mead Hotel which, despite its 2-star rating, is walker-friendly. Lunches and snacks are excellent. The building dates from 1891 and was the summer residence of Edward Fox, proprietor of the Ryde to Yarmouth railway company.

After passing beneath the small footbridge, turn right along Turf Walk (which the Victorians called the Grass Promenade). Continue uphill on Cliff Road, round the right-hand bend, then as the road swings left take path T16 on the right. Beyond the barrier the way is tree-lined for 200m before becoming wide and grassy. Carry on climbing gently, following the coast path sign just after the National Trust information board on your right. With magnificent views back along the north coast, walk up the heather and gorse clad slopes to the Bronze Age tumulus at the summit of Headen Warren, complete with explanatory display.

Go left to the end of the wooden rail and turn right for more spectacular views; this time ahead are The Needles. Further on the coast path is signed down left but better views are gained by carrying on to just before the old gun emplacement then doubling back left and descending the track to an unmade road. This leads down to the main Alum Bay access road, along which turn right.

A stormy winter's day on the coast path at Shippards Chine

Carisbrooke, the Island's only castle, dates from Norman times

On the River Medina stands Newport, the Island's administrative, commercial and cultural centre

Tranquil countryside on the Hamstead Trail near Wellow

The Needles Pleasure Park owes its existence to Alum Bay's famous coloured sands of which the cliffs are composed. Although interest had begun as early as 1830, by the late 19th century ever increasing numbers of visitors were arriving at the pier (since demolished) by steamer from south coast resorts. In various combinations, minerals such as Limonite (yellow and brown), Haematite (red) and Glauconite (green) have stained the sand grains, producing up to 20 different colours (best seen in sunshine after heavy rain). Sand shapes from Isle of Wight holidays adorn many a mantlepiece nationwide and the popularity of these novelties continues unabated, with a 'fill your own' facility now available. Up to 30 tons of sand per annum are removed in this way but approximately 80% of that would be washed away into the sea by natural erosion.

Marconi used Alum Bay to carry out his pioneering wireless experiments, enlisting the help of Totland postmaster Mr Garlick in 1897. On returning from America two years later aboard the *St Paul*, Marconi contacted The Needles from a distance of some 70 miles (113km).

Elsewhere in the Pleasure Park are a chair-lift to the beach (which can also be reached by a stepped path), a glass-blowing studio, gift shops, bar and restaurant, stalls and entertainments, all aimed at family holidaymakers. For some walkers it may all be anathema, in which case escape or complete avoidance is easily achieved!

Follow the road up past the toilets and coach park and walk through the barrier gate to the westbound lane which leaves from a right-hand corner by a garden full of gnomes! (A short-cut on the left - T25 - could be used if the weather is very rough.) In about 30m join the path on the right (T29a) and take a look back for superb views of Alum Bay cliffs. From a stile on the left further along, a chalky path (T24) slants uphill past coastguard cottages where, at the narrow road, a little time can be spent inspecting the old gun emplacements of the Needles New Battery which can be found by continuing ahead for a short distance.

With an hour or more to spare, a visit to the National Trust's Old Battery is well worthwhile. Constructed originally in 1861-63 in response to a French invasion scare, the fortification was extended at the end of the 19th century. In fact its location in Channel approaches to Portsmouth was always a vital one and The Needles defensive position retained an operational capability right up until the 1950s. The Old Battery provides a vivid impression of coastal defence systems from Victorian times onwards.

Carry on round a corner in the ridgetop access road and you will reach the concrete remains of an engine-testing site for the *Black Knight* and *Blue Streak* rockets, used during the mid-1950s before Britain's rocket research programme was abandoned. Steps to your right lead down to a spectacular viewpoint over The Needles from high above Scratchell's Bay.

To continue from the steps, walk up the path in front of you towards the radio masts, cross the stile then head slightly left for the best views on both sides of West High Down, 463ft (141m) above the waves. The way now makes a bee-line for the Tennyson Monument some 1½ miles (2.5km) distant. It's a pleasant, if often breezy, stretch of walking of firm turf, culminating at the summit of Tennyson Down where the trig pillar is dwarfed by the 38ft (12m) high Cornish granite memorial to one of England's most celebrated poets.

As you proceed in the same direction downhill towards Freshwater Bay, the Island's west coast is visible all the way along to St Catherine's Point, including the dramatically sudden transition from chalk to yellow clays and sandstones. Above tiny Watcombe Bay you reach a gate and a lane leading left past Fort Redoubt tea-rooms to the B3322 road at Freshwater Bay.

Alfred, Lord Tennyson lived at nearby Farringford House (now a hotel), his work inspired by proximity to his beloved coast and downs. Tennyson's popularity drew a host of eminent visitors, from aristocrats to architects, scientists, scholars and especially artists and fellow writers. Long after Tennyson's death the area continued to attract artists and intellectuals as well as ordinary folk who, today, flock here for the stunning scenery and bracing air.

Turn left beside the B3322 to see the Island's only thatched church. Built in 1908, St Agnes fulfilled the needs of a then swelling local community.

From behind the seafront at Freshwater Bay, take Coastguard Road heading north into path F32. Before long you are treading

Freshwater Bay

protective boardwalks in Afton Marsh Nature Reserve, a Site of Special Scientific Interest and an important reed-bed habitat for a rich variety of birds, plants and insects.

Either branch in the path will bring you out to the minor road at Black Bridge. Turn right then left beside the stream which, after a small bridge, runs along on your left. In just under ½ mile (800m) cross the main A3055 road into Hooke Hill but in only 50m turn right into a residential road called The Crundles. Almost immediately fork right along by a fence (F38) and follow the path as it weaves mysteriously through reed beds past unseen water channels in the ancient valley of the Yar. Beyond the blocked-up road bridge ahead the river is tidal. Alternatively, use the old railway trackbed.

The River Yar once rose in hills far to the south, draining into what was then the River Solent before Wight had become a true island. This explains how a river that runs for a paltry 3 miles (5km) today can boast such a broad and developed estuary.

Turn left along the road past a wartime bunker and bear right

just before the Red Lion pub alongside All Saints churchyard which contains the grave of Tennyson's wife, Emily. Heading due north, the way soon joins a tarred lane (F1) for about 500m before veering left over a stile just before Kings Manor Farm. Swing right behind the farmhouse and after passing through a tree enclosure bear left up a field track. Curving right this becomes grassier and drops gently to a stream footbridge in trees to the right.

Walk up field headlands and savour the delightful path dipping through Saltern Wood. You emerge at a rough road, turn left then turn right along the pavement at the main A3054 road, returning over the Yar Bridge to the start at Yarmouth.

WALK 10: A CIRCULAR HIKE FROM WHALE CHINE ON THE ISLAND'S WEST COAST

Whale Chine - Bucks Farm - Shorwell - Brighstone Down - Strawberry Lane - Chilton Green - Coast Path back to Whale Chine.
15½ miles (25km). Start Grid Ref: 469784

Exploring countryside and downland on the more exposed, south-west facing side of the Island; returning along the coast path above dramatically eroding cliffs.

The walk starts and finishes at Whale Chine which has a car park and is on the Island Explorer No 7 bus route.

'Chine' is a local name for a coastal ravine, formed when a stream cuts through the soft clays and sandstones at the edge of land. Wind and weathering remove further material, scooping out a deep little valley. Some chines are small-scale features while others such as Blackgang Chine (before landslips destroyed it) reach a significant size. Whale Chine is one of the most sensational examples - so deep and precipitous that the sun rarely penetrates its depths. Its bare walls, scoured by strong winds off the sea, lead down to a wild shingle beach, reached by a flight of 126 timber steps.

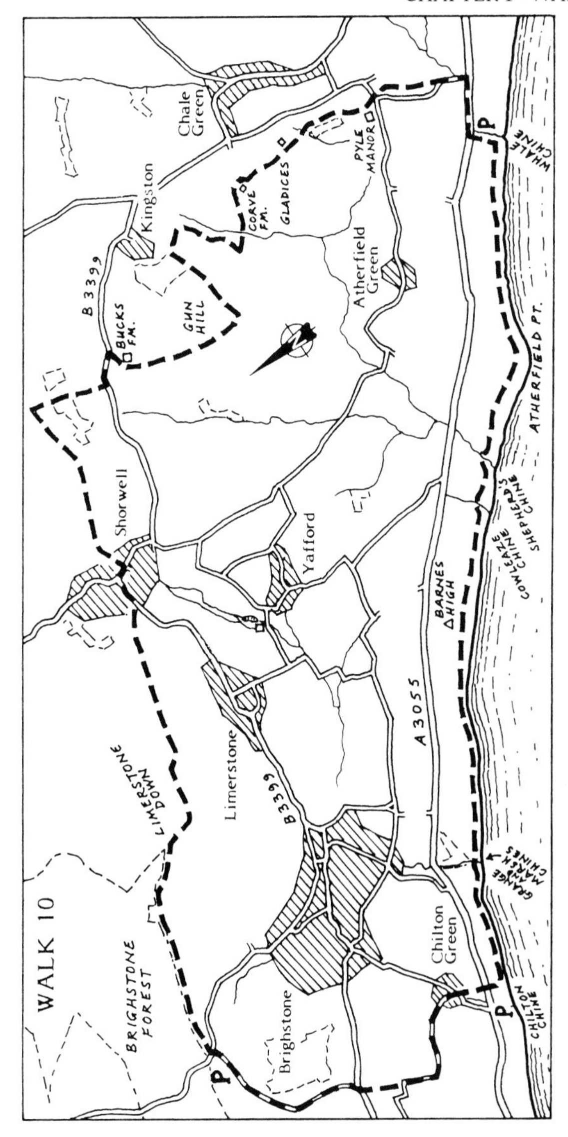
WALK 10
BRIGHSTONE FOREST
Brighstone
LIMERSTONE DOWN
Limerstone
B3399
Shorwell
B 3399
BUCKS FM.
GUN HILL
Kingston
Chale Green
CORVE FM.
GLADICES
PYLE MANOR
Atherfield Green
Yafford
A3055
BARNES HIGH
Chilton Green
CHILTON CHINE
GRANGE MARSH CHINES
COWLEAZE CHINE
SHEPHERD'S CHINE
ATHERFIELD PT.
WHALE CHINE
P
P
P

The chine is thought to take its name from a 63ft (19m) whale stranded here in Chale Bay in 1758.

Leave Whale Chine car park, heading south-east beside the A3055 Military Road and in about 500m turn left into Southdown Lane. At a left bend keep straight ahead uphill (C22) and continue along the ridgetop. When you reach an opening, go half-left, dropping to Chale Lane and turning right along it. At the T-junction just ahead walk straight across and through a small gate, signed 'Pyle' (C20).

The way now crosses a lawn behind Pyle Manor and passes through a large gate into Windmill Copse. Beyond a high deer fence on your right you reach a marshy area equipped with boardwalks then cross a stile into a small paddock. At the next stile keep right through a gate (by some old cars) and you will come out into a lane at Gladices. Turn left for about 50m and at the end of the hedge on your right turn right beside a drainage ditch towards Corve Farm. Approaching the farm you walk up a short, tree-lined track before bearing right between brick and stone barns. Keep left past two fuel tanks then swing right and left to come round the back of the last barn (path SW33). In 50m turn left again (a field ditch now on your left).

At the end of the field turn right for about 100m then cross a stile on your left which can be difficult to spot. Walk ahead to the fence and turn sharp right (SW38), continuing round the same field edge to another stile through the trees. Once over the small footbridge you veer left and arrive at a broad track.

Looking right (north-east) will reveal the little 13th century church at Kingston, perched on its knoll above a 17th century manor house and farm.

The way now heads west along the track (SW56) beside Kingston Copse for about 1/2 mile (800m) then bears right (north) beneath Gun Hill along another wide track (SW54), passing Bucks Farm and reaching the B3399 road.

Turn left along the road and in 400m take a right turn (SW47). After about 300m you will cross a track, continuing via Sheard's Copse to the top of the hill. Here the way turns left (SW11) downhill towards Shorwell, passing through two gates, running along by a hedge and eventually turning left through a gate into

the final field. At the right-hand bottom corner you will emerge onto the B3399 road.

Along to the right stands Shorwell village. Turn left at the mini-roundabout into (appropriately named) Walkers Lane and you will discover the Crown Inn, a 'walker-friendly' establishment with its own trout stream - an excellent place at which to break the walk for lunch.

Surrounded by patches of woodland and set back from the coast in a hollow of the downs, Shorwell exudes considerable olde-worlde charm. St Peter's Church contains a beautifully restored medieval fresco of Christ being carried across a river by St Christopher. The church's interior is divided by slender pillars into three chapels, one for each of the village's manor houses - Northcourt, Westcourt and Wolverton. Less than a mile downstream to the south-west stands Yafford Mill, still in working order and set in 36 acres of countryside with collections of waterfowl and rare breeds of domestic animals.

To resume the walk, carry on west for about 300m along the B3399 and turn right by the last cottage (SW6). In 15m you go through a gate and head diagonally left uphill to a small gate by a hedge in the field's top left-hand corner. Continue along the ridge, passing through three gates then veering right past wind-shaped trees. At the next gate turn left - fence on your left, hill on your right. Ignoring all the gateways overlooking the Limerstone valley, follow the path as it swings right and rises to the top of Limerstone Down.

Here you will turn left along an ancient stony trackway (BS10) which drops steadily beside the edge of Brighstone Forest to meet the Brighstone-Calbourne road at a car park. Bear left into Strawberry Lane.

(About 1/2 mile (800m) down the lane there is short detour, if time and energy allow, to visit the Longstone which is situated 500m due west at the edge of forestry on Mottistone Common. The path climbs gently past Castle Hill, crossing a stile to reach this imposing prehistoric megalith. The 13ft (4m) high sandstone pillar, and an adjacent one lying flat, formed part of the entrance to a neolithic long barrow, or burial chamber, built some 5000 years ago.)

At the end of Strawberry Lane cross the B3399 road into path BS101 then follow twisting Hoxall Lane towards the coast. At Chilton Green turn off left onto BS68 which takes you to the main A3055 coast road.

This so-called Military Road was constructed in the 1860s to link coastal fortifications at a time when the threat of a French invasion seemed very real (although it never materialised). Until the road was built, this exposed western part of the Island was particularly isolated. What settlements there are sprung up a mile or so inland from the eroding, storm-lashed cliffs and are collectively known as Back o' Wight.

Cross the Military Road and take the path to the cliffs between a holiday centre and Isle of Wight Pearl.

The latter houses a comprehensive collection of pearl jewellery, along with production demonstrations, a personalised design service and a (perhaps welcome!) cafe. Admission is free.

A couple of hundred metres back west, the coast path came inland round Chilton Chine, one of the many such features along this stretch of coastline. The sandstones and mudstones which comprise this sector of the Island contain quite numerous fossilised dinosaur bones and footprints - especially those of Iguanadon. It seems likely that such creatures were as common hereabouts 120 million years ago as cattle are today! Furthermore, it is reckoned that their embedded fossils are washed out of the rocks by the sea faster then collectors can save them.

Now turn left along the clifftops above a wild shingle beach. The path quickly passes another holiday centre (mostly converted World War II POW camps) and just beyond Grange Farm camping and caravan site reaches Marsh Chine. The stream itself is spanned by a footbridge but because the chine is badly eroded there's an often muddy scramble up the far side. The way continues outside field fences and within a mile or so rises to the marvellous viewpoint of Barnes High at 174ft (53m) above the sea.

No walker on this part of the coast can ignore the rampant erosion taking place. Here in Brighstone Bay the high cliffs are cracking and slumping seawards at an alarming rate, with as much as 20 inches (0.5m) of farmland lost every year. An underlying layer of Gault clay, known locally as 'blue slipper', is to blame. Percolating springs and rainwater cause the clay surface to act as a lubricant, destabilising the land resting on top; gravity does the rest! The whole process is well beyond man's control and graphically illustrates the relentless power of the elements.

After passing Cowleaze Chine there's another muddy little scramble, this time the other side of Shepherd's Chine (where there's a seasonal cafe at the holiday centre). Alternatively you can cross the chine a little way inland. The onward trail now reaches Atherfield Point and Rocks at the western end of Chale Bay, an infamous lee shore upon which many a vessel foundered in the days of sail.

All along this remote coast, smuggling and wrecking (deliberately luring ships onto rocks for their cargo) were rife in the 18th and 19th centuries. On a more contemporary note, local crab and lobster fishermen do manage to work these uninviting waters; the tall pole and rope above Fishing Cove allows them to haul up their catch, while a little further on steps cut into the soft cliff face provide access to small boats beached on the lower undercliff.

Striding out along gently rising clifftops you soon arrive back at Whale Chine and the end of this circular walk.

CHAPTER 2

The Official Trails

Walk 11: The Freshwater Way
Walk 12: The Nunwell Trail
Walk 13: The Hamstead Trail
Walk 14: The Shepherds Trail
Walk 15: The Stenbury Trail
Walk 16: The Bembridge Trail
Walk 17: The Tennyson Trail
Walk 18: The Worsley Trail

THE TRAILS

The Isle of Wight Council have created and officially designated 8 trails for use by walkers and, on some stretches, by cyclists and horse-riders. The trails combine footpaths, bridleways, ancient tracks and highways, unclassified roads and a few sections of classified road. A ninth trail - the Freshwater Way - is too short in itself to be included officially but because it is often walked as part of a longer circular route it appears in this chapter. The coast path, being a long-distance, multi-day affair appears in a separate chapter (although of course individual shorter sections of it can always be enjoyed on their own).

It has been the Council's policy to waymark their trails with red paint flashes on gates, trees, posts etc. but often these are either indistinct or absent altogether just when you need them most! Each trail has a logo too, but again their appearance is inconsistent. To be fair, waymarking is notoriously difficult to maintain as pathside infrastructure changes and petty vandalism and the elements take their toll. The trails are marked on OS maps (most helpfully on the 1:25,000 Outdoor Leisure Sheet 29) but on the ground some quite intricate navigation is required at times when waymarking is sketchy. The following route descriptions should, however, remove any doubts about which way to go!

Considering that the trails have been established for several decades and are widely publicised in descriptive leaflets at Tourist Information offices, they are surprisingly little walked. Surprisingly because they are all exceptional fine linear rambles exploiting the Island's immensely varied character by linking places north to south, east to west. And along the way there is a wealth of historical, ecological and cultural detail to savour.

In a few locations some of the trails overlap, running 'in tandem' for short distances on their cross-country routes to different destinations. Indeed, it is virtually impossible on such a relatively small island to avoid repeating the best sections of trail here and there.

The trails are arranged in ascending order of length but walkers seeking more challenging distances could well link these trails, or parts of them, together. In fact, armed with a map and the detailed path descriptions contained in this guidebook, there is virtually no limit to the creation of new individualised routes.

WALK 11: THE FRESHWATER WAY

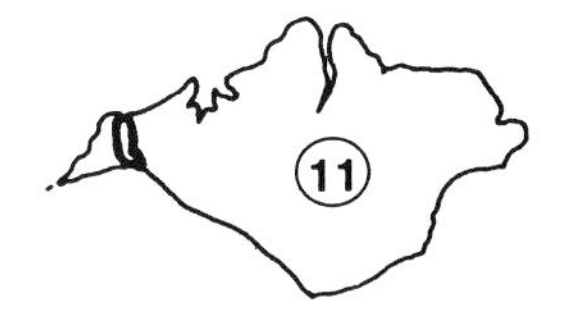

Yarmouth to Freshwater Bay circular.
8 miles (13km)

The designated Freshwater Way runs down the Yar's west shore, samples the coastal downland and Afton Marsh before retracing its steps north. As a variant for the outward leg of the walk we suggest setting off from Yarmouth along the disused railway trackbed on the east shore.

By around 6000BC, rising sea levels had finally broken through the great ridge of chalk that once continued westwards into Dorset, and Wight was truly an island. The River Yar had previously drained into what was then the River Solent; it must have risen far to the south for no river forms such a broad estuary as the Yar's after a journey of only 3 miles (5km)! With its rivermouth flooded to create a natural harbour, the Yar graphically illustrates how landscapes have changed in recent geological times.

Despite, or perhaps because of, its compact size, Yarmouth has great visitor appeal. A variety of shops and eating places can be discovered by wandering through the narrow streets dominated by the 17th century church tower behind the square. But it is a town with a history too.

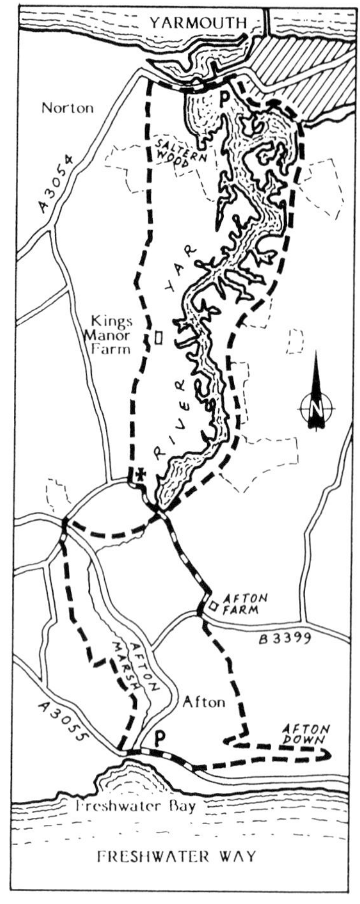

In common with other Island market towns, Yarmouth had suffered at the hands of the French since medieval times. As part of his strategy to counter the threat, Henry VIII ordered the building of a seafront castle. Squat, massively constructed and equipped to accommodate the heavier cannon of the period, Yarmouth castle has survived intact down the centuries so that today you can visit the Master Gunner's quarters and scan the wide Solent panormama just as those Tudor gunners did 450 years ago. Except that the scene has changed somewhat! Yarmouth is the docking point for the Lymington ferry and the harbour is a colourful forest of yacht masts and hulls, backed by a busy boatyard and overseen by the imposing presence of 'Arun' class lifeboat *Joy and John Wade*.

In 1667 Sir John Holmes, Governor of the Island, had the castle moat drained and built a large residence nearby in which he entertained Charles II; it is now the George Hotel. In and around Yarmouth's picturesque square stand the old town hall, rebuilt in 1764, and a number of fine 18th century buildings. The pier is Victorian, intended for the steamer trade and now a marvellous viewpoint.

Start from the large car park east of the rivermouth near the ferry terminal (Grid Ref: 354895). To begin with you can either walk inland along the grassy estuary shore; or you can turn south off the main A3054 into Mill Road. Both routes lead quickly to a tarmac path past houses which crosses an arm of the Yar near the old tide mill, complete with sluices. Prior to the construction of Yarmouth's modern harbour, there was sufficient depth of water at the mill for cargoes of grain to be unloaded there.

At a bench you bear right to join a pedestrian and cycle route along the trackbed of the former Freshwater, Yarmouth and Newport Railway which carried passengers on this most scenic of lines from 1889 until 1953. The trackway snakes along the estuary shore whose habitats are shared by seabirds, waders, ducks and geese, depending on the season. In the patches of woodland passed through you may catch a glimpse of red squirrels.

There are footpaths off the trail to Thorley and Willmingham before it arrives at a road opposite Freshwater Church - the estuary's tidal limit. Turn left along The Causeway road and at Afton Farm you will meet the B3399 (bus stop). Turn left and in 20m cross over to enter a track on the right (Manor Road). In 50m fork left (bridleway F31) onto a field path heading towards the base of Afton Down where, just beyond a gate, you encounter a cross-track.

Here the Pilgrims Way (F32) heads east, but the Freshwater Way turns up right (west) for 100m before doubling back left (east). Higher up on Afton Down beside golf links, the chalky bridleway swings right to join the Tennyson Trail. At this point the Freshwater Way begins its return leg to Yarmouth by bearing due west downhill on F33, the old highway from Carisbrooke. As you stride out down the breezy slopes ahead, there are superb coastal and inland views.

A lane lower down leads out to the A3055 Military Road. Turn right and follow the verge down into Freshwater Bay.

This tiny, semicircular cove, formed where the original River Yar had cut through the chalk hills on its journey north, can seem an elemental place when a heavy swell roars against the cliffs and stacks bounding it on both sides. When the West Wight forts were built as part of Lord Palmerston's coastal defences in the mid 19th century, so much shingle was dredged from the beach for use in construction that the sea broke through into the low-lying Yar valley. For a time Freshwater and the western peninsula became a separate island. To prevent a recurrence, the bay is backed by a very substantial sea wall and promenade.

Famous residents of Freshwater Bay include Alfred, Lord Tennyson who bought Farringford just to the west (now a hotel) and entertained many contemporary celebrities; and Julia Cameron, the pioneer portrait photographer who lived at Dimbola in the main street near the coastal path turning to Tennyson Down. Famous for its artists and writers, Freshwater attracted increasing numbers of visitors and remains a popular beauty spot to this day. Summertime brings throngs of sightseers who are catered for by several hotels, cafes and shops.

Behind the seafront take Coastguard Lane leading north onto path F32. You are soon treading sections of boardwalk through Afton Marsh Nature Reserve.

This Site of Special Scientific Interest is an important reed-bed habitat for a rich variety of plants, insects and birds, including reed and sedge warblers and kingfishers. Owned by South Wight Borough Council, the Reserve is currently managed in conjunction with the Countryside Management Service.

Where the path splits, either branch will bring you out to the road near Black Bridge. Turn left then right into Easton Lane and in about 400m watch for a stile on the right, sometimes obscured by greenery. Walk along the top of the fields behind houses (on F37), following overhead wires and passing through a gate into a path between fence and trees. Posts lead the way across a private garden and another gate takes you past the back doors of houses and out to the road opposite Stroud playing fields.

Turn right along to the main A3055 at a foodstore, cross the road straight ahead and in only 50m up Hooke Hill turn right into The Crundles, a residential road. Almost immediately fork right

on path F38 along by a fence. The trail weaves between high reed beds and unseen water channels - an intimate encounter with the Yar environment before, at the blocked road bridge ahead, it becomes tidal. Alternatively, use the old railway trackbed.

Turn left along the road past a wartime bunker and bear right just before the Red Lion pub, alongside All Saints Church graveyard wherein lies buried Emily, Tennyson's wife. Soon on a tarred lane (F1), the Way continues due north, a field's width away from the Yar, until just short of Kings Manor Farm you go over a stile on the left and bear right behind the farm buildings. After passing through a planted tree enclosure you turn left up a field track which curves right, becomes grassier and fenced and drops gently to a footbridge over a stream in trees off to the right of the main track.

Walk up the field headland and cross a stile to the other side of the hedge. The Way drops prettily through Saltern Wood and meets a rough road. Turn left and this will lead you to the pavement flanking the A3054. The walk's starting point is a simple 500m away over Yar Bridge from where there are comprehensive views of the estuary and harbour.

WALK 12:
THE NUNWELL TRAIL

Ryde to Sandown.
8 miles (13km)

Just as the Hamstead Trail traverses the Island's western sector, so the Nunwell Trail makes a similar crossing in the east. From the busy seaside town and ferry port of Ryde, suburban roads give way to lowland countryside past farms and copses to Nunwell House, the walk's focal point. Climbing over the ridge of chalk downs which extend along the length of the Island brings the trail down to Alverstone hamlet in the marshy valley of the East Yar

river. A further hour's easy walking and you arrive at the traditional family resort of Sandown. The Nunwell Trail officially begins and ends at railway stations, facilitating a straightforward return to the start by using the Island Line's ex-London Underground electric trains.

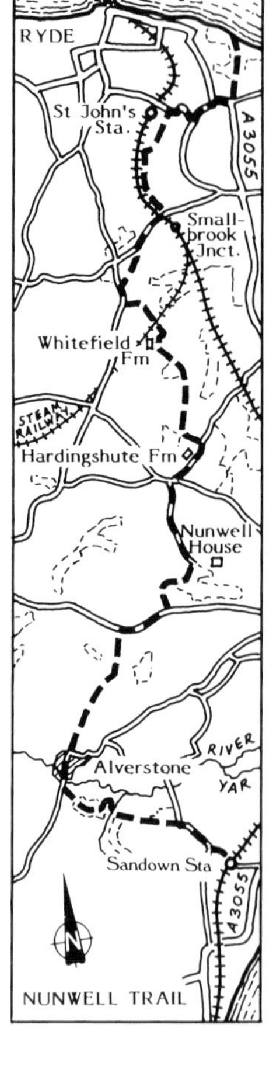

Ryde, 'Gateway to the Island', is a bustling place. In addition to catering for holidaymakers who flock here in the summer, the town also fleetingly hosts many thousands of visitors from mainland UK who arrive by ferry, catamaran or hovercraft en route for other Island destinations.

The town developed rapidly after the pier was built in 1824, saving steamer passengers an exposed ride by horse and carriage over the vast sand flats that extend out from the shore at low tide. Forty years later the railway came, accelerating the growth of Victorian resorts such as Ryde and Shanklin which it linked. There are miles of sandy beaches, a busy town centre sloping down to the sea, impressive Victorian terraces, now mostly hotels, and good leisure amenities on the long, reclaimed seafront. Wide views of the Solent with its three forts are animated by an endless procession of shipping, from huge oil tankers and naval vessels to yachts and hovercraft. The latter will whisk you across the water to Southsea in just 9 minutes!

Whilst starting at St John's Station south of the town (Grid Ref: 596919) may prove convenient for some, others may prefer Esplanade Station by the Pier (Grid Ref: 594929). In fact the following route description guides you along the seafront on the coastal path, reaching the Nunwell Trail's official start at St John's Station via Appley Park - a much more attractive beginning

than traffic-choked town streets.

From the Pier set off east past the Ice Rink, harbour and bowling greens seaward of the main Esplanade road. In summer a tractor-hauled Dotto Train plies along the prom. Keep close to the shore along North Walk, with swimming pool and boating lake on your right, until you reach the Inshore Rescue Lookout post adjacent to Appley Beach. Here you need to take Appley Lane up past the car park; it rises, tree-lined, to the B3330 Appley Road. Turn right alongside the A3055 for 200m then bear left, back on the B3330. Follow this road (St John's Hill) down, and just past a left-hand bend watch out for Oakfield's High Street over on your left. Pass a few shops and continue to the far end where you turn down right (Slade Road) to find bridleway R54 on the left. (Walkers starting from St John's Station simply go up St John's Hill and turn right into the High Street.)

Held between trees at first, the track soon emerges into the open beside the railway line where you may well encounter one of the ex-Piccadilly Line trains clattering by. At the road bridge ahead turn right along Smallbrook Lane.

Four hundred metres beyond the road bridge lies Smallbrook Junction, an important cross-platform interchange between British Rail's Island Line and the privately owned Isle of Wight Steam Railway. On steam operating days the two contrasting railways can be linked (but there is no road or footpath access to Smallbrook Junction station).

Closed in 1966 by the infamous Dr Beeching and re-opened in 1971, the steam branch line, run mainly by volunteers, uses locomotives and rolling stock of exceptional vintage. Skilfully restored, many examples are over 100 years old. The principal station and operational centre is situated at Havenstreet, a couple of miles to the east of Smallbrook. There you will find an interesting museum-cum-gallery, a souvenir and book shop, refreshment bar and picnic area, children's adventure playground, as well as all the sights, sounds and smells of a functioning steam railway. The line runs for 5 miles (8km) between Smallbrook Junction and Wootton via Ashey and Havenstreet.

Smallbrook Lane provides a none-too-pleasant 500m without a verge to walk on. However, a diversion introduced in recent

years cuts the corner to Ashey Road by using path R50 over a stile on the left. Initially you are on an untidy bank (at the time of writing) above a playing field but by maintaining the same south-westerly direction you pass a sports centre and stadium before veering half-right at some caravans to reach the Ashey Road.

Turn left, past Oak Cottage livery stables, and at Kerry Cottage turn left into bridleway R35 for Brading Down. The track twists and turns past a bungalow before crossing the railway branch line. At two large oak trees ahead, go through a field gate and turn right to Whitefield farm, passing between the barns and bearing left at a signed junction. A right turn, back on the bridleway, takes you straight over fields and up the edge of a small wood where a field gate keeps you on course towards distant Brading Down, now with a hedge on your left. Continue up the next field with hedge to your right and at the corner of Broadley Copse turn sharp left along to the country lane which is reached near a charming little duckpond. The trail turns right here, past Hardingshute Farm to a road junction with West Lane (leading to nearby Brading). Turn right then immediately left into Nunwell Farm Lane. A little further on two paths lead off to the west, while the long-distance Bembridge Trail, having come down past the farm, heads east across fields towards Brading. The Nunwell Trail continues on the lane to the half-timbered West Lodge where it veers up right (bridleway N59) beside a wood.

Below you, though unseen, stands Nunwell House. It was the seat of the Oglander family since Norman times when, upon William the Conqueror's instigation, Richard d'Oglandres became lord of the manor here. A well known 17th century Oglander - the royalist and diarist Sir John - is buried in Brading's St Mary's Church and commemorated there by a wooden effigy. As a guest of Sir John, Charles I spent his last night of freedom at Nunwell House in November 1647 before his incarceration in Carisbrooke Castle and subsequent execution. Nunwell House itself, present home of the Aylmer family, is not easy to view from a distance, being surrounded by 6 acres of landscaped grounds. It is, however, open to the public on some days during the summer and contains a military museum.

A gate at the top of the short bridleway leads out onto a track

running beneath glorious beech woods on the steep flanks of Nunwell Down. Turn right and in 100m fork left, climbing round Nunwell Down onto the crest of Brading Down to meet the main Newport to Brading road.

Not only are views from here quite magnificent, taking in the whole of west Wight, Spithead and the Solent, but the chalk ridge itself is of interest for its grassland flora.

Turn right along the verge and in 500m take the fenced bridleway on the left for Alverstone. A mile or so of steady descent brings the trail to the access lane for Southview Nursery and, further down, the Alverstone Road.

Alverstone hamlet sits in the middle of a long stretch of copses, wetlands and tributary streams surrounding the East Yar river. In spring and summer the water plants and wildflowers for which the area is locally renowned brighten the marshes, while reed beds shelter wading birds and warblers.

Walk south along the road for about 150m, crossing the disused railway trackbed; beyond a bridge turn left at a gate (NC42). The way curves right over a meadow and through two stiles, rising to become a delightful terraced path beneath sweet-chestnut and oak trees on steep hillside. At a sign for Sandown opposite a house, turn sharp left and follow the trail's big loop, passing a path to Adgestone. To resume its easterly progress, the trail turns left through a gate and crosses a footbridge over the marshy course of Scotchells Brook, a tributary of the nearby Yar.

You now climb to a gate and keep to the main route through oak woods, haunt of owl and nightingale. To your right, behind the trees, appears the golf course on Lake Common and soon after you reach a lane near a water pumping station.

Turn right, walking along the lane for about 400m to a right bend. Here the Nunwell Trail carries straight ahead along a narrow footpath beside a playing field. Approaching the railway line, cross the road and go through the underpass, turning left towards Sandown Station which is now directly in front of you - the official end of the trail (Grid Ref: 593845). Those wishing to return direct to Ryde can catch a train and be there in 25 minutes! Others who wish to explore Sandown first can continue down Station Avenue almost to the seafront about ½ mile (800m) away.

With an enviable sunshine record, plenty of accommodation and amenities, and a safe sandy beach, little wonder that Sandown has established itself as a traditional family holiday resort.

Of special interest to walkers will be the Isle of Wight Geological Museum above the Library at the eastern end of the High Street. Elsewhere, old barracks and forts around which the town grew up have found other uses; best known is Sandown Zoo, famous for its big cats. There are numerous local walks - along the seafront in both directions, or inland to Yaverland and Brading. Within the town itself, all west of the Pavilion Theatre and well worth visiting, can be found Los Altos Park, Ferncliff Gardens and the clifftop Battery Gardens.

WALK 13: THE HAMSTEAD TRAIL

Newtown Bay to Brook Bay.
8 miles (13km)

This north-to-south crossing of the Island's western sector makes an ideal half-day walk. Alternatively, by lingering to watch wildlife and take in all the views, perhaps with a picnic thrown in for good measure, it could occupy a very enjoyable day. The route starts from the Solent coast by threading the banks of the River Newtown's estuary before striking off cross-country along often wooded tracks to the tiny hamlet of Wellow at roughly the halfway point. Field paths through lovely rolling countryside take you to the foot of the downs and a climb to Bronze Age barrows overlooking the entire west coast and much of the north coast too in one magnificent panorama. A final descent on coastbound bridleways brings you out at the coarse sandy beach and low cliffs of Brook Bay.

Reaching the official start of the Hamstead Trail near Hamstead Point (Grid Ref: 405920) is somewhat problematic! Served only by unsurfaced roads and tracks, the communities west of the

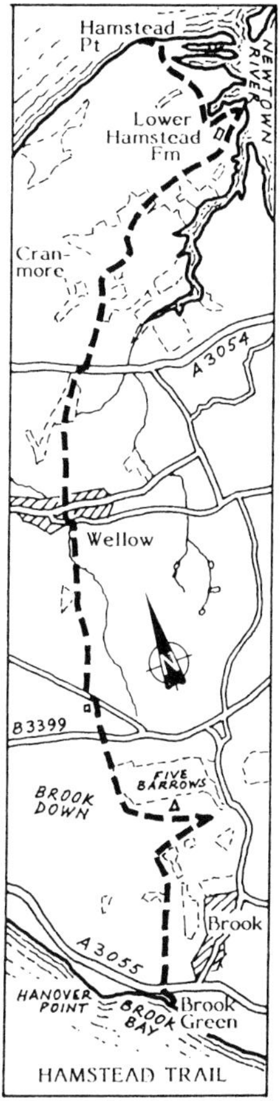

Newtown river are some of the most remote on the Island. One possibility would be to start at Bouldner, just east of Yarmouth, and walk along the coast path to Hamstead Cliffs. This would add about 3 miles (5km) to the route.

Hamstead Cliffs contain several Sites of Special Scientific Interest for it is here that fossil-rich clay strata from the Oligocene period are exposed more accessibly than anywhere else on earth. Marine erosion is mainly responsible and it is advisable not to wander seawards from the path onto the adjacent slumping undercliff.

Initially the trail hugs the backshore, bright with sea pinks next to the Solent's glittering waters. It passes a small Celtic cross on the right - a memorial to two men tragically drowned just offshore in 1932. Once round Hamstead Point, watch for steps in the bank (S3) at a 'Permanent Footpath Diversion' sign. The field path leads to a long timber footbridge spanning a creek. Next, angle half-left across pasture, over a stile in trees and turn right along the field edge to the head of a marshy inlet which is crossed on a series of boardwalks.

HAMSTEAD TRAIL

Swinging east, the way shadows the estuary banks in fields and reaches a stony track. To your left are slipways and a small quay for yachts. A brickyard once stood here at Western Haven, associated with the Hamstead estate under the ownership of the architect John Nash. Bricks and locally produced salt were transported across the Solent from here and from Newtown quay opposite - busy times, quite unlike today's peaceful seclusion.

You now turn right (south-west) along a shady track (S28) past Lower Hamstead Farm. It undulates gently through conifer forest and eventually meets a north-south cross track. Turn left and in

150m fork right on S29. This takes you past Silver Glade Caravan Park to another junction at Solent Road post box. Fork left past bungalows, once again on a rough but motorable road typical of this area.

When you reach the A3054, turn right and in 20m cross the road and take a stile into a belt of woodland. (NB: Woods marked on the Outdoor Leisure map have been partially cleared.) Go straight ahead then angle slightly right over the field to pick up the next stile in trees at the far side (now on S8 to Wellow).

Weaving through woods which are quite overgrown in summer, you'll emerge in a field; keep along by the right-hand edge with open views of tree-topped downland. Further field edges are followed in the same direction, crossing the undergrowth-choked dismantled railway and leading into Wellow.

Such a sleepy hamlet! Yet this little cluster of stone farm buildings and cottages was once a hideaway for contraband on the smuggling route from west and south Wight to the mainland.

Cross the B3401 to a cottage, walk over tiny Thorley Brook and continue along the residential lane, turning left at County Lane. In 50m turn right on bridleway S19 which heads off south over a vast crop field towards Hummet Copse. As you gradually gain height there are marvellous views back north to the Solent coast. Go through the gate to the left of the trees; further on, beyond a disused quarry, the trail reaches Broad Lane, the country road from Thorley to Shalcombe.

Here you turn left and in 50m fork right on bridleway S10, at first a tarmac driveway to The Quarries. Leave it after 100m by carrying straight on up the hedge-lined, grassy track, crossing the B3401 road and continuing uphill onto Wellow Down. The narrow path now follows the edge of a wood on the left and after passing through 2 gates you are veering south-east to meet the Tennyson Trail on the crest of Brook Down.

If visibility is good, leave the main track and take the detour path over Five Barrows. The trig pillar stands rather incongruously amongst the prehistoric burial mounds at 538ft (164m) above sea level. Long ago, before woodland was cleared and land cultivated, these chalk downs provided the only safe trade route for our Iron and Bronze Age ancestors. Burying their dead on this ridgeway and other hills reflects the importance they attached to such places. The panorama is indeed 360 degrees, with the entire west coast from Tennyson Down to St Catherine's Point featuring prominently. In early summer the springy turf of these chalk downs, protected by the National Trust and undisturbed for many years, supports numerous wildflower species such as cowslips, harebells and several varieties of orchid; these, in turn, attract clouds of butterflies.

Walk south from Five Burrows back onto the main track as it descends towards the Brook to Chessell road. The track's continuation as it climbs Pay Down is clearly visible ahead. Before reaching the bottom of the slope, the Hamstead Trail doubles sharply back to the right (west). Once on this path you will soon top a rise with Tennyson Down in the distance; keep left here. The path now drops gently beside a wood, crosses a stile and arrives at a corner facing open fields. Turn left but not down the main track. Instead take the grassy ramp just above it and go through a rickety gate. The way continues south down the rather overgrown ancient road between hedges (BS86a) to a gate and lane at Dunsbury Farm. In order to circumvent the farm complex, the trail turns right then left and follows the lane as it sweeps south-west past a few houses.

Although 'olde worlde' Brook village itself isn't visited by the Hamstead Trail, it lies very close, an ancient settlement mentioned in the Domesday Book. Brook contains two buildings of note, both named on the Outdoor Leisure map. Brooke House is associated with the 19th century Italian patriot, Giuseppe Garibaldi (of squashed-fly biscuit fame?!) who planted an oak tree there. Brook Hill House, set on a wooded hill to the north-east above the little church, was once the home of the author J.B. Priestley. It was also owned by the Seely family, great local benefactors who built schools, helped establish a library service and provided Seely Hall in the village as a reading room and exhibition space.

Back on the trail's final leg - when the tarmac ends, continue straight ahead along the grassy bridleway to a house. Cross the lane and walk through a field to a stile at the A3055 Military Road where the trail officially ends (Grid Ref: 384836).

A short distance to the left you can take path BS51 from the car park down Brook Chine. Over to the left stands a scattering of cottages at Brook Green and one of the Island's earliest lifeboat stations, built here in 1860 and in service for 53 years. (For details of the Coastal Path which passes Brook Bay, please refer to the relevant section of the long-distance Coastal Path walk.)

Yellow-brown, slumping cliffs of clay and sand along this eroding part of the coast are renowned for their butterflies and fossils. It is said that at one time fossilised dinosaur bones were so common that they were used by villagers as doorstops! On the same theme, the fossilised stumps of a conifer 'log-jam' in an ancient river are exposed off Hanover Point at very low spring tides.

The conspicuous stone pillar is of much more recent origin. It was built during the Napoleonic Wars as a marker for the cannon at Fort Redoubt on the west side of Freshwater Bay: firing only to seaward of the marker was meant to ensure the safety of those on land.

WALK 14: THE SHEPHERDS TRAIL

Carisbrooke to
Shepherd's Chine.
9 miles (15km)

Although not long, this trail is likely to take most walkers the better part of a day. Of all 9 officially designated walking routes, the Shepherds Trail is the most rural, weaving through the deepest countryside and passing nowhere larger than Chillerton village at about halfway. There are sections of ancient trackway interspersed with field paths, bridleways and a few country lanes on this peaceful walk far from the madding crowd. Careful route finding is necessary in places and with no refreshments available, food and drink will need to be carried.

The Shepherds Trail's official starting point is Whitcombe Cross (Grid Ref: 487874) just south of Carisbrooke Castle. Because it is so close, an hour or two spent looking around the castle first will probably appeal to many walkers.

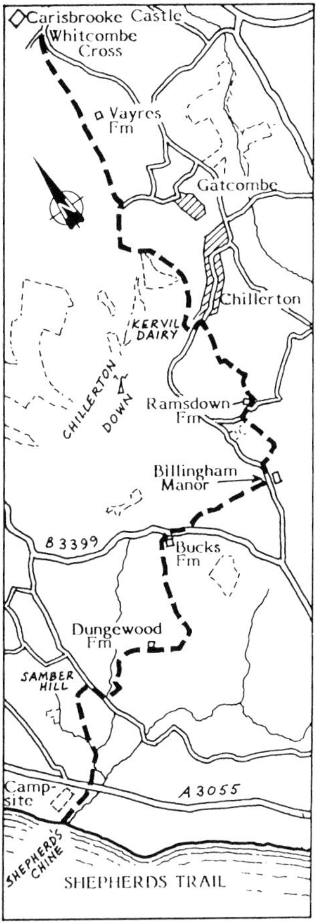

Following the Norman invasion of 1066, William the Conqueror's new regime included equipping the Isle of Wight as a defensive outpost, a role it would play for many years to come. The first Island lordship was granted to a friend, William FitzOsbern, and Carisbrooke Castle was built on a steep chalk spur overlooking the Bowcombe valley through which flows Lukely Brook. For much of its time the official residence of the Island's governor, the castle today is one of Wight's great historical showpieces, with wonderfully preserved ramparts, governor's appartments, domestic buildings and gateway, all maintained by English Heritage. In 1817 the poet John Keats, greatly impressed, wrote: "I have not seen many specimens of ruins. I don't think, however, I shall ever see one to surpass Carisbrooke Castle".

From the castle car park turn south-east through a handgate into Carisbrooke Walk and turn down the steep defensive bank off the first corner. This leads into a path tightly hugged between hedges, first dropping then rising to Froglands Lane. Turn left to the road at Whitcombe Cross. The trail now turns sharp right - not along the road but onto bridleway N108 for Gatcombe which runs parallel to the road at first.

Soon you are walking in an old sunken trackway, a tunnel through a hidden world of ferns, tree roots and earthy banks. This is Dark Lane, an excellent example of a medieval 'hollow way'. During the strengthening of Carisbrooke Castle by the addition of its great stone ramparts in the early 1100s, building stone was carted along this very route from quarries around Gat Cliff near Godshill, and near Gatcombe.

Eventually you will emerge, blinking, into open fields encircled by distant hills with the TV mast on Chillerton Down a conspicuous feature. Ignoring the left turn to Vayres Farm, the trail continues along field headlands through handgates and reaches low cliffs where the land's strata is bared above the tiny village of Gatcombe nestling in a fold of the downs.

Cross the track ahead and descend through a copse and past the Isle of Wight Hunt kennels to reach a country lane. Turn right then follow Newbarn Lane as it curves to the left (south-west). In about 400m the lane veers sharp right to Newbarn Farm and the downs but the Shepherds Trail turns left (south-east). The chalky bridleway (G6) now climbs to the neck of Tolt Copse, joining a track coming in from the right. Fifty metres ahead turn right down a field edge (still on G6). One's impression here is of penetrating typically English countryside of the most beautiful kind; crop fields and pasture on gently sloping hillsides are overlooked by dark-shadowed woods of oak, beech and chestnut. At a gate you have a glimpse of Chillerton village down to your left, in contrast to the graceful swell of Chillerton Down topped by its TV mast now less than a mile away. Rounded hollows on the flanks of the down are old chalk pits. **Soon the sunken track descends to a country road at the southern end of Chillerton village, the only settlement of any size passed through on the Shepherds Trail.**

Though composed of predominantly modern buildings today, Chillerton and neighbouring Gatcombe both appear in the Domesday census of 1086. They share a lovely little 13th century, gargoyled church - that of St Olave situated near Gatcombe House. Its fascinating interior includes stained glass designs from the 19th century Pre-Raphaelite period. Gatcombe House itself, best viewed from the east, was put up in 1750 for the Worsley family of Appuldurcombe House, near Godshill. Both church and house can be reached from Chillerton by a pleasant detour (a mile each way) through fields and woods past Sheat Manor.

Turn left along the Chillerton Road at Kervil Dairy and in 150m go right into Hollow lane (G15a). Beyond Hollow Lane Cottage the old bridleway lives up to its name, deeply overhung with tree roots and vegetation. Steadily gaining 220ft (67m) of height, the trail arrives at a corner of open fields. Keep ahead under telegraph wires to reach a cross-track at right angles on the ridgetop.

Bridleway G15a now turns right and descends gently past an old barn and through Ramsdown Farm. At the lane turn right; about 200m after it swings left, look out for a grassy path heading south-east down a field edge on the left. (This short stretch of country lane just walked is shared with the Worsley Trail.) You soon pass Berry Copse, descending a little then veering west to meet the road near West Billingham Farm. Turn left and in 200m turn right (SW43).

Behind you stands haunted Billingham Manor, the pre-war home of the author J.B. Priestley (who later bought Brooke Hill House further west near the Hamstead Trail). We don't know whether Priestley ever saw the ghostly head of Charles I which reputedly appeared whenever an execution took place at the Island's Parkhurst Prison!

Walking due west you now follow a grassy track along field boundaries; it jinks to the right at one point but westerly progress is quickly resumed. Gradually converging with the B3399, the trail crosses a final field to a white house and turns right along the roadside. In 200m turn left onto bridleway SW54, passing to the right of Bucks Farm holiday cottages on a broad, stony drive. Past the farm it bears left (south-west), becoming a sandy field track with the English Channel in sight ahead.

After 1km you reach a cross-track and turn right (SW56); this ancient trackway swings north-west between hedges and drops towards Dungewood Farm where it becomes the metalled Dungewood Lane. Several bends later at the T-junction, turn right on the Atherfield Road and in 300m turn left through an opening, heading due west across a large field on Samber Hill. A signpost for path SW22a indicates a left turn down the field track. Where it bends to the right, keep straight on with a ditch to your left. Follow the field headland to the right and traverse the last

field to arrive at the A3055 Military Road. Cross over and take the footpath below the campsite running seaward down Shepherd's Chine whose meandering stream is flanked by unstable, landslip-prone banks (Grid Ref: 447798).

'Chine' is a local name for the narrow ravines which form such a distinctive feature of the Island's southern coastline. Stream beds cut into the soft clays and sandstones are scooped out and enlarged by the action of strong winds. Most dramatic of all is Whale Chine, just to the south, its walls precipitous and bare, but most other chines, in various stages of evolution, are vegetated. Along with the slumped undercliffs, these habitats provide shelter for small birds and represent one of the main breeding areas for the Glanville Fritillary butterfly which feeds off ribwort plantain and is unique to the Isle of Wight and the Channel Islands.

WALK 15:
THE STENBURY TRAIL

Newport to Ventnor Botanic Gardens.
11 miles (18km)

Like the Bembridge Trail, the Stenbury Trail begins at Shide on the south-eastern outskirts of Newport. A disused railway trackbed sets you on course south to Blackwater where farm lanes and tracks through gentle countryside lead on to the much-visited, picturesque village of Godshill, famous for its model village. An old coach road and a short section in tandem with the Worsley Trail beneath Gat Cliff brings the way beneath Appuldurcombe and Stenbury downs which are climbed for an exhilarating stretch of high level walking with wonderful views. For its finale the trail descends from the hilltops and drops through the Undercliff near St Lawrence to end at Ventnor Botanic Gardens. A southerly aspect, sheltered from north winds, supports species that would not survive a mainland winter.

As well as having a fascinating history, aspects of which are described at the start of the Bembridge Trail, Newport is also the Isle of Wight's modern administrative and shopping centre. No longer are 'beast markets' held in St James's Square, but a stall market may be browsed around each Tuesday and Friday. Elsewhere in the town are many familiar chain stores and individual retail shops; there are pubs, cafes, restaurants and hotels too. The Tourist Information Centre is situated near the bus station on South Street.

From St Thomas' Church walk south along Town Lane, cross South Street into Church Litten and turn left on Medina Avenue. This curves southward from the junction with St George's Approach and passes the entrance to Cypress Road, the location of Newport's Roman Villa.

Built on or near an earlier Iron Age settlement, the original Roman farmstead would almost certainly have kept flocks of sheep on the nearby chalk downs. Although at the time there were no significant towns or roads, trade was nevertheless important, hence the siting of Wight's Roman villas near seaports. Within Newport's villa can be found a reconstructed Roman kitchen and an interesting centrally-heated bath system.

From the end of Medina Avenue turn left and in about 150m, opposite the 'Barley Mow' pub, set off along the trackbed of the dismantled railway which is also a route for cyclists. In a little over a mile you cross a small bridge where the River Medina, accompanied closely since Shide,

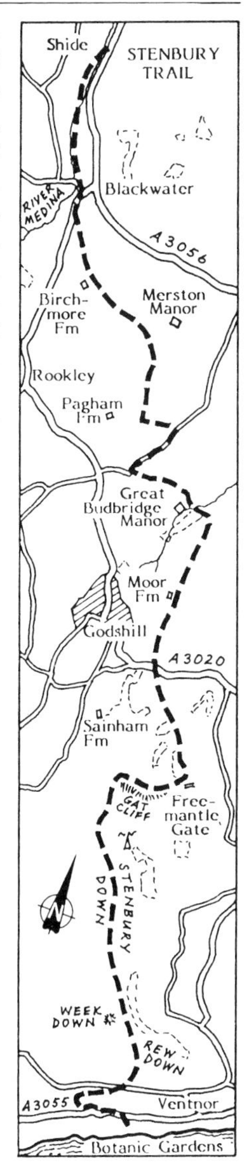

meanders away to the south-west.

Turn left along Sandy Lane to reach Blackwater Bridge opposite a garage and turn right along the A3020 through the village. Watch for a left fork into an access lane by a thatched house (Bridleway SA36). Follow this lane south-east, forking left to pass Birchmore Farm. The lane narrows to pass Stenbury House then becomes a track. Shortly beyond a path on the left to Merston Manor, you reach a field lane at right-angles.
NB: The next short field section may not be waymarked and is subject to crop planting. Carry straight ahead towards the field boundary, veering right along by a drainage ditch. Pass through a couple of gates and bear south-south-east until you reach bridleway SA35 a little way east of Pagham Farm. Now turn left and follow the bridleway to Merston Lane opposite Alma Cottage. A right turn here gives you about 600m of road walking; at a sharp right bend the trail heads due east on a field track (A32). There's a small jink before you cross the disused railway (a branch of the one followed from Shide to Blackwater) and soon you are walking past a row of conifers screening glasshouses at Great Budbridge Manor. Bear right at the junction ahead on the A49 to Godshill, past a gateway revealing the fine old manor house reflected in its foreground lake. The way now swings east again, crosses the infant River Yar and veers right (south) from a wood on a straightforward sandy field track to Moor Farm (GL46) and onwards to meet the A3020 Shanklin Road just east of Godshill.

During holiday periods visitors flock here to view the delightful model village, built to 1/10th scale and based on both Shanklin and Godshill itself. The Natural History Centre, with its collection of minerals and fossils and its marine aquariums, all contained in a 17th century coaching house, provides another fascinating venue. As indeed does the Nostalgic Toy Museum displaying largely pre-war models.

There is, however, another side to Godshill than all the attractions, pubs and tea-rooms, one that is perhaps best appreciated out of season. Rows of thatched, stone-built houses line the main street leading up to lovely All Saints Church. Nearby Old Bell Cottage was once a pub! Legend has it that the church's original masons began laying its foundations on a flatter site but each morning the stones

Looking west over Whitwell to St Catherine's Down from Stenbury Down

had mysteriously transported themselves to the hilltop. Believing a power greater than Man had ordained this strange phenomenon, the builders eventually gave in and constructed the church where it stands today. Inside, a unique medieval fresco, rediscovered under old paint in Victorian times, depicts Christ crucified on a three-branched lily.

The Stenbury Trail doesn't actually venture into Godshill but at the main road turns left then immediately right onto the former coaching drive leading towards Appuldurcombe House. Keep straight on past a path left to Redhill Lane and one right to Sainham. The sandy track continues gently uphill to Freemantle Gate.

This imposing, 3-arched gateway bears above its central arch a griffin, or wyvern - a mythical dragon adopted by the Worsleys of Appuldurcombe as its family insignia. As well as the Griffin pub, many other connections with Appuldurcombe can be found in Godshill.

Don't pass through the gateway but instead turn up right beside the edge of Freemantle Copse on bridleway GL49 to Stenbury. Beyond a handgate the trail continues up a field by the old Appuldurcombe estate wall, following it along through a muddy hollow in pasture beneath Gat Cliff. In fact a spur path leads off to the left where a short but stiff climb brings you to the Worsley Monument, a granite obelisk put up in 1774 by Sir Richard Worsley of Appuldurcombe House in memory of his grandfather, Sir Robert. Interestingly, Gat Cliff was a major source of building stone for Carisbrooke Castle.

Continue along the top edge of the pasture field until you reach a handgate. Here, walk down ahead into the copse and pass through a high deer gate on the track coming in from Sainham Deer Park, established to breed red deer in 1987. Go straight across and through the next gate, still on GL49 for Stenbury Down. The trail curves left (south), climbs a little then contours along field headlands beneath the flanks of Appuldurcombe Down with wide views to westward.

Before long the path makes a determined, if muddy, ascent onto Stenbury Down, reaching the top adjacent to a radio station mast. With a feeling of being on top of the world, the delightful grassy path heads along to the next mast but about 200m before reaching it, go through a handgate on the left in a hedge corner to join a surfaced access lane. Follow the lane until it veers sharp left down towards Wroxall and from then on keep straight ahead by the hedge on GL51.

At a field gate ahead, keep left now on V61 to Upper Ventnor along the crest of Stenbury and Week downs from where much of the southern Island can be seen, including, far to the west, the swell of St Catherine's Down. Beyond a path on the right to St Lawrence, you are on V38. A tumulus marks the summit of Week Down at 690ft (210m) above sea level and then you are alongside golf links on Rew Down.

The Stenbury Trail now descends through gorse and low, scrubby woods, passing several turnings left towards Ventnor. Finally on V56 above a sports field, you reach the Whitwell Road appropriately at a 'Welcome to Ventnor' road sign! Turn right and

The Medieval Pepper Pot lighthouse on St Catherine's Hill

The beached paddle steamer *Ryde Queen*

Walkers at the Longstone, a megalith dating from the New Stone Ag

Ventnor seafront

in 150m cross the road into bridleway V73 which, as Paradise Walk, slants down through luxuriant woods below the richly weathered limestone crags of the Undercliff. The bridleway eventually bears down left into Inglewood Park bungalow estate. Walk down the road where a short-cut path on the right quickly reaches the A3055. Turn left and in 300m you will arrive at Ventnor Botanic Gardens, southern terminus of the Stenbury Trail (Grid Ref: 547768).

Sheltered by the downs from cold north and north-easterly airstreams and enjoying an exceptionally mild climate, the 22 acres of gardens provide ideal conditions for many sub-tropical plants and shrubs. It is all set out around the walled terraces and lawns of what was once the Royal National Hospital for Diseases of the Chest. Established in 1868, the huge hospital catered for the many serious chest complaints that in pre-drug therapy times were treated mainly by rest and fresh air. Patients worked out of doors in the gardens which, with generous donations of plants and trees, developed and flourished. However, by the 1960s the hospital had become virtually obsolete. It was demolished and within its neglected grounds were born the present wonderful gardens.

Themed botanical displays embrace species from the Mediterranean, South Africa, Australasia and the Americas. Amongst other features you will find a medicinal herb garden, alpines, Japanese terraces and extensive mixed borders. In 1987 the Temperate House was opened, its extensive range of Southern Hemisphere species being continually added to by seeds sent from other similar establishments across the world.

The centrally situated Garden Tavern cafe/bar will satisfy the inner man at the end of a day's hike; children can let off steam at the large play area on the Garden's west side not far from the coast path.

In the car park can be found a Museum of Smuggling History. Do not be deceived by the tiny entrance building: the museum itself is housed in the old hospital's subterranean vaults and cellars, an eerily atmospheric venue for tableaux covering over 700 years of smuggling methods and collected artefacts.

WALK 16:
THE BEMBRIDGE TRAIL

Newport to Bembridge.
13 miles (21km)

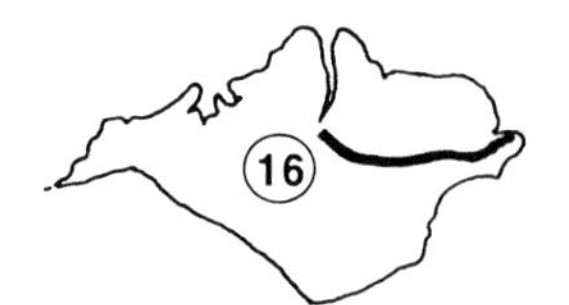

From the Island's busy capital, the trail sets off south on urban roads for Shide and a climb over St George's Down. Beyond Arreton's famous manor house and craft village, tracks lead east beside arable fields beneath and parallel to the chalk ridge of Arreton and Mersley downs to Knighton hamlet. From here you walk through delightful countryside of copses and hilly fields before climbing up and over the chalk downland to Brading, a popular village with several attractions. The trail's concluding section has a markedly different character as it traverses the low-lying flood plain of the River Yar with its water meadows and wetlands. Arrival at Bembridge is heralded by a splendidly

preserved 18th century windmill.

In 1180 Richard de Redvers, Earl of Devon, granted the fledgling settlement of Newport its first Charter. Already a straight road existed from Carisbrook Castle to the Quay (High Street) and other streets were arranged in a grid around three squares used as market places.

The town was burned down during a French raid in 1377. Two hundred years later the Plague took a heavy toll of life but Newport's fortunes would soon revive. In the 17th century the town became England's first line of defence against France in the Napoleonic wars. As more and more soldiers arrived to man the garrison, requiring supplies of all kinds, so trade prospered. New mills were built, along with many fine Georgian merchants' houses and the markets for corn, meat and other commodities flourished.

Today Newport remains a busy, sometimes congested, shopping centre, in contrast with most other parts of the Island. But its narrow streets, little riverside quays and historic buildings are well worth exploring. Of particular interest are the Town Hall, designed by John Nash and built in 1816; St Thomas' Parish Church containing some notable old tombs; Church Litten Park, south of the centre and reached through a great Tudor archway; and the Quay Arts Centre down at the end of elegant Quay Street. The Tourist Information Office is situated near the bus station on South Street.

Officially the Bembridge Trail starts at Shide (grid ref: 504881), but this point is easily reached from Newport centre where

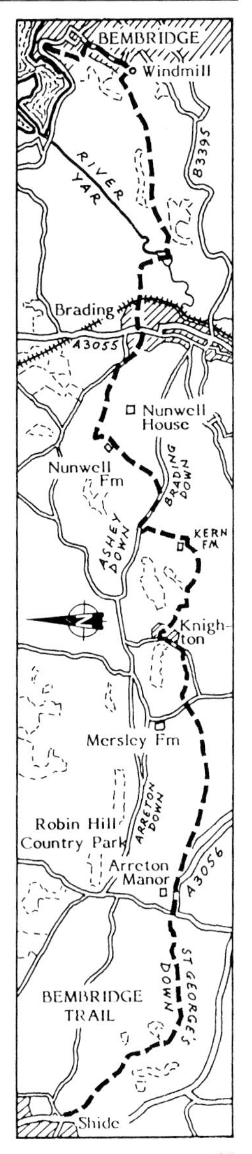

most walkers set out. From St Thomas' Square walk south along Town Lane, across South Street and into Church Litten. Turn left onto Medina Avenue and follow it curving south. On your left along Cypress Road can be found Newport's fascinating Roman villa remains. **At the end of Medina Avenue, turn left over the River Medina by the Barley Mow pub to reach the main A3020 road at Shide. Opposite, by the Blackwater Road sign, is the entrance to St George's Lane and the trail's official start.**

Within the last generation, Shide's quarry was a working enterprise. Nowadays it is a Nature Reserve, its chalk floor a haven for orchids and butterflies.

St George's Lane climbs south-east onto gorse and scrub dotted downs. Beyond Newport Golf Club's clubhouse continue south-east on the Old Highway (A28), parallel to more recently made heavy vehicle access for gravel workings. The trail rises then narrows pleasantly through bushes and trees to a path junction. The ancient way on your left leads past Great East Standen Manor, a farm with a history dating back to the Norman Conquest. Keep ahead, downhill through trees, still on the A28 to Arreton Cross. Here you join the A3056 eastbound for about 500m through the straggling village of Arreton.

To your left stands a quintessentially English scene of manor house, church, village and inn. Most of Arreton Manor dates from the early 17th century but a dwelling on the site itself, nestling under the Island's chalk spine, was mentioned in AD885 in Alfred the Great's will. The building is mainly Elizabethan and has been owned and lived in at various times by royalty from Henry VIII to Charles I. Inside, twisting stone steps lead down to 14th century rooms - part of the original farmhouse built by monks from Quarr Abbey. As well as its architectural beauty and historic associations, there are attractions of other kinds too: a Museum of Childhood, a lace collection, and the National Wireless Museum. Refreshments are available, as they are at the nearby White Lion pub. Before moving on, do look round massively built, 12th century St George's Church containing fascinating details; and the adjacent Arreton Craft Village.

From the White Lion walk along the pavement and branch left on bridleway A9, passing Arreton's primary school. Soon you are

Haseley Manor

walking on a grassy track along field headlands. The soil hereabouts is some of the most fertile on the whole Island, yielding a range of crops from wheat, barley and vegetables to 'pick your own' fruit, garlic and glasshouse tomatoes.

Five hundred metres to the south along Shepherd's Lane bridleway stands Haseley Manor. If you have time, visiting it is a 'must'; if not, then earmark a visit for a separate occasion. Once one of the most important houses on Wight, Haseley gradually became eclipsed by larger buildings until it was finally forgotten. When Raymond Young, the present owner, acquired the manor house in 1976 it had been empty for two years but neglected for much longer. The place was a virtual ruin - dilapidated, leaking, stripped of everything saleable and inhabited by mice and birds. Mr Young and his late wife, Krystyna, only discovered the house's historic significance during the purchase process. Twenty years of dedicated restoration, funded solely by admission fees and pottery sales since 1978, has transformed Haseley into the magnificent complex we witness today. And its history, even older and richer than at first thought, has been verified by experts. There are beautiful gardens, a children's play area, Wight's largest pottery studio still producing designs originated by Krystyna Young, as well as a sweet factory, gift shop and cafe.

Back on the Bembridge Trail, more fields are threaded along until you reach a country lane just south of Mersley Farm. Turn left here and in 100m turn right onto footpath NC1 to Mersley Down and Knighton. Beyond a little stream, bear right along by a hedge and note the conspicuous seamark atop Ashey Down, a navigational aid for shipping.

At the next lane turn left to pass Knighton Farm and Gardens. Then, at the bottom of Knighton Shute, turn right (NC45) to Kern and Alverstone. Past Knighton Waterworks buildings the motorable lane takes you up to Po House where you turn sharp right on a rough track. At the bottom turn left and walk up through a copse and cross the sandpit track ahead.

Now on a well defined field track, continue towards Kern Farm but just before you reach the farmhouse, turn right at a gate (signed Alverstone), pass a bungalow and turn left to join the rutted track heading straight up the flank of Ashey Down. There's a little jink at old chalk pits near the top then you arrive at a gate and the road. Turn right along a good verge path for about 750m and watch for bridleway B26 on the left.

This is Brading Down, a superb viewpoint - south over Shanklin, Sandown and the Arreton valley; north to the Solent and Spithead. Further along the road on lovely chalk grassland is a popular picnic area.

Follow the field edge which bears right and drops to a hollow. Go through a field gate on your left and keep left where the track divides ahead. The trail now descends gently over the next field and passes to the right of Nunwell Farm buildings. Turn left on the lane past the farm entrance and in 200m leave to the right on footpath B23 towards Brading. (There's a junction here with the Nunwell Trail.) Aim for a leaning oak tree across the field, go over the wooden footbridge and stile and continue straight ahead (just south of east).

Nunwell House, up to your right - another historic building with Conquest associations - is open to the public at certain times.

It is described in more detail on the Nunwell Trail.

Passing New Farm, the way crosses the next two fields, following a line of trees and emerging on West Lane. Turning right takes you past Nunwell House public entrance and first right after the Lodge is Doctors Lane, running beside a bungalow estate. A left fork along Cross Street brings you to Brading High Street which, unfortunately, is also the busy A3055.

The north end of the village is dominated by a justly celebrated Wax Museum. It is housed in the now brightly painted but basically Early Tudor Rectory Mansion, reputedly Wight's oldest house dating from 1228 and a one-time inn and smugglers' den to boot!

Founded by Graham Osborn-smith, the Wax Museum traces the Island's history in a series of exquisitely detailed and imaginatively lit tableaux. A separate entrance off the old galleried Queen's Bower Courtyard leads to a Chamber of Horrors graphically depicting man's inhumanity to man. Gruesome, yes, and not for the faint-hearted, yet every one of the instruments of torture was put to use in less civilised bygone eras. Adjoining the Wax Museum is Animal World, a highly recommended exhibition of taxidermy and preserved creatures including some mind-boggling 'freaks of nature'!

Across the High Street will be found the fascinating Lilliput Antique Doll and Toy Museum. Nearby stands Brading's Town Hall, complete with barred gaol, stocks and whipping post. South of the village centre are a Roman villa with beautiful mosaic floors, and Morton Manor whose terraced gardens lead to a vineyard producing a very good white wine. The final stage of a longish walk may not be the best time to savour all that Brading has to offer, strongly suggesting a separate visit.

Walk north up the High Street. Just beyond the Wax Museum, St Mary's Church contains some particularly fine wooded effigies of the Oglander family who occupied Nunwell House from Norman times until 1980.

The trail now turns east along Quay Lane. Following years of piecemeal land reclamation the mouth of the East Yar river was finally dammed at St Helens in 1877, blocking the tidal flow and creating a vast expanse of water meadow and reed beds. It also left the ancient, rumbustuous seaport of Bradynge high and dry: strange to think that only 100 years ago ships moored at the bottom of Quay Lane, here at the head of a picturesque sea inlet known as Brading Haven. Sea shells can still be found in the adjacent marshland.

Walk past bungalows, over the railway line and go through a gate to the right of a house at the disused railway crossing. The trail continues half-right along a low grassy embankment (Footpath B3 for Brading) and crosses two channels in the River Yar on sluice bridges. At the second, keep left on a pretty path through Centurion's Copse and over Centurion's Hill.

The site is associated not as you might expect with a Roman soldier but with a small chapel that once stood here dedicated to an 8th century abbot called St Urian. It is not hard to imagine how over the years his name has corrupted to Centurion.

Reaching a path junction, bear left (BB20) and a little further on left again through trees. In the absence of any path at a large crop field ahead, walk straight across, keeping right of a lone tree to a stile at the far side. Over to your right stands the Yarborough monument on Culver Down and immediately beyond it the sea.

The way proceeds straightforwardly over several more fields and draws alongside Bembridge Airport where the possibility of very low-flying light aircraft can never be ruled out! Path BB20 now heads for Bembridge Windmill on the skyline, climbing away from the floodbank up a pasture field. At the top go over the stile and turn right along by the hedge.

Built in 1700, the windmill is the Island's only surviving example in working order, thanks to careful restoration by the National Trust. Housed in a four-storeyed tower of local stone some 30ft (9m) high, much of the original wooden machinery remains intact. Display panels explain the milling process to visitors. (Open April to October.)

Beyond the windmill turn left along a track to the top of Bembridge High Street and walk down it, taking the path to Bembridge Point from opposite The Courtyard. It threads through woods to reach houses on Station Road. Continue past the Row Barge and the Pilot Boat pub and at the road end cross over to the Royal Spithead Hotel (bus stop) where the Bembridge Trail meets the Coast Path and terminates. (Grid Ref: 643886)

Bembridge village, nowadays set between the sea and the

drained remnants of Brading Haven, was once no more than a fishing hamlet whose impoverished inhabitants indulged in a little smuggling to enrich their lives. Only when wealthy Victorians began building villas and large hotels here, aided by the newly arrived railway, did Bembridge grow into a fashionable resort. It remains a large and prosperous, tree-studded settlement, its peaceful, shallow harbour contained by the 19th century embankment along which now runs the B3395 to St Helens. Houseboats, colourful and individualistic, line the southern bank while small craft of all kinds come and go with the tide.

Bembridge has a modest shopping street and an excellent maritime museum - the Shipwreck Centre - crammed full of historic finds, models and pictures. Bembridge lifeboat, a 'Tyne' class vessel, is kept in readiness at the end of a very long jetty on the east shore.

WALK 17: THE TENNYSON TRAIL

Alum Bay to Carisbrooke.
$14^{1}/_{2}$ miles (23.5km)

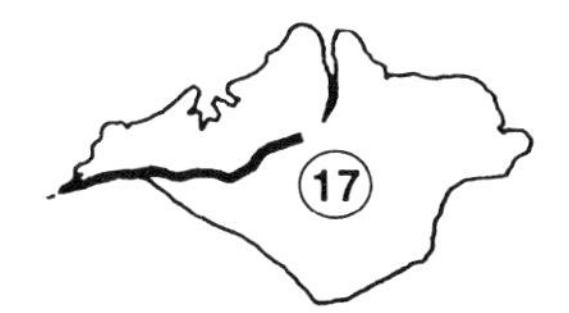

Few would dispute that the Isle of Wight's westernmost tip provides sensational walking and thrilling scenery. In tandem with the coast path which follows the same line as far as Freshwater, the Tennyson Trail takes you past Alum Bay's colourful cliffs to the famous Needles. There the trail doubles back east along Tennyson Down above high cliffs, remaining on the Island's west-to-east chalk ridge. Brighstone Forest is reached and after a woodland section you emerge onto field tracks across open downland with marvellous views of rolling countryside. Eventually the trail descends to Carisbrooke, not far from its great Norman castle.

As early as 1830 Alum Bay had become an essential ingredient in any visit to the Isle of Wight. The nearest hotel stood $^{3}/_{4}$ mile

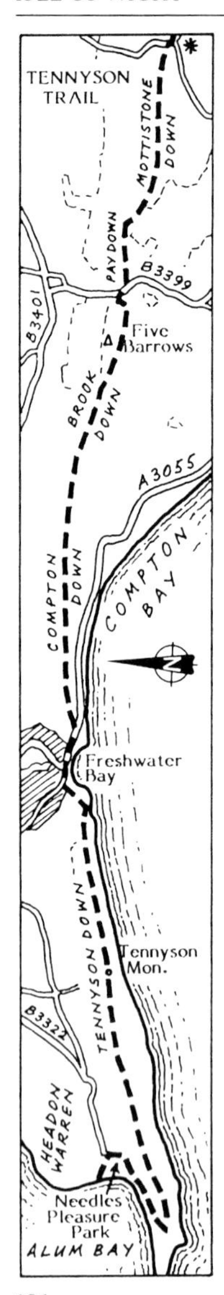

(1.25km) inland from the Chine which was then reached along a rough track. As holidaymaking grew more widespread, excursion steamers plied between Alum Bay and the nearby south coast resorts of Bournemouth, Southampton, Portsmouth and Southsea, as well as Cowes and Ryde. In 1873 a pier was built for passengers at Alum Bay but was dismantled as a defensive measure during World War II.

Until 1920 a good path descended to the beach but erosion here - as along all the Island's west coast - has eaten back the cliffs. It is not unusual for today's steps to need repair or replacing annually.

Alum Bay's world famous coloured sands have been the focus of attention for visitors since the early 1800s. Sunshine after heavy rain accentuates the remarkable hues, grouped into white, black, red, green and yellow-brown and formed by various minerals such as haematite, glauconite, limonite and carbon. Natural erosion removes far more material from the cliffs than does periodic and sensitive excavation, despite a booming trade in sand-filled glass shapes that started in Victorian times. These souvenirs may be purchased ready-filled or you can do it yourself with help from the experts.

Elsewhere in the Needles Pleasure Park will be found a glass blowing studio, numerous family entertainments, a cafe and a bar and the Marconi Memorial. Pioneering experiments with radio transmission to ships were carried out by Marconi in the late 1800s from the Royal Needles Hotel here at Alum Bay. It was destroyed by fire in 1909.

If you started on the beach at Alum Bay, climb the steps (or return by chairlift!) to the clifftops and follow the road up past Alum

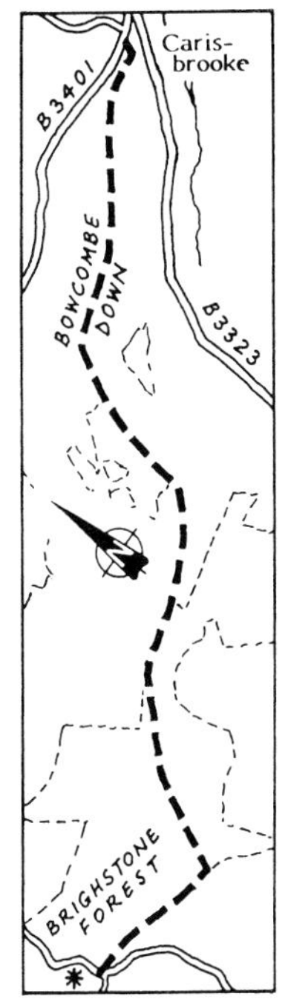

Bay Glass to the east of the main car park. Beyond a National Trust sign to the Needles Battery and a garden full of gnomes, the lane swings right. As you walk beside it there are increasingly fine views back to the coloured cliffs.

In about 600m bear left on a chalky path slanting up towards West High Down. The trail passes some Coastguard cottages before reaching the top of the downs where a detour down to the right could be taken for spectacular views of the Needles from a fenced corner high above Scratchell's Bay. (The Needles Battery itself, well worth visiting, is situated a little further west. For details see the relevant section of the Coast Path.)

Although a thin path runs outside a wire fence it is perilously close to the unstable cliff edge in one or two places. The main trail takes a safer line along the grassy crest some 460ft (140m) above the sea. This is a designated bird sanctuary for nesting seabirds, while kestrels and even the occasional buzzard can be seen hovering and soaring in the updraughts. Rare wildflowers, grasses and small chalkland plants, including pyramid and bee orchids, thrive here in spite of exposure to frequent and strong, salt-laden winds.

Except in a sea mist, the Tennyson Monument beckons from afar and half an hour's brisk walking brings you up to this granite Celtic cross and adjacent trig pillar at 482ft (147m) - the site of an earlier Armada beacon.

Alfred, Lord Tennyson, after whom the downs (and the trail) are named, was Queen Victoria's favourite Poet Laureate. Such was his genius and popularity that from improvished beginnings he became one of the wealthiest poets the country had ever known. He was able to buy Farringford House, a late 18th century Gothic mansion north of the downs near Freshwater Bay, which he could see from his study window. Tennyson loved nature and was fond of walking regularly across his beloved downs where he famously declared the air to be "worth sixpence a pint!"

During his heyday in the latter half of the 19th century, Tennyson's reputation attracted to Farringford House (now a hotel) a succession of illustrious Victorians, among them Charles Darwin, the Prince Consort, Garibaldi, Lewis Carroll, Anthony Trollope and Charles Kingsley.

The trail descends east from the monument with commanding views over Yarmouth, the Solent and the Hampshire coast; the English Channel; and West Wight right along to St Catherine's Point. The crumbling cliff edge should be approached with caution.

From Fort Redoubt tea-rooms (in the old Palmerston fortification against a possible French landing), just beyond tiny Watcombe Bay, a lane leads to the road (toilets, bus stop). Here a right turn takes you quickly to the little promenade at Freshwater Bay backed by cafes and a car park. A 500m diversion left, however, leads to beautiful St Agnes Church, dating from 1908 when the Bay community had swelled with artists, writers and a steady stream of visitors. It is the Island's only thatched church.

Freshwater Bay, a horseshoe-shaped scoop in the line of chalk cliffs, has a pebbly beach and its own miniature version of The Needles. Arch Rock collapsed a few years ago, however, dating published photographs of the Bay. A few fishing boats are usually moored offshore and in springtime nesting seabirds all but smother the sea stacks.

The Tennyson Trail now detaches itself from the Coast Path by heading up the A3055 Military Road. About 100m beyond Southdown Road, it bears left on S33 - the Old Highway to Carisbrooke, climbing the spine of Afton Down across the middle of a golf course. At a fork keep left (right is the Freshwater Way) and the grassy bridleway will take you along the top of Compton Down, with superb views of the coast in both directions. Once the golf links are behind you the trail passes a junction left with the Hamstead Trail and reaches Brook Down where a short detour gives access to Five Barrows.

The prehistoric ridgeway you are following once represented a dry, safe route above swamps and forests and was used as a trading route by our Stone and Bronze Age ancestors as long ago as 3000BC. More than 240 Bronze Age burial mounds, or long barrows, have been identified on the Island, nearly all on the chalk downs where many, like Five Barrows, are well preserved.

From the trig pillar at 538ft (164m) above sea level, return to the chalk track which descends via a gate on the left and a short lane to the B3399. Turn right across the road and almost immediately turn left through a gate into a bridleway signed Newport, Brighstone and Shorwell. A steady climb up Pay Down to a corner of woodland, through another gate and you are on course for the tumuli-crowned summit of Mottistone Down.

Flanked by the mixed woodland of Brighstone Forest, the grassy, gorse-lined bridleway now drops gently east to the National Trust's Brighstone car park off the road from Calbourne to Brighstone village. Once again, turn right across the road and left into stony bridleway BS10 (Newport and Shorwell). It gains height gradually and in a little over 1km there is an important junction. The Worsley Trail sets off south-east along the downs, while the Tennyson Trail branches off left on BS54 - the Old Highway to Carisbrooke.

Walking through Brighstone Forest contrasts sharply with the open, airy character of the route so far. Forestry Commission woodlands are found throughout the Island, totalling 1500 hectares, and Brighstone Forest was planted in the 1940s. As felling proceeds - some 8000 tons of timber are harvested annually - conifers are being largely replaced by beech and sycamore, with oak on the clay lowland soils.

Follow the trail north-east, gently uphill through the forest which is clear-felled in places; you soon pass the cross-track BS8 (Calbourne and Brighstone Road). Ignore turnings off and you will eventually come to a gate at the end of a row of hawthorns. With the forest now behind you, the remainder of the trail provides easy walking on undulating field tracks along a broad chalk ridge above the fertile Bowcombe valley.

On bridleway 136A you quickly reach a path crossroads alongside Monkham Copse. Both right-hand forks lead to Bowcombe (N135 and N136), while N131 leads left to Rowbridge Lane. The Tennyson Trail itself gradually swings further north

beside extraordinary flint-strewn fields on Boscombe Down and at the site of a tumulus veers right (east-north-east). Bowcombe hamlet lies down to the right, while ahead on the left there once lay a racecourse. **Keep straight on along a field edge and over the final path junction (left on N125 to the Blacksmith's Arms pub on the Newport to Calbourne road; right on N126 to Plaish and the Newport to Shorwell road).**

The ancient road you are now treading (N123) is initially little more than an earthy pathway between bushes and low trees but lower down it widens into a track (Down Lane) which drops to emerge at a house on the left called Castle Crag. Here you join Nodgham Lane leading down to the main B3401 at Carisbrooke where the trail ends (Grid Ref: 482882).

Although the main road hill does nothing to enhance your appreciation of Carisbrooke, it's an interesting place, new in parts but with rows of attractive cottages and old stone houses, particularly in Castle Street by the ford over picturesque Lukely Brook. The Church of St Mary the Virgin, dating from the 12th century, is one of the Island's finest. An impressive 15th century tower outside is rivalled inside by massive Norman pillars.

Carisbrooke Castle frowns from a chalk spur behind the village and is reached by a narrow footpath off Millers Lane. There is evidence that this commanding site was a stronghold even in Roman and Saxon times. Originally built by the Norman de Redvers family, the castle was further fortified in the early 1100s by the addition of the massive stone ramparts we see today.

Captured only once - in 1136 when the wells dried up in a drought - Carisbrooke Castle was well able to withstand attack by archery and early handguns. However, the 16th century development of more powerful cannon so threatened the old medieval walls that a ring of outer artillery fortifications was installed.

Lords of the Isle of Wight, right from the first, William Fitz Osbern, have traditionally occupied Carisbrooke Castle. The last resident Governor to do so was Queen Victoria's daughter, Princess Beatrice, whose term of office ended in 1944.

Carisbrooke's most famous occupant of all was King Charles I, imprisoned here from November 1647 to September 1648 when he

Carisbrooke Castle

was taken to Whitehall to be hanged. A daring escape plan was foiled, so the story goes, when he became stuck between the bars of his window trying to climb out!

The self same battlements walked round for exercise by Charles I are enjoyed by visitors today on a tour of this immensely evocative edifice set in 7 acres of grounds. As well as wide views and intriguing architectural details, the Great Hall contains the Isle of Wight Museum. But perhaps most captivating of all - a little piece of living history - can be found in the courtyard well-house. The 161ft (49m) deep well taps an underground stream, endowing it with a reliability the other well - up in the massive shell-keep - never had. For four centuries the winding wheel has been turned on the treadmill principle by donkeys. Today's happy animals work an easy shift system for the benefit and enjoyment of visitors, but it is worth remembering that without this vital water supply the castle would probably never have been a viable stronghold against medieval siege tactics.

WALK 18: THE WORSLEY TRAIL

Brighstone Forest to Shanklin.
15 miles (24km)

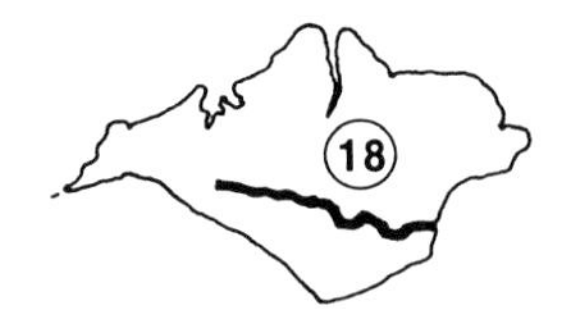

High level walking along chalk downland at first gives way to paths and lanes through beautiful, undulating countryside which at times can seem surprisingly remote. Picturesque Godshill with its famous model village provides a natural refreshment stop before you continue to the Worsley Monument and unsurpassed, Island-wide views. Beyond Wroxhall, a final climb over St Martin's Down brings the trail to its conclusion at Shanklin. Besides the popular seafront and town centre areas, be sure to visit the thatched cottages and tea-rooms of Shanklin Old Village, as well as nearby Shanklin Chine.

Officially the Worsley Trail begins near the south-east corner

of Brighstone Forest, at a junction with the Tennyson Trail which branches off north-east on its way towards Carisbrooke. However, the obvious practical starting point is the National Trust's Brighstone car park just off the road midway between Calbourne and Brighstone (Grid Ref: 420845). Alternatively you could start at Brighstone village and join the Worsley Trail by taking any of the paths and bridleways climbing north from the Limerstone Road.

Across the road from Brighstone car park, take the ancient stony trackway heading east (BS10 to Shorwell) which climbs beside the forest edge onto Brighstone Down. In a little over 1km you reach the Tennyson Trail turn-off on the left - the Old Highway signed BS54.

The Worsley Trail now levels off along Limerstone Down. Over to the right stands a topograph identifying the many landmarks visible from this wonderful spot high above Wight's west coast.

There is no mistaking the way which follows a broad track along Fore Down. Adjacent to a quarry there's rough tarmac underfoot and you veer south-east by an old wartime bunker on Renham Down, finally dropping to the B3323.

Just down the 'shute' to your right, nestling beneath the downs and surrounded by woods, stands the pretty village of Shorwell. Ancient St Peter's Church contains a beautifully restored medieval fresco depicting a diminutive Christ being carried across a river by St Christopher. Arcades of slender pillars divide three chapels, one for each of the village's impressive manor

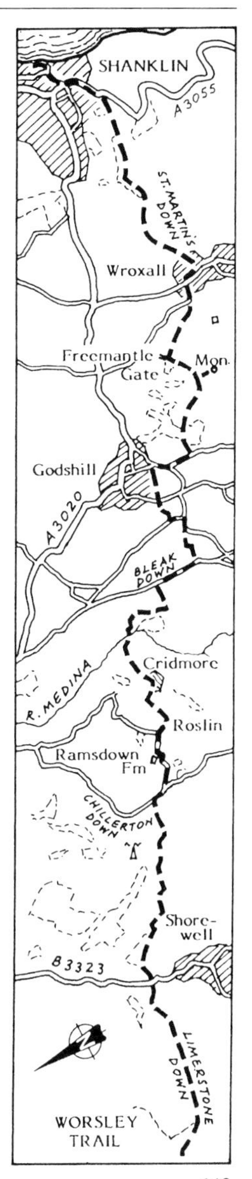

houses, namely Northcourt, Westcourt and Wolverton. The latter, now a working farm, is reputedly haunted by the ghost of a murdered minstrel. There's a pub too - the Crown - set beside the same stream that flows through Yafford Mill not far to the south-west of Shorwell.

Across the road the way climbs into bridleway SW49 (signed Chillerton) which heads for Lorden Copse and swings right (south-east) alongside the trees. In fact the path does a little jink but continue south-east towards the now conspicuous TV mast on Chillerton Down. Shortly after a left turn you join the main track leading downhill towards New Barn Farm. Halfway down (about 150m before the farm buildings) watch for footpath SW15 on the left which climbs a steep bank to a wooden gate.

The trail now follows the bottom edge of a field below Northcourt Down, with a hedge on your right. Pass through a gate and follow the field boundary downhill. Turning east, the rough path threads through brambles, thistles and other uncomfortable species, with the added delights of gluey mud in wet weather! There are several trods along this rugged stretch of hillside and for a while you are accompanied by overhead power lines. However, beyond a handgate the going eases considerably. As you pass old quarry pits the TV transmitter mast at 548ft (167m) on the downs above is barely a stone's throw away.

From a National Trust sign at the next handgate the track veers south-east then east, with superb views ranging right back over the route so far. Meeting the country road, turn right and at the top of the rise (bus stop) fork left on a quiet lane flanking Berry Hill. In good visibility you can see ahead to the distinctive profiles of Appuldurcombe Down and Gat Cliff upon which stands the Worsley Monument, still a couple of hours distant.

As the lane swings north-east you pass first an intersection with the Shepherds Trail, then Ramsdown Farm. Lower down, fork right into the 'No Entry' lane leading to Roslin and turn left (on G14) between the first buildings you come to - a cottage and a barn. This is the farm road to Cridmore but keep left past some timber sheds (G24), soon after which the lane reverts to a stony field track between hedges.

The next couple of miles or so potentially pose navigational

problems for the trail doesn't correspond exactly with the map; however, the following directions will help. Go through the metal gate and walk ahead across the field, a hedge to your right. Turn right at the next field and continue in a south-easterly direction with a fence on your right. When you are about 50m away from scrubby woodland ahead, strike left (east) to find stiles and a railway sleeper footbridge over the infant River Medina which runs through an area nearby known as The Wilderness.

Walk up the field edge ahead and follow it round to the right. Unless it is planted with crops you can short-cut across to a telegraph pole, continuing due south down the narrow field to its far end and into a track. About 100m along it, watch carefully for a stile on the left. The trail now climbs east up a field headland, turning right along the top edge to a stile exit onto the Bleak Down road. Follow the road south, with outstanding views, for about ½ mile (800m) and turn off left (GL15) at a right-hand bend. The trail doesn't take the track you'd expect but keeps straight ahead beside the gorse and wire fence. It dips downhill, past Upper Elliotts over to the right, and aims for the field's bottom left-hand corner. Here you will find two handgates and a bridleway leading east along a field boundary, with Godshill church an eye-catching landmark. You soon reach the country road at a corner of Beacon Alley.

Turn left and then left again along Bagwich Lane for about 200m. Beyond Lavender's Farm entrance a track on the right leads into a hedged path winding down to a footbridge in the grounds of a ruined 13th century mill. Cross the bridge and turn left along the bank of the infant River Yar, veering off right beside Bridgecourt's garden and across a field to the Whitwell Road. Directly opposite a bridleway (GL21) strikes up the centre of a crop field, bringing you out to Sheepwash Lane. Here, technically, the Worsley Trail shuns Godshill and heads south. However, having traversed some of Wight's loneliest countryside, few walkers will be able to resist the attractions of this celebrated and welcoming village. To reach it simply turn left then right down Church Hollow.

There's no denying Godshill is a tourist honeypot! Pubs and tea-rooms adorn its main street of thatched cottages beneath the crowning presence of All Saints Church. The nostalgic Toy Museum and the Natural History Centre are both worth visiting, but the renowned Model Village, set in 1½ acres of the Old Vicarage Gardens, remains Godshill's showpiece. Based on Old Shanklin and Godshill itself, the original attraction opened in 1952. The 1/10th scale buildings are made from coloured cement which weathers well and appears natural. Even the thatch is authentic miniature! Hundreds of tiny trees and shrubs have been painstakingly 'coaxed' into small-scale specimens, adding to the illusions of reality in a tiny world.

Shady Hollow Lane from the south-eastern end of Godshill village will reconnect you with Sheepwash Lane and the Worsley Trail. Walk due south, forking left at the junction with Meryl Lane and passing the livery stables at Cleveland Farm and the entrance drive to Sainham Deer Farm. Just before the top of the hill turn left into a field and walk to the left along its edge (GL56), then uphill to join an eastbound track alongside the wood above Sainham Farm. The track, uphill between fences, passes through two deer-proof gates and takes you up though woods to a junction.

The Worsley Trail goes across to a handgate (GL49) and up into rough pasture beside the old stone wall of Appuldurcombe estate. For the first time on this hike the east coast is in sight at Culver Cliff and if you take the steep spur path on the right (GL63) up to the top of Gat Cliff, the panorama is more spectacular still, spanning as it does the whole girth of the Island from distant Tennyson Down. Here on an outcrop of Upper Greensand stands an obelisk of Cornish granite.

The Worsley Monument, after which this trail is named, was put up in 1774 by Sir Richard Worsley of Appuldurcombe in memory of his grandfather, Sir Robert. All but the restored façade of Appuldurcombe House, once a fine Palladian-style mansion with grounds landscaped by none other than Capability Brown, is now ruinous. Even the Worsley obelisk was shortened by lightning damage in 1831 but was restored in 1978.

Returning to the main trail you descend beside Freemantle Copse, taking a thin path to a stile on the right at Freemantle Gate. This impressive stone archway with its Ionic columns and the Worsley family's crest formed the estate's main entrance during the

18th century. **Go through the side gate and in 100m, at a 'Private Road' sign, fork left (GL44) down three fields on a bee-line towards Wroxall. At Appuldurcombe Road, turn left - down and up - to emerge on the B3327 in Wroxall.**

Originally just a small agricultural settlement, the village was transformed when the railway arrived. Owing to the stubborn refusal by Lord Yarborough of Appuldurcombe to permit the new line to cross his land, a substantial tunnel had to be excavated under St Boniface Down a mile to the south. Cottages to accommodate the workers were built in Wroxall's main street and St John's Church was constructed using stone from the tunnel boring.

Cross the road to climb the steps and bank opposite, turning right along the disused railway trackbed and rejoining the road at a bridge. Here the trail turns left onto pedestrianised Castle Road and follows the lane up past houses to a stile on the right.

The next section of trail climbs onto the flanks of St Martin's Down but doesn't traverse the top, though a detour that does is suggested. Once over the stile, height is gained with a hedge on your left and the next stile leads into a field with a line of trees. By following its right-hand boundary (or cutting across north-east), you will reach a yellow-waymarked stile in the far corner.

This is the site of the now disappeared Cooke's Castle, a folly ruin incorporated into the landscape by Capability Brown to improve Sir Richard Worsley's view from Appuldurcombe House!

Now the path weaves through hillside woods, joining a bridleway from the left, and climbs across a sloping field. Ignore the prominent path up a hillock ahead (although this can be taken to reach the summit of St Martin's Down for marvellous views; rejoin the trail on a footpath descending north). Keeping below the field fence initially, the trail then continues above woods in a generally easterly direction for about $^{1}/_{2}$ mile (800m).

With Shanklin and Sandown beckoning, height gained must now be lost! The way, sometimes stepped, is easy enough to follow and brings you down through woods at first then through crop fields and pasture to the churchyard of St Blasius (patron saint of wool combers) - Shanklin's Old Parish Church. (Bus stop.) Turn left and walk down the road to Shanklin Old Village. The fountain bears an inscription by the American narrative poet,

Henry Wadsworth Longfellow:

'O traveller, stay they weary feet;
Drink of this fountain, pure and sweet;
It flows for rich and poor the same.
Then go thy way, remembering still
The wayside well beneath the hill,
The cup of water in His name.'

In Longfellow's day Shanklin was little more than a fishing hamlet at the head of a dramatic chine. Nowadays visitors are more likely to plump for a cream tea in this quaint but popularised corner of Shanklin.

Satisfaction at having completed the Worsley Trail will be rounded off by continuing downhill and dipping a toe in the English Channel! (Grid Ref: 586812)

CHAPTER 3

The Coastal Path

WALK 19: THE COASTAL PATH

Around the Island.
71 1/2 miles (115km)

Because the Isle of Wight is roughly diamond shaped, the coastal path divides itself neatly into four distinctive sections - one for each side of the diamond. This works well as a device for describing the terrain and scenery but is less useful for splitting up the walk into practical day stages.

For one thing, covering 17 miles (27km) on each of four consecutive days is rather too ambitious for the majority of walkers: the going may be easy enough in some places but it is tougher or more complex in others. Despite the Island's enviable sunshine record, English Channel weather can also be wet and windy and there's nothing like a gale to slow your progress along a coastal path!

Many walkers tackling the entire route choose to return to their base accommodation each night, so time must also be built in for transport. But the most compelling argument against rushing the walk is that so much would be missed along the way. Completing the route in 5 or 6 days will add flexibility. You will be able to fully appreciate the magnificent scenery and take an hour or two out to visit places of interest. There will also be time to enjoy a relaxed meal and refreshments. And if the weather's unkind, a little less distance one day can be readily made up the next.

Being circular, the coastal path can, of course, be started anywhere. However, as with most long-distance routes, there are 'obvious' stages - based mainly on the availability of transport and accommodation at the end of the day. The stages used below will not necessarily suit everyone's requirements. Just as stronger walkers will be quite capable of exceeding the suggested daily mileages, so walkers with different priorities may prefer a more leisurely pace.

For its size, the Isle of Wight boasts an extraordinarily varied coastline. This is due partly to underlying geology and partly to the Island's location in the English Channel. The great chalk ridge running west to east from The Needles to Culver Cliff produces not only lofty downland but also high cliffs of outstanding beauty. Along the lower-lying north coast, river estuaries bite deep inland, though only one - the Newtown River - actually forces the coastal path to make a significant detour. South and east Wight, being sheltered from the prevailing winds and weather, support the larger seaside resorts. In contrast, dramatic erosion by the elements and a thinner scattering of settlements endow the west coast with a wilder, lonelier ambience. Throughout the coastal walk there is an unfolding wealth of detail and viewpoints to relish as the path weaves its way along cliff and foreshore, through woodland and village, past tidal marsh and harbour.

STAGE 1:

West Cowes to Yarmouth.
16 miles (26.5km)

Westwards from Cowes and neighbouring Gurnard, developed seafront gives way to a rough cliff path. At Thorness Bay begins a detour on field paths and country lanes round arms of the Newtown River estuary, once one of the Island's busiest ports and now an important Nature Reserve. Returning to the shore at Hamstead Point, the coastal path threads fields and woods above spectacularly eroding Bouldnor Cliffs, renowned for fossils, before arriving at the historic town and harbour of Yarmouth, terminal for the Lymington car ferry.

At the very hub of the yachting world for well over a century and a half, Cowes has become a household name. During Cowes Week (the first week of August each year), yachting activity reaches its zenith with an internationally famous festival. But throughout the summer and even in the winter, craft of all shapes and sizes can be seen racing or cruising in The Solent. Indeed, a unique feature of the Cowes scene is the proximity of participant and spectator. Go to The Parade, Princes Green or The Esplanade in June and you will witness the start of the Island Sailing Club's 'Round the Island Race' involving over a thousand yachts and the largest of its kind in the world. Walking along the shore of the western Solent presents endless opportunities for viewing both small craft and larger commercial vessels plying these busy waters.

Until Henry VIII's edict to build a coastal fortress at the mouth of the River Medina, West Cowe (as it became known) was just a collection of fishermen's huts. Today, Cowes' importance as the Island's (arguably Britain's) premier yachting centre is indisputable. The pedestrianised High Street, winding along behind the clubs, jetties and dinghy moorings of the marina, contains numerous shops selling nautical gear, as well as pubs, cafes and restaurants. Town Quay, not far from the Tourist Information Office, is Red Funnel's terminal for their popular 'Red Jet' catamaran passenger service to Southampton, taking just 22 minutes for the crossing. (Arrival by Red Funnel car ferry is at East Cowes, joined to West Cowes by a chain ferry for vehicles and passengers - the so-called Floating Bridge.) Before setting off, Cowes Maritime Museum is well worth seeing for its model ships, prints and paintings.

Start by walking along the High Street, passing the Royal Ocean Racing Club and the Island Sailing Club, and follow Watch House Lane (named after the Customs House) down to a broad square overlooking The Solent called The Parade. A little further west the promenade narrows to pass Cowes Castle (incorporating parts of the original West Cowe) - home of the Royal Yacht Squadron. The cannon are from William IV's yacht *Royal Adelaide*.

Above a pebble beach the seafront widens again to accommodate the grassy banks of Princes Green, donated by the railway baron George Stephenson and a favourite spot for watching shipping. There are refreshment huts too.

Soon you are approaching Egypt Point, the Island's

northernmost tip marked by a small automatic lighthouse. Follow the prom along to Gurnard. (A gurnard, or gurnet, from which the village takes its name, is a sea-fish with a heavily armoured head and finger-like pectoral fins.) **Keep seaward of the beach huts at east Gurnard then turn left just before the Sailing Club. Not far up the hill road take the footpath on the right (Winding Way) which comes out onto Shore Road. Turn right to join Worsley Road, then right again down Solent View Road and past the Sealights pub on the little seafront, a landing place pre-dating Cowes. The one-time marshland is now covered by chalets. Once over Gurnard Luck rivermouth with its small boat moorings, the coastal path bears right along a gravel track which it soon leaves to the left (CS16) to pass seaward of fields and chalets.**

Rounding a minor headland at Gurnard Ledge you are walking above an extensive area of slumped cliffs, overgrown now with vegetation; there are good views ahead to the Newtown estuary. The path itself is subsiding quite badly in places but eventually leads down to sea level at a track from Whippance Farm and a signpost by a marshy stream outlet in Thorness Bay.

The beach of mud and sand is frequented by flocks of birds such as oyster catchers, redshanks and ringed plovers; also in summer by water sports enthusiasts!

The coastal path now heads half-right and continues along the top of the beach, a muddle of shingle, sand,

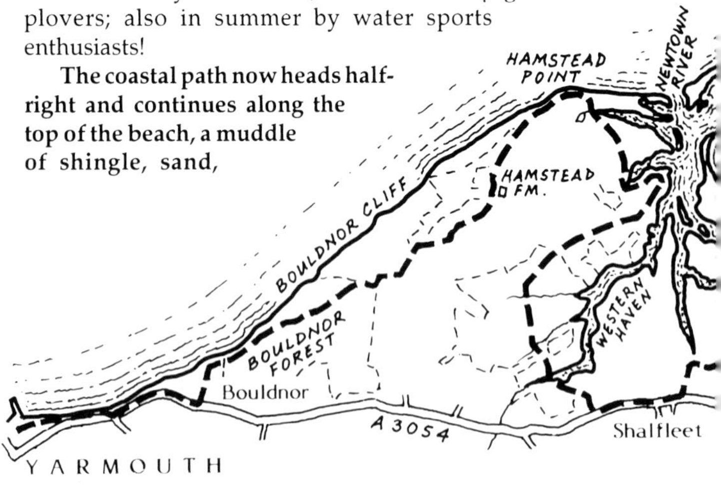

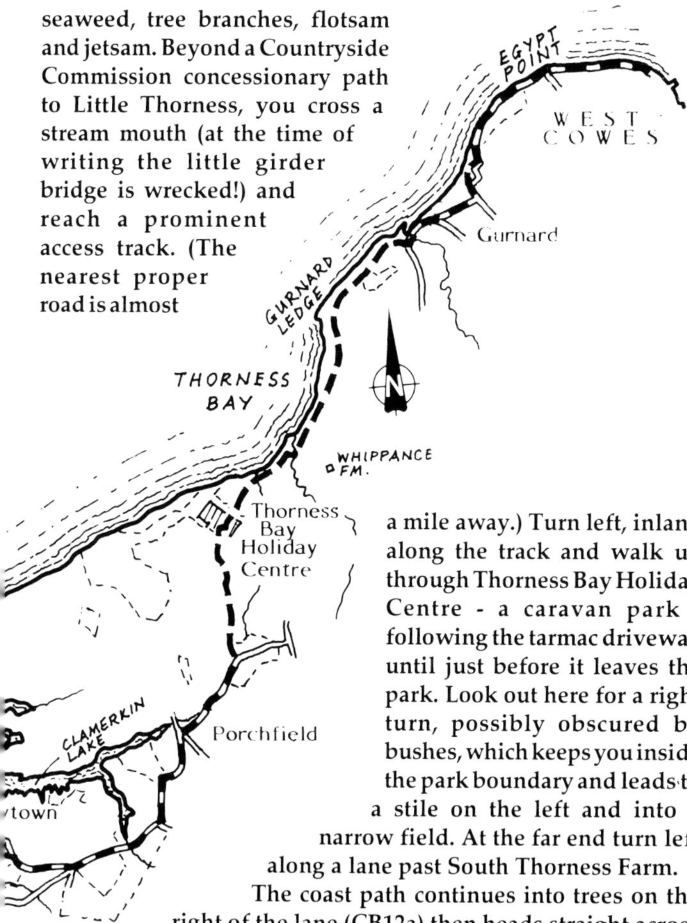

seaweed, tree branches, flotsam and jetsam. Beyond a Countryside Commission concessionary path to Little Thorness, you cross a stream mouth (at the time of writing the little girder bridge is wrecked!) and reach a prominent access track. (The nearest proper road is almost a mile away.) Turn left, inland along the track and walk up through Thorness Bay Holiday Centre - a caravan park - following the tarmac driveway until just before it leaves the park. Look out here for a right turn, possibly obscured by bushes, which keeps you inside the park boundary and leads to a stile on the left and into a narrow field. At the far end turn left along a lane past South Thorness Farm.

The coast path continues into trees on the right of the lane (CB12a) then heads straight across two small fields. Keep left along the edge of the next one and in the same direction along further field edges past a wood to meet a country road. Turn right towards Porchfield. Set in pastoral countryside, the little village is served by a shop, a chapel and a pub - the Sportsman's Rest - which makes an excellent lunch break on this fairly long day of walking.

Next the road crosses Rodge Brook and passes Jersey Training Camp for Volunteer Reserve and Cadet Forces. Ignore Colemans Lane on the left and continue past the entrance to Clamerkin Farm Park. As well as B&B and camping, there's a tea room, a picnic area, short local walks beside the creek, and a family-orientated farm park with pens of friendly animals.

The route eventually forks right towards Newtown, passes Old Vicarage Lane on the left and takes to a footpath on the left (marked Newtown/National Trust) which leads across narrow fields through a series of hedge gaps and stiles roughly parallel to the road. Before long you regain the road at Newtown and turn left to the Old Town Hall.

Founded by the Bishop of Winchester in the mid-13th century and planned on a grid pattern, Newtown rapidly became a thriving community, more important then than Newport. A century later local industries included oyster farming (recently enjoying a revival), salt production and a busy, safe harbour capable of docking up to 50 large vessels. However, Newtown's prosperity drew attacks from the French during the Hundred Years War, culminating in the disastrous raid of 1377 when the town was burned down and never really recovered.

Despite its decline and the ascendancy of Newport and Yarmouth as Wight's major towns, Newtown, as a 'Rotten Borough', continued to send two Members of Parliament to Westminster right up until the first Reform Act of 1832 which put an end to that anomaly! Its buildings already decimated, the little town slipped further into obscurity with the demise of its salt industry and the closing of the inn in 1916. The Georgian town hall, put up in 1699 by public subscription but no longer needed for parliamentary elections, became first a school then a dwelling. Acquired by the National Trust in 1933, it was used temporarily as a youth hostel. After the war, ivy-clad and falling into decay, the building required extensive renovation. This has been carried out and this isolated remnant of a once flourishing settlement is open to visitors during the summer months; it contains many exhibits of historical interest.

The National Trust also owns the Newtown River estuary, now an important Nature Reserve, as well as 220 acres (89 hectares) of adjacent fields and oak woodlands.

Newtown itself has changed little over the past three centuries, although grass has transformed some of the old streets and backyards into tiny fields. The church may be disappointingly 19th century, but the original village pump and the stone built pub (now a house) bearing the town arms can still be seen.

Despite efforts to reclaim the main marsh dating back over 300 years, the sea has prevailed. You can, however, walk out over a long timber causeway to the old Quay and relish this delectable spot whose complete solitude is broken only by the occasional passing yacht and the activities of fishermen.

The coast path continues along the lane past the Old Town Hall and over Causeway Lake, one of the Newtown river's many tidal arms. At the road junction ahead, turn right and take the concessionary footpath just inside the field boundary, avoiding the tarmac along to Corf Farm. Immediately beyond the buildings, turn right into a lane and at the far end keep right on a path through trees which curves round over a footbridge across the end of Shalfleet Lake and emerges by the old mill (now a house) and a car park. Now bear left along past Shalfleet Manor Farm to reach the A3054 at the 18th century New Inn. (With its local seafood, this would make a good alternative lunch stop to Porchfield.)

Perhaps because Shalfleet lies on a busy route to west Wight, many visitors simply pass through, never stopping to explore its feudal cluster of church, manor, pub, brewhouse and stone built cottages, all set around a crossroads beside the Caul Bourne. St Michael's church tower, massively constructed by the Normans as a retreat against French raiders (its walls are 5ft - 1.5m - thick!), contributes to a simple stone interior - a modern day retreat of a different kind from traffic and heat on a summer's day! A short walk to the north beside the creek brings you to a tiny 17th century quay, once bustling with the comings and goings of boats carrying grain, coal and other commodities.

Follow the A3054 verge for about 1/2 mile (800m) and watch out for a stile on the right (S11 - Lower Hamstead and Yarmouth). The field edge path leads round to a plank bridge over a creek in Nunneys Wood. Bear right through trees, keeping to the main path, and you will quickly reach a broad stony track. Turn right, crossing the bridge over Ningwood Lake, and continue ahead,

gently uphill through woods. You pass a junction with the Hamstead Trail on the left (S29), then in a further 150m fork right (Creek Farm), now joining the Hamstead Trail on a track through conifers.

(If time presses, you could short-cut the section round Hamstead Point by continuing straight on along the northbound track, veering left past the entrance to Hamstead Farm and regaining the coast path about 150m further on at Woodcote Cottage.)

The main route stays on the shady track past Lower Hamstead Farm to a jetty at Western Haven - another one-time busy quay with a brickworks and salt pans but now just a quiet anchorage for pleasure craft.

Cross the stile on the left (S3) and follow the creek's shore. Muddy shallows are traversed on sections of boardwalk and then you keep to the left of a field boundary before crossing a stile in trees on the left. Now angle north-west over a pasture field to a stile in the far corner where a long timber footbridge will be seen spanning a creek. Low woods and steps take you to the backshore shingle path at Hamstead Point, with marvellous views of The Solent and Newtown Bay.

At Hamstead Ledge, the coast path slants up inland along field edges above vegetated, pine-fringed cliffs comprising several Sites of Special Scientific Interest. They are unique for exposures of fossil-rich Oligocene rocks some 60 million years old.

A stile directs you onto a track past Hamstead Farm and Woodcote Cottage and the coast path continues (as S1) across fields towards Yarmouth. After passing beneath overhead wires, keep right along the top field edge, over the driveway to West Hamstead Farm, and on past a bungalow to a junction and a Permanent Footpath Diversion. Here you branch left on an unsurfaced lane (still S1) called Seaview Road, leading into Cranmore Avenue. Almost immediately, turn right along West Close, a gravel track, and as you approach houses ahead veer sharp left down a narrow footpath which skirts the properties through trees.

The coast path now enters the Forestry Commission's Bouldnor Forest and proceeds in a generally south-west direction through

delightful mixed woodland, separated from the sea by the slumped and eroded Bouldnor Cliff. Ignore tracks off to the left and you will emerge directly above a foreshore ravaged by marine erosion, the beach littered with the skeletons of dead and falling trees. In fact, to by-pass a small landslip the coast path dives back into deep conifers before regaining the shoreline and passing through reedbeds at the top of a little shingle bay.

Stay on the main path, signified by a finger post, and you will reach a Forestry Commission signboard. Turn left to the A3054 at Bouldnor and walk westwards along the pavement. Beyond the Thorley road junction it's preferable to follow the sea wall, backed by pleasant grassy banks, into Yarmouth.

Attractive narrow streets lead straight to the square and there is no shortage of shops and eating places for the weary walker. This charming harbour town is dominated by the imposing tower of 17th century St James Church which is visible for miles around. Inside stands a marble statue of Sir Robert Holmes, the Island's Governor in the mid-1600s, but it is part-deception! The body is a scuplted depiction of King Louis XIV of France, discovered unfinished in a captured French vessel. His vanity kindled, Sir Robert had the statue brought to Yarmouth and a likeness of his own head grafted on!

There's no better place from which to enjoy the often glorious Solent sunset colours than the gardens of The George Hotel adjacent to Yarmouth Castle; it was originally the official residence of Sir Robert Holmes whose bedroom is marked by a plaque.

STAGE 2:

Yarmouth to Freshwater Bay.
$9^{1/2}$ miles (15.5km)

Napoleonic forts, woods and holiday villages lead on towards Wight's westernmost tip. Beyond the bathing resorts of Colwell and Totland, the way crosses Headon Warren heathland to reach the famous coloured sands of Alum Bay, complete with clifftop entertainments and crafts complex. Although the coast path doesn't officially take you there, the Needles Old Battery is well worth a visit for its historical interest and viewpoints over The Needles themselves. Turning east, the route rises along the gorse-patched turf of West High Down and Tennyson Down above precipitous

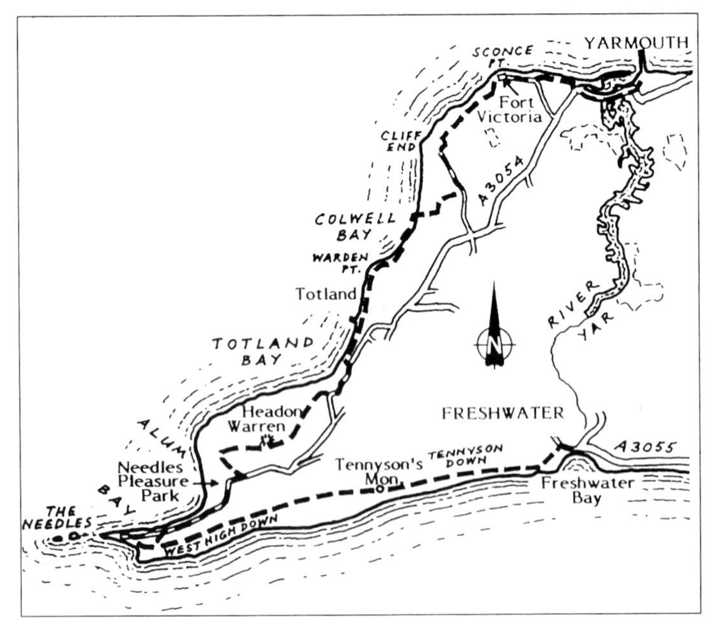

een Victoria's beloved Osborne House, her family's country retreat for nearly half a century

alking the southern coast near Woody Point towards distant Ventnor

Admiring the view north-east from Bonchurch Down to the chalk bastio
Culver Cliff

12th century St George's Church beneath the downs near Arreton Mar

The historic town and ferry port of Yarmouth, gateway to West Wight

chalk cliffs, passes the Tennyson Monument at the summit then drops gently to the little seafront promenade at Freshwater Bay.

Yarmouth harbour, once much more extensive than it is today, is nevertheless a bustling place; in summer you can take boat trips for sightseeing and fishing. **The coast path heads west across the new Yar bridge, opened in 1987; there are good views of the estuary saltings. In summer, however, a pleasant alternative is to take the little passenger ferry over to Norton Spit.**

The main roadside routing passes a boatyard and where the road bends left at Hallett's Shute, turns off right towards Fort Victoria and Colwell. Here at the western end of Norton Spit the two exits from Yarmouth join. You are now atop the low sea wall past villas and (at the time of writing) the Wayfarers Cafe. Steps on the left and a narrow path through sycamores lead to the minor road along to Fort Victoria but it is also possible to reach it by continuing along the shingle foreshore past an old jetty.

The L-shaped, single storey casements at Fort Victoria are all that remains of an original triangular structure built between 1852-55 to protect the very narrow neck of The Solent here. Like many others of its time the fort never saw action and became known as one of Lord Palmerston's 'follies'. The true extent of the site is demonstrated by reconstructed, low perimeter walls around the car park; included were massive barracks, demolished in 1969. Today, amongst the visitor attractions, will be found a Planetarium, a Maritime Heritage exhibition, an excellent Marine Aquarium and a good cafe. Nearby Sconce Point provides wonderful views of shipping and birdlife.

Walk round to the lawns between fort and shore and in the far corner, opposite a pit built in 1888 for an experimental 'see-saw' searchlight, you will find the onward coast path, doubling as a Nature Trail in Fort Victoria Country Park. It turns up into delightful, mature woodland containing ferns, honeysuckle and wild clematis. Turn right along the overgrown cobbled roadway, built by the army at the end of the 19th century to link Fort Victoria with Fort Albert at Cliff End (now a private residence). As you walk through the woods above landslipped cliffs there are glimpses of Hurst Castle less than a mile away on the mainland next to a white lighthouse: this, like Yarmouth Castle, was another of Henry VIII's coastal defences.

Eventually the path mounts steps and narrows, arriving at the perimeter fence of a holiday bungalow estate which is followed round to Monks Lane. Turn left downhill and up through a little valley and at the top of the rise bear right (F9), now en route for Alum Bay. Walk straight ahead through Bramble Chine holiday centre and take the footpath on the left leading to a track junction. Providing the tide is not too high, path F13 can be followed down to the shore; otherwise, keep left on F10 to Yarmouth Road, Totland, via Brambles Farm. In 300m turn right back to the coast at Colwell Chine. (The old clifftop path has been washed away by erosion, hence the inland detour.) Both the beach route and detour are reunited at Colwell's modest seawall prom, backed by beach huts, cafes and a lifeguard lookout.

You now walk round Warden Point - a reef of black rocks where slumping yellow cliffs threaten to engulf the sea wall. Beyond Totland's pier with its entertainments and cafe, look for steps on the left by the Waterfront Bar and licensed restaurant. (Both the Waterfront and the Sentry Mead Hotel, just inland,

welcome walkers and are very well positioned for a lunch stop.)

At the top of the steps, turn right on Turf Walk and carry on uphill past houses. Path T17 for Alum Bay leaves on the right and takes you round Warren Cottage before reaching the heather and gorse clad slopes of Headon Warren. Fork right for spectacular views back along the north coast; the left fork runs parallel, while several other stony paths criss-cross Headon Hill. At the summit (fenced for conservation at the author's last visit), stands one of Wight's few prehistoric burial mounds on heathland - this one dating from farmers of the early Bronze Age around 1500BC.

Coming over past the tumulus, a dramatic view of cliff-girt Alum Bay and The Needles bursts upon you. The soil underfoot is composed of acid sands and gravels supporting markedly different flora and fauna from the lime-rich downlands across the bay.

Towards the end of the Headon Hill ridge, the coast path descends narrowly to the left, stepped in places, skirts a pitch and putt course and arrives at a gate onto a track. Turn left then right to The Needles Pleasure Park.

This entertainments and crafts complex owes its existence to the world famous coloured sands of Alum Bay. In 1830 the bay was already an essential component of Island holidays, despite in those days being remote and difficult to reach (the nearest hotel stood $^{3}/_{4}$ mile - 1km - inland and further progress westwards was along a rough track). Thirty years later the Royal Hotel was built on the clifftop but burned down in 1909. During the late 1800s, excursion steamers from English Channel resorts brought in ever increasing numbers of visitors and a pier was constructed to facilitate the landing of passengers; it was considered a security risk during World War II and duly dismantled.

It is usually possible to walk down a stepped path to the beach 165ft (50m) below (the path was a much more prominent affair prior to erosion in the chine over the last 75 years or so). Above your head, less energetic visitors are whisked down by chairlift. It was opened in April 1973, has a design capacity of 1000 passengers per hour in each direction and proved an instant success. To date, well over 10 million people have been carried.

Now, as it has been for almost two centuries, the main reason for a descent is to view the multi-coloured cliffs. Individual sand grains have been stained by various minerals such as haematite (red), glauconite (green), carbon (grey and black) and limonite (yellow and brown). Differing concentrations and mixture produce gradations of these primary hues. The result are vertical bands of up to 20 recognisable colours, especially intensified in sunshine after heavy rain.

Staff from the Sand Shapes operation which markets ready-filled glass shapes as well as 'fill your own' excavate coloured sand from the cliffs for refining. They are keen to point out that the material they remove pales into insignificance beside the process of natural erosion.

There are boat trips from the beach and elsewhere in the Pleasure Park will be found a glass-blowing studio, gift shop, bar and restaurant, as well as entertainment for all the family. Marconi's pioneering work with radio transmission here is commemorated by a memorial at the clifftop end of the Park.

The coast path continues up the coach park road and turns right into the westbound National Trust lane at a cottage garden full of gnomes! (A short-cut off the corner on the left (T25) leads to Freshwater Bay in 2½ miles - 4km.) Follow the lane, or the path along its seaward bank, and you will obtain magnificent views back to Alum Bay. From a stile on the left, a chalky path slants uphill to some Coastguard cottages on West High Down, above which the official route heads east. Walkers wishing to visit the Needles Old Battery (open April to October) should continue along the lane to pass under the archway and over the drawbridge.

Supporting her aggressive foreign policy in the late 1850s, France became the world's first nation to develop ironclad warships. With the Napoleonic wars still a recent memory and our coastal defences virtually unchanged since Trafalgar, Britain experienced a real invasion scare. Lord Palmerston's government responded with the building of our own ironclad fleet and with innumerable south coast fortifications including, in 1861-63, the Needles Point Battery to help protect Portsmouth.

Old Needles Battery (as it is now known) provides us with an intriguing insight into the evolution of coastal defence systems from Victorian times onwards. Two of the original six guns can be inspected, as well as a restored shell-filling laboratory, an exhibition and many other features. Ultimately the chalk geology of Needles Point proved too fragile for the firing of rifled, muzzle-loaded guns and the New Needles Battery was constructed higher up on the site of the old lighthouse in 1893; by 1895 the connecting road to Alum Bay had also been built.

At the Old Battery, a spiral staircase from the parade ground (resident were one officer, two NCOs and 21 men), followed by a 200ft (61m) long tunnel through the chalk, leads to a spectacular searchlight emplacement excavated in 1899. From this very westernmost tip on the Island you have a wonderful view of the south coast from Barton to Hengitsbury Head as well as an intimate perspective over The Needles Rocks with their seabird colonies. (NB: An informative leaflet - 'The Needles Batteries' - is published by the National Trust and available locally.)

The chalk stacks themselves are thought to take their name from a 120ft (36m) high tapering pinnacle known as Lot's Wife which collapsed into the sea with a thunderous roar in 1764. On the summit of West High Down stood the original, cone-shaped lighthouse, put up in 1785; however, at 462ft (141m) above the waves it was frequently obscured by sea mist. In 1859 it was abandoned in favour of the present structure which, now fully automatic and complete with helipad, hugs the base of the most seaward stack.

On your return to the coastal path on the downland summit, walk a little way south above Scratchell's Bay. Not only will you discover a thrilling viewpoint over precipitous cliffs to The Needles from a little fenced corner, but here stand the concrete remains of an engine-testing site for Britain's *Black Knight* and *Blue Streak* rockets, in use in the mid-1950s before the rocket research programme was discontinued. The entire headland was acquired by the National Trust in 1975 and much of the restoration work was carried out by volunteers.

Although a narrow path does run along the cliff edge outside a wire fence (rather precariously in places), the official route now takes to the crest of West High Down towards the Tennyson Monument some 1½ miles (2.5km) distant. Here you are walking 460ft (140m) above the waves; crannies and ledges on the great sea cliffs below are favourite nesting places for seabirds, while the downland itself supports many quite rare grasses and flowers, despite being an exposed location.

Built on the summit of the downs at 482ft (147m), the granite monument in the form of a Celtic cross stands as a memorial to one of England's most famous poets - the great Poet Laureate of the Victorian age. Tennyson rented and later bought nearby Farringford House (now a hotel); from its windows he could gaze out over the bay framed by Afton Down. His love of nature and some of the Victorian romantic ideals are encapsulated in poetry written at Farringford, including *Idylls of the King* and *Maud*. During the latter half of the 19th century, Tennyson's immense popularity attracted eminent people from other walks of life - royalty, scientists, artists, scholars, architects - and lasting relationships were forged with Island residents. The so-called Tennyson Circle flourished between 1865 and 1874 until Tennyson's wife, Emily, fell ill and was unable to continue her vital secretarial role. She was subsequently wheeled out onto the downs on innumerable occasions to partake of the bracing, invigorating sea air which Tennyson declared "worth sixpence a pint".

In clear visibility the views up here are tremendous, embracing the entire western peninsula. As you begin the descent towards Freshwater, the west coast is in sight all the way along to St Catherine's Point, with the geological transition from chalk to the clays and sandstones especially dramatic.

A broad swathe of green turf leads straightforwardly downhill past tiny Watcombe Bay where you reach a lane connecting to the road at Freshwater Bay. Up on the headland to your right stands another of Lord Palmerston's fortifications against a feared French attack - Fort Redoubt. It is now converted to holiday flats and a tea room with sensational views from the little balcony.

Freshwater Bay, once heavily patronised by fans of Alfred, Lord Tennyson who, it is said, even climbed trees at Farringford to get a glimpse of him, eventually reverted to a more normal village after the decline of the Tennyson Circle. Today, new development has virtually linked it to the busier town of Freshwater. Only a robust sea wall prevents the sea from inundating the low-lying River Yar valley with its wetland and estuary habitats. As well as an inshore rescue boat, the little seafront settlement offers all the basic amenities that walkers need and good bus links to the rest of the Island.

STAGE 3:

Freshwater Bay to Chale.
12 miles (19km)

After an initial continuation of walking along high chalk cliffs, this stage becomes dominated by a geological transition to softer clays, making for a very different and less stable coastline. Shadowed by the Military Road and passing near a few small villages, the path nevertheless has a wilder, rougher character, heightened throughout by proximity to the crumbling cliff edge. This whole shore is renowned for its shipwrecks and fossils. Stream mouths eroded into ravines called 'chines' interrupt smooth progress but create interesting focal points in a walk of wide horizons next to the restless sea.

At the east end of the sea wall prom, steps lead up to the clifftops above sea stacks (Arch Rock collapsed a few years ago). Never far from the A3055 Military Road, the coast path gently climbs grassy slopes, passes a small memorial obelisk and rises to meet the road on Compton Down. The terrain here is very steep and there is even concern that the road itself may be threatened by subsidence.

Soon after starting to descend you hop over a stile on the right and quickly encounter the sudden shift from chalk to Wealden and Lower Greensand clays. Heavy soils inland are given over mostly to rough pasture while the yellow-brown cliff edge is dangerously unstable. At a gate, although there are steps down to the popular beach here at the northern end of Compton Bay, the coast path has been re-routed at a higher level due to landslip. Even the new path line is subject to cracking and slippage, so watchfulness is essential, as indeed it is right along the west coast.

A large chunk of the National Trust car park at Shippards Chine slipped away in 1993, underlining the drastic rate of erosion which cuts back the coastline relentlessly each year. Flanked by the coast road, shallow Shippards Chine is the main access point for beachgoers in Compton Bay during the holiday season.

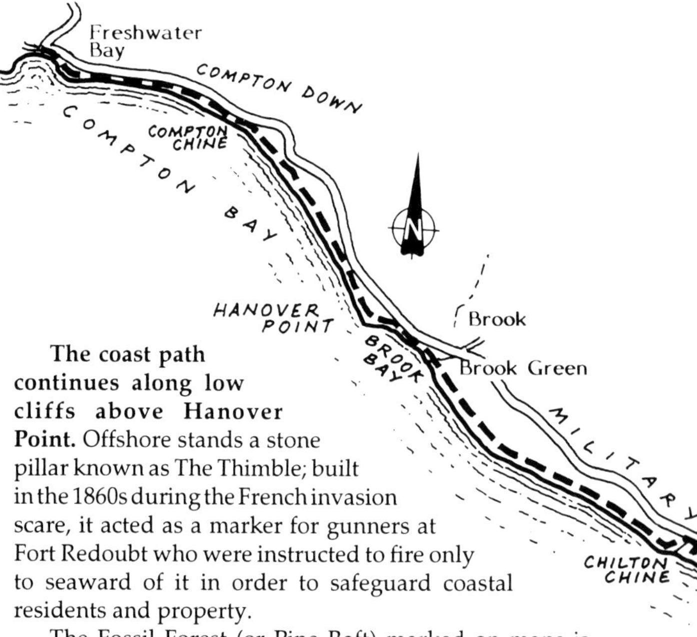

The coast path continues along low cliffs above Hanover Point. Offshore stands a stone pillar known as The Thimble; built in the 1860s during the French invasion scare, it acted as a marker for gunners at Fort Redoubt who were instructed to fire only to seaward of it in order to safeguard coastal residents and property.

The Fossil Forest (or Pine Raft) marked on maps is visible at low tide as a jumble of weed-covered fossilised conifer logs scattered around a sandstone reef. It is thought to be the result of a log jam in an ancient flooded river rather than the site of a forest per se.

Brook Chine has a small car park, an emergency telephone and a National Trust information board. A stile leads on towards the row of Coastguard cottages at Brook Green: keep seaward of the thatched end one, past the old lifeboat house, to resume clifftop walking. (From across the Military Road the Hampstead Trail begins on its way to the north coast.)

(NB: Walkers ready for a lunchtime break would do well to detour a little inland to the Sun Inn, a 500-year-old thatched pub at Hulverstone. Walk up the road to Brook, turn right opposite Badger Lane, walk past Downton Farm, bearing north-east past Downton Cottage over stiled fields to a private garden leading into the road at Hulverstone. The Sun is just along to the left.)

Onwards from Brook Green you traverse a large cattle pasture above Roughland Cliff, part of the Mottistone Estate. The path then threads along a strip of untouched grassland outside fields, with the nearby cliff edge a graphic lesson in coastal erosion! Slumping levels in the Undercliff create temporary habitats for a variety of wildlife. **At Chilton Chine the path detours inland round a holiday centre.** Next door stands Isle of Wight Pearl, one of the largest assemblies of pearl jewellery in the country, complete with in-house personalised designs, production demonstrations and a cafe (free admission).

Not long ago the bones of a 33ft (10m) long dinosaur were unearthed near Chilton Chine, one of many such creatures that frequented this area some 120 million years ago and whose bones and footprints - especially those of Iguanadon - are embedded in the sandstones and mudstones. They are washed out to sea faster than collectors can save them!

(Brighstone village lies just inland, an alternative lunch stop to Hulverstone. Take the path signed 'Chilton Green', pass the duckpond and Chilton Farm Cottages, and walk up Chilton Lane, turning right at the main road. In addition to the Three Bishops pub are pretty thatched cottages, a tea garden

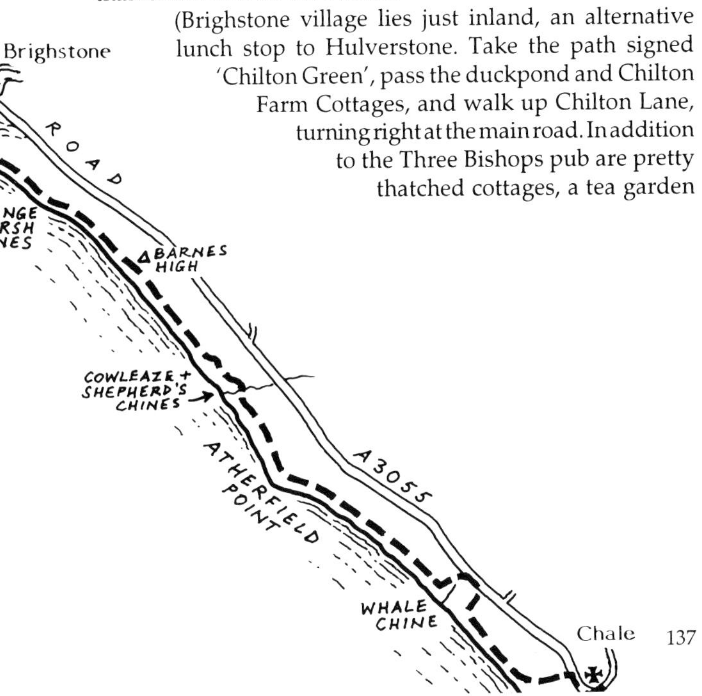

and a small Norman church. The old thatched Post Office is especially picturesque and there is a museum to look round too.)

Until the construction of the Military Road in the 1860s this western sector of the Island, often buffetted by wind and waves and with no safe anchorages, would have been very isolated. The row of modest settlements which grew up here a mile or so inland from the eroding cliffs became known as Back o' Wight, sheltered to some extent from the worst of the winter storms.

Having flanked the holiday centre and returned to the sea, the coast path continues along the cliff edge above a wild, shingle beach and passes another holiday camp (used to house POWs during World War II). At Grange Farm camping and caravan site, there follows a down-and-up over the footbridge in Marsh Chine (badly eroded and very muddy in wet weather) before the trail resumes progress outside field fences - often electric to keep livestock well back. Beyond shallow Barnes Chine a more significant climb brings you onto the marvellous viewpoint of Barnes High at 174ft (53m) above sea level.

Coastal erosion is at its most raw and spectacular, with the cliffs below your feet cracking, slipping and generally collapsing seawards. The culprit is a layer of Gault Clay known locally, and with graphic accuracy, as 'Blue Slipper'. Spring and rain water percolating down lubricates the clay surface, causing it to slide forward and destabilise the land resting on top. Prolonged dry spells simply create more cracks in the upper layers of porous rock and soil, allowing even greater moisture penetration during the next heavy rains. It is a process that man is unable to control. Yet, according to at least one local farmer, the accelerating rate of erosion over recent decades is of man's own making. He recalls as a young boy playing on a steep shingle bank running all along the base of these cliffs. It absorbed much of the waves' energy but was dredged from just offshore between the wars, leaving the cliffs far more vulnerable to wave damage. Whatever the reason, there can be no doubting that man is firmly in retreat.

After Cowleaze Chine, another muddy little scramble ensues from the holiday camp-cum-campsite at Shepherd's Chine (seasonal cafe). Alternatively, walk a little way inland and cross the meandering stream bed there before picking your way up the

opposite bank. In fact the Shepherds Trail begins here, heading away north-east to Carisbrooke through some of the most peaceful countryside on Wight.

As well as offering shelter for small birds, plants and insects, the inaccessible, slumped undercliffs on this coastline provide a breeding habitat for the Glanville Fritillary butterfly which is unique to the Isle of Wight and the Channel Islands.

The onward trail now rounds Atherfield Point, moving from Brighstone Bay to Chale Bay, though the change is almost indiscernible for you are still heading resolutely south-east towards the great bastion of Gore Cliff above Blackgang Chine.

In the days of sail, smuggling and wrecking (the deliberate luring of ships onto rocks for their cargo) were rife in west Wight. However, the natural elements took their toll too and innumerable ships foundered in south-westerly gales on this wild and dangerous lee shore. During a severe storm on October 11th, 1836, the fully rigged East Indiaman *Clarendon* was driven under Blackgang cliffs and quickly broke up in gigantic seas. Of 27 aboard, only 3 survived. The disaster so shocked the Islanders that a new lighthouse was speedily put up on St Catherine's Point to the south of Chale Bay and began warning shipping in 1840.

Striding out along the clifftops you may notice a number of small fishing boats beached on the lower undercliff, ready to be launched by winch in favourable conditions.

Before long the trail reaches Whale Chine, deepest and most dramatic of all the chines on this coast, its bare, precipitous sides sculpted by the wind into pinnacles and ridges. It is thought to have been named after the stranding in 1758 of a 63ft (19m) whale.

A hundred and twenty-six timber steps lead down to the beach (unsuitable for bathing) but there is no way out the other side. Instead the coast path turns inland to the Military Road (a mere track in the 19th century but surfaced during the 1930s and now a supremely scenic road). Turn right past the car park and in about 300m watch for the seaward path on the right. The terrain becomes more overgrown and rougher now - poor land outside crop fields but brightened by colourful plants and flowers. Planks lead over drainage ditches as you head straight for Chale Church and emerge opposite the entrance to the Wight Mouse Inn and

Clarendon Hotel. Turn right along the A3055 verge to reach Chale and the end of this stage.

St Andrew's churchyard contains, as you would expect, the graves of many mariners, among them those who perished in the *Clarendon* wreck. Here on elevated ground there are wide views back along the coast just walked. Chale itself is linked inland to Chale Green by a mile-long straggle of farms and cottages astride the Newport Road.

STAGE 4:

Chale to Shanklin.
11 miles (18km)

After the coast path has passed Blackgang Chine and rounded St Catherine's Point there is an almost immediate change from the exposure and sparsely settled open-ness of the west coast to the sheltered lushness of the old-established Undercliff along the south coast. Facing the sun and protected from cold northerly winds, vegetation and humans thrive! At first the path hugs the crest of the Undercliff before descending to the shoreline and being re-routed in places: even here the sea is winning its battle with the land. There are many visitor attractions along the way as

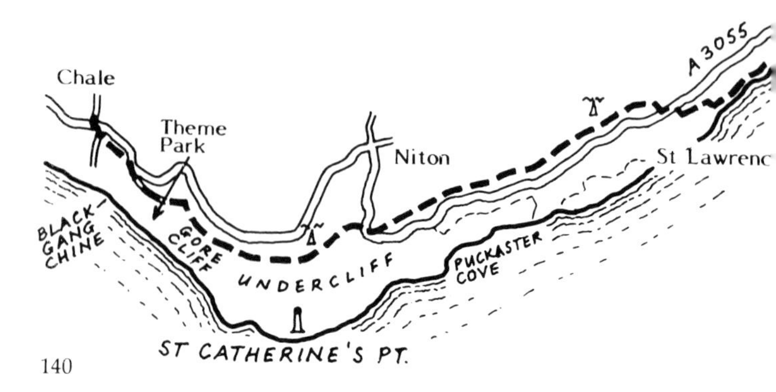

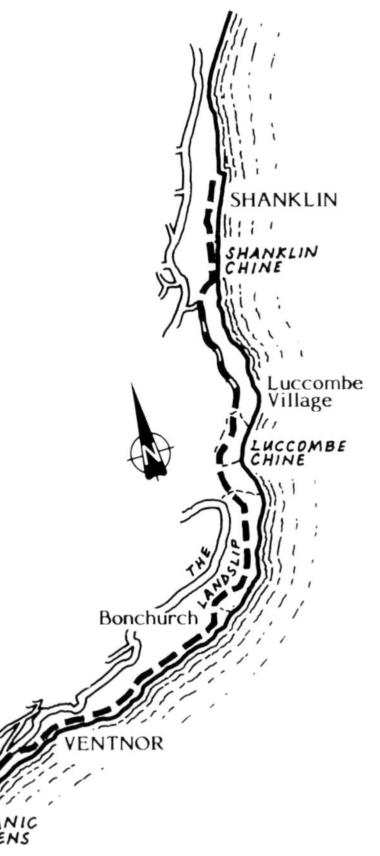

you walk through the Victorian resort of Ventnor nestling beneath St Boniface Down, thread through the Undercliff past Luccombe Village and arrive at the popular seaside town of Shanklin.

Just beyond Chale church, turn right along The Terrace (signed 'Pedestrians to Blackgang'). This by-road once boasted five Victorian villas but only three remain and they too are doomed eventually to fall into the sea. **Take bridleway C15 on the left, a pretty, wooded pathway that leads back to the road higher up. Turn right along the verge and whether or not you are visiting the theme park, branch down right. The coast path continues from the top right-hand corner of the large car park ahead, where a stile and steps lead up to Windy Corner atop Gore Cliff - one of the Island's most spectacular viewpoints.**

Gazing north-west takes in the chalk cliffs of Tennyson Down, The Needles and even the Dorset coast beyond. Closer at hand, set out among the trees, lies Blackgang Theme Park.

The site may not be on every walker's agenda and any visit will certainly occupy at least 2 or 3 hours: perhaps it is best left for a non-walking day? However, the geology and history of the place merits more than just a passing mention.

In the early 19th century Blackgang Chine was by a wide margin

Blackgang Theme Park - a modern version of clifftop attractions dating back 150 years

the grandest such feature on the Island. Reaching over 500ft (152m) above the sea and extending back 3/4 mile (1200m), its stream outlet formed a waterfall down to the beach. No-one had cause to visit the desolate chine except for mackerel fishermen and probably smugglers whose name became adopted. It was not until the early 1840s that Alexander Dabell, son of a Nottingham lace-maker who had come over to set up a lace-making factory in Newport, recognised the tourist potential of the chine. An inveterate entrepreneur, Alexander landscaped gardens on the clifftop, constructed a stepped path to the shore and even exhibited the skeleton of a large fin whale that had stranded on The Needles. With the revenue earned from visiting holidaymakers, Blackgang Chine's scenic gardens were expanded and in due course the business passed down through generations of the Dabell family.

Already serious coastal erosion was taking place, just as it had been since the end of the last Ice Age. The lower road lasted only until 1860, the beach path until 1913. By the 1960s, themed tableaux - educational as well as entertaining - were drawing in the crowds. Today's fantasy theme park represents a logical progression in response to the changing tastes and interests of visitors.

Nature, however, remains oblivious to the success or otherwise of man's ventures. While the west coast cliffs generally are retreating at an average of 20 inches (0.5m) a year, the Blackgang area is estimated to have lost 8-10ft (2m) a year over the past half-century. By any yardstick this is an extraordinary phenomenon. Major recent landslips have occurred in 1978 and in January 1994, the latter responsible for the loss of part of the public road, some adjacent properties, caravans and vehicles, as well as a portion of the theme park itself. At the time of writing the aftermath is still evident in the form of tumbled roads and pathways ending in sheer drops, scattered house contents and even wrecked cars.

For many years Blackgang's owners have adopted a policy of 'managed retreat', acknowledging that large scale civil engineering measures to arrest erosion are totally unrealistic. Attractions within the park are moved when necessary to ensure the public's safety but there can be little doubt that in the long term the whole enterprise will slip away into the waves.

In the meantime there is much to absorb and enjoy. Adjacent to the theme park stands Blackgang Sawmill tracing the history and techniques of timber-use from felling and steam sawing to such crafts as coopering, shipbuilding and domestic carpentry. Next door stands St Catherine's Quay, a maritime museum par excellence. Among the exhibits are the original whale skeleton and a 'Liverpool' class lifeboat - the RNLI's 36ft (11m) *Friendly Forester*, built on the Island in 1953 and instrumental in saving some 89 lives. (This reminds us that Chale Bay, Atherfield Ledge and the infamous St Catherine's Race off the headland have claimed over 250 ships in the last 200 years. Before then, and mostly unrecorded, thousands of vessels and countless mariners crewing them met their end on this treacherous stretch of coast open to the full force of Atlantic storms.)

Before continuing the coastal walk, ponder these lines penned by Wilhemina Smith in the 1930s:

'Some ramblers start at Ventnor and walk it, all the way;
Others go from Shanklin (I did the other day).
And if I must be truthful, I went by motor car,
But for stalwart, honest hikers the distance isn't far!

And oh! when you get there you'll gasp out your delight;
This Chine is quite unusual, a most impressive sight.
Blue clay and yellow sandstone towering above the sea;
Silent, grim and scornful - gigantic masonry!'

Take the ascending pathway to the Observation Peak.
On the wooden platform stand - but do not speak.
'Tis the best feature of this Blackgang Chine.
In this lovely Island, no view half as fine
As seen from this pinnacle when the day is clear:
Boldly stand The Needles - and Dorset's coast draws near.'

From Windy Corner the coast path begins its gradual turn towards the east, once again on chalk cliffs. Below, a much more extensive and vegetated undercliff stretches down to brown shingle foreshore and is penetrated by several paths including the old Sandrock Road which continues to be vulnerable to landslip. **Soon you come abreast the gleaming white buildings of St Catherine's lighthouse, set on green, wildlife-rich hillocks and hummocks at the Island's**

On the coast path above St Catherine's lighthouse

southernmost tip. Opened in 1840 following the tragic loss of the *Clarendon* at Blackgang, its present light has a range of 18 miles (29km).

Passing telecommunication masts, the trail proceeds along field edges into an old walled track descending to the A3055 at Barrack Shute which connects the upper and lower parts of Niton. The upper village, with its old thatched stone houses, 12th century church, pub (The White Lion) and shops, expanded seawards in the 19th century when wealthy visitors discovered the attractions of the Undercliff and built their summer residences there.

About 20m down the road to the right, turn left into bridleway NT31, keeping right for St Lawrence and soon branching left on the coast path. The following section takes a straightforward line east along the inner cliffs at the edge of the downs, well back from the coast. There are airy views over the Undercliff and rolling

countryside inland. Coming over a rise and passing more aerial masts across pasture, you reach the intersection with St Rhadegund's Path and turn right (V8).

Medieval pilgrims arriving by sea at Puckaster Cove (a little to the west and once a busy port) walked up over the downs this way to take the holy well waters of Our Lady and St Rhadegund at Whitwell. The path retains its ancient name to this day and the well has never run dry.

The stepped path takes you down to a road. Cross over into a residential estate and branch left on a tarmac pathway to reach the main A3055 coast road.

You have descended to the base of a prominent cliff line of Upper Greensand where the Undercliff originally broke away. Between cliff and shore are many minor escarpments separated by deep gulleys, each being a piece of Upper Greensand which broke off and slid forward on the 'Blue Slipper', tilting back as they did so into a steep northern slope. Small movements do take place occasionally but the principal formation of the Undercliff occurred in distant times and it is now relatively stable.

Turn left along the road then right into Woolverton Road and take the path on the right through a gate and continue down to a track. At the time of writing a diversion bears left here owing to erosion at Woody Bay. In about 200m turn right past bungalows to reach the clifftops. Not far ahead, from a rise at Woody Point, is your first view of Ventnor.

The path now runs along outside the perimeter fence of the Rare Breeds and Waterfowl Park. Its 30 acres contain a fascinating array of creatures from the domestic to the exotic, including otters, miniature horses, deer, guanacos, pygmy goats, wallabies, coloured turkeys and over 100 bird species. There is also a Temperate Waterfall House, gift shop and lakeside cafe.

Within a short distance the trail skirts the seaward edge of Ventnor's Steephill Botanic Gardens. Like Blackgang, they and the nearby Museum of Smuggling History deserve a separate visit. Set out around the 22-acre grounds of the erstwhile Royal National Hospital for Diseases of the Chest, rendered obsolete by the 1960s through new drugs and treatments, the gardens are a marvellous sight. Themed borders feature plants from around the world and there are plenty of corners in which to relax and soak up the almost

Mediterranean ambience. The Garden Tavern cafe/bar might well be of interest at this stage of the walk!

At Steephill Cove (tea gardens) another erosion diversion takes you left to the main road pavement for about 1/2 mile (800m) before a right turn heads back seaward. The onward path leads down to grassy terraces in Ventnor Park, passes a car park and arrives at Ventnor's seafront prom.

West of the resort, a £1 million coastal protection scheme involving the reinforcement of the cliff base with carboniferous limestone from the Mendip Hills was completed in 1992. It seems unlikely to be a final solution.

Ventnor grew up from beginnings as a health resort for wealthy Victorians and some of that genteel, old-fashioned character remains in its handsome villas and terraces of substantial properties stacked onto the steep southern face of St Boniface Down. All the resort amenities you would expect to find are here but without the brash modern development that so often blights holiday towns. Unfortunately the pier has burned down. Both the Heritage Centre and the Longshoremen's Museum are well worth visiting, while delicious crab sandwiches are served in the Spyglass pub. The original spa waters are used in the local brewery recipe.

If, however, your sights are set on reaching the end of the stage at Shanklin, continue past the Winter Gardens and boating lake along The Esplanade. Beyond little Wheelers Bay a broad sea wall carries the coast path beneath chalk cliffs renowned for their rare plants and nesting seabirds. Continue past Bonchurch Pottery and bear left up behind a row of houses to tiny Bonchurch Old Church of Norman origin. Turn right here, along past a sports field and Carigdene Farm.

You next walk through The Landslip, densely overgrown with a veritable jungle of creeper-hung trees, moss covered rocks and shadowy fissures, mostly created by major landslips in 1810 and 1928. Sections of boardwalk protect fragile habitats from tramping feet.

The walled track continues from an information board and crosses above Luccombe Chine which can be explored by a steep path on the right. The delightful coast path track now heads north past a tea garden and reaches Luccombe Road; keep straight on past the old Shanklin Hospital and turn right by Rylstone Gardens

into Popham Road. Steps lead down to Appley Beach where you bear left along the foreshore path, past the Chine's outlet with its cottage pub. Reaching the Esplanade, turn left up zig-zags past the Chine Inn and veer right along Keats Green and Eastcliff Promenade.

For anyone interested in natural beauty, geology and history, Shanklin Chine is a 'must'. On payment of a modest fee you can wander down a delightful shady path into the depths of a chine quite unlike those on the exposed west coast. Here the ravine is lushly wooded - a haven for ferns, mosses and woodland wildlife; its little stream provides the moisture and falls in a 40ft (12m) waterfall. The Chine's story includes the Victorian Experience, shipwrecks and smuggling and the World War II era when Commandos trained here and Pluto ('Pipe Line Under The Ocean' which supplied fuel for the D-Day landings) was laid down the chine. Apart from the scenery, Heritage Centre and gift shop, there's a Victorian Tea Garden.

From the top of the Chine you can wander through picturesque Shanklin Old Village, a cluster of thatched cottages whose modest origins as a fishing hamlet have been comprehensively transformed by a plethora of eating and drinking places, stalls and gift shops catering unashamedly for holidaymakers who flock here during the season.

Running north above the Chine is Keats Green, named after the poet who stayed at Eglantine Cottage (now Keats Cottage, 76 High Street) in 1819 to improve his failing health and take in 'the wideness of the Sea'. Even in those early days the Chine was a popular sight, a fact reflected in Keats' wish that he had a penny for every visitor entering! Tragically, within 2 years the poet had died at the age of 26. There are fine coastal views from the green which is connected by lift to the seafront.

Shanklin developed rapidly once the railway arrived and the pier was built in 1891; as a result the main part of the town, set on its coastal hillside, is Victorian and Edwardian in character. One of Shanklin's great attractions is its long, safe, sandy beach and all the usual holiday amenities; another is its proximity to splendid walking country, with paths radiating west and south across beautiful downland. A storm destroyed Shanklin's pier in 1987.

STAGE 5:

Shanklin to Ryde.
15 miles (24km)

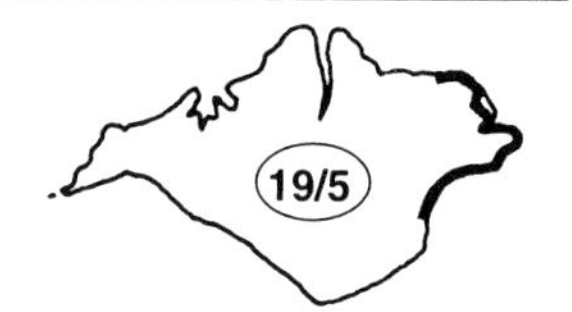

From the bustling seaside resorts of Shanklin and Sandown the coast path rises over chalk down on Culver Cliff then weaves along low shoreline above rock ledges round the Foreland at Bembridge. Passing the lifeboat station there's a roadside detour to St Helens to cross the broad rivermouth estuary of Bembridge Harbour. Field paths just inland lead to Nettlestone Point where the seawall prom is taken all the way along to Puckpool Point and onwards to Ryde Pier, with extensive views over the Spithead offshore forts and busy shipping lanes. A longer stage than most but on the easier, more sheltered eastern coastline with plenty of interest along the way.

There can be no equivocation about the initial 3 or 4 miles (5km) of this stage: it's basically a leisurely stroll around Sandown Bay, for much of the time along seafront promenade.

Sandown's gently-shelving, sandy bathing beach and enviable sunshine record have established it as the Island's largest traditional family resort. There's also more in the way of entertainments than at neighbouring Shanklin, from fish and chips, candy floss and amusement arcades to bingo, discos and the Pavilion Theatre. Several of the old 19th century barracks and forts around which the town developed now house attractions, among them the large Leisure Centre and Sandown's famous zoo. It's not all razzmatazz: Battery and Ferncliff Gardens provide flower-framed views of the Bay, there are quiet corners and open spaces in Los Altos Park, and above the Library in the High Street is a fascinating geological and dinosaur museum.

Walk north along the prom past the pierhead and war memorial. There's a little jink to the left then you're passing the zoo and going through a car park at Yaverland to pick up a coast path sign to Bembridge; other notices warn of cliff falls. The well walked path climbs gently behind slumping cliffs of soft, fossil-bearing

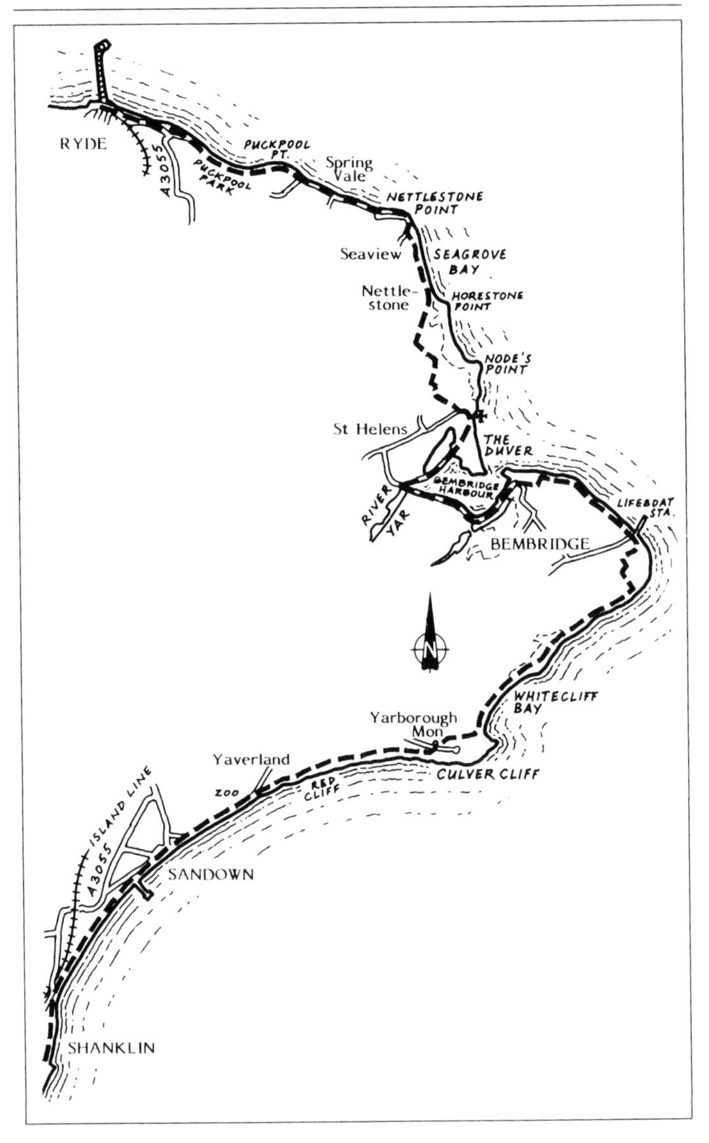

RYDE
A3055
PUCKPOOL PT.
PUCKPOOL PARK
Spring Vale
NETTLESTONE POINT
Seaview
SEAGROVE BAY
Nettle-stone
HORESTONE POINT
NODE'S POINT
St Helens
THE DUVER
BEMBRIDGE HARBOUR
RIVER YAR
BEMBRIDGE
LIFEBOAT STA.
N
WHITECLIFF BAY
Yarborough Mon
Yaverland
ZOO
RED CLIFF
CULVER CLIFF
ISLAND LINE
A3055
SANDOWN
SHANKLIN

red sandstone towards the monument on Culver Cliff - the day's first objective. Angling across open grass and through incongruously isolated iron gateposts, the trail continues to gain height and offer ever wider views back along the coast.

Culver Cliff forms the easternmost bastion of the great chalk ridge stretching right across the Island from Tennyson Down in the west. The stone needle on its summit was constructed in 1849 to the memory of Charles Pelham, Earl of Yarborough and inaugural commodore of the Royal Yacht Squadron.

From the handgate, bear left up to the road at the crest of Culver Down, cross over (left of a pub and cafe) and head half-right down to a stile. Beyond, you join a steeper chalky path towards Whitecliff Bay. Waymarks guide you outside properties, round the back of a landslip, past chalets and over little footbridges until you reach a large caravan park with a bridge over its beach slipway. There are superb views back to Culver Cliff.

Now the trail begins to thread through scrubby woods, crosses a few minor slips and passes Bembridge School, founded in 1919. Ahead lies more landslipped terrain with slumped ground and tumbled trees. The soft clays of the Palaeogene beds covering northern Wight are heavy to work inland; on the coast the earth appears to flow when saturated, drying out like lava. **Occasional views through a clifftop screen of foliage and sections of boardwalk characterise the onwards path, with small fishermen's huts located in the undercliff as you approach Bembridge.** Weed-covered limestone ledges running out from shore provide food for over-wintering birds such as purple sandpipers and sanderling.

The trail soon comes past a beach cafe to the Crab & Lobster pub, an old smugglers' haunt. Walk left across its car park and turn inland along unsurfaced residential Beachfield Road. In about 200m turn right then swing left into Foreland Farm Lane. In 100m take the tree-lined path on the right past a golf course to emerge at Bembridge Holiday Village where a left turn along Fishermen's Walk takes you to the lifeboat station jetty and adjacent car park and cafe at Lane End.

Bembridge's lifeboat, 'Tyne' class *Sir Max Aitken III*, serves an exceptionally busy stretch of water used by ferries, cargo ships, Royal Navy vessels and leisure craft of all descriptions.

Large enough to be a town really, thanks to much post-war building, Bembridge village sits on the Island's east tip at the mouth of the East Yar river. A curious collection of ageing houseboats occupies the margins of its shallow tidal harbour which is contained by a 19th century embankment now carrying the B3395. Here small craft come and go with the tide. Appropriately for a nautical centre such as this, Bembridge contains a fascinating maritime museum crammed full of historic shipwreck finds, models and pictures.

Developed originally by wealthy Victorians who extended the railway line here, the place remains today prosperous and peaceful. Non-sailors will know Bembridge best for its splendid windmill set on a hill to the west. Careful restoration of this the Island's sole surviving example gives us a rare first-hand glimpse of 18th century milling technology. It is owned and cared for by the National Trust.

To continue the coast path, walk on along the sea wall from the lifeboat jetty. The trail then basically follows the sandy shore for about 1/2 mile (800m) before bearing inland (just before the concrete groyne) as a woodland walk beneath a steep, overgrown cliff-face. This soon becomes a hedged path leading to a track - Dulcie Avenue. Turn left then in about 75m turn right into Pump Lane (BB3). Meeting the B3395, you can easily stroll out to Bembridge Point for the wide views.

Bembridge is strategically placed for a lunch break and there are several establishments on or near the path; the Row Barge especially welcomes walkers. It is situated just along the road opposite Pump Lane. (Incidentally, the Bembridge Trail ends here, having crossed the Island from Newport.)

The coast path now follows the B3395 (Embankment Road) past various small marine businesses and colourful houseboats, right along to the Yar bridge.

The harbour used to be much more extensive but was dammed in 1877 in order to connect Bembridge with St Helens. This blocked the tidal flow and created a vast expanse of freshwater marsh, reed beds and meadow, leaving high and dry the ancient port of Brading at the head of an inlet known as Brading Haven. St Helens, whose spring water was once highly valued by mariners for its exceptional keeping properties, was formerly an important port accessible to the fleet anchored at nearby Spithead.

Cross the Yar bridge and turn sharp right along Latimer Road. At the end, beyond garages, stands a sign for the onward coast path (R108) to Seaview. Walk straight ahead to the little quayside and bear left behind Mill House to reach the footpath over the Causeway, one of the 18th century dams that were used to impound water at each tide to power the mill. It's an exhilarating stretch, especially at high tide. The Causeway ends at The Duver, a spit of open grassland, scrub and marsh containing well over 250 plant species. Access is unrestricted as it is owned by the National Trust, but the coast path keeps left over St Helens Common - until 1961 the site of the Royal Isle of Wight Golf Club. It's well worth detouring over to the seawall for coastal views, a cafe and, further along to the left, the remains of St Helens Church. It was badly damaged by the sea in 1550 and again in 1703 but restoration was never considered economic at such an exposed location. The ruined tower, however, has been consolidated and is now painted white to seaward as a daymark for shipping.

The trail temporarily leaves the actual shoreline now for a couple of miles, mainly due to private property. Walk inland from the church tower for about 150m to a tarmac road. Cross the stile on your right (R85), walk up a marshy field to the top right-hand corner stile and continue up the next field to double telegraph poles where you meet an access lane. Turn right, passing Nodes Park Holiday Camp, and go through a gateway onto the Priory Hotel's driveway. At the next gateposts turn left onto bridleway R84 and the end turn right (R74). This track comes down to residential Ferniclose Road heading towards the sea. Pass Gully Road on your left and just before reaching the beach toilets at Seagrove Bay, go left (R105) into a tarred path between garden fences. This continues as a track (Pier Road) between woods and seafront houses leading to Seaview village and shops. Bear right to regain the shore at Nettlestone Point.

Seaview's narrow, seaward-sloping streets and alleyways evoke a few echoes from its Edwardian heyday as a rather more select alternative to Ryde. Large, secluded villas were built and steamers from the mainland berthed at the chain pier (which was subsequently destroyed by a severe storm in 1951).

Walking up this east coast it is virtually impossible - except in

Good views of The Solent forts from Nettlestone Point on the east coast

the most persistent of sea mists - to ignore the offshore granite forts sitting squat and defiant in the approaches to Portsmouth. St Helens Fort is clearly visible from Bembridge northwards, while from Seaview, No Man's Land Fort and House Sand Fort rise from the sea not far distant; the fourth fort, Spitbank, lies nearer the mainland shore off Southsea. Like so many of the Island's coastal defences, they were built between 1860 and 1880 against the imagined threat of a French invasion under Napoleon III and became known as 'Palmerston Follies'.

At ebb tide it's possible to walk from St Helens to Seaview along the rocky/sandy shoreline but care should be taken not to get cut off at Horestone Point.

From the interesting rock formations at Nettlestone Point the coast path takes to the seafront Esplanade, passes The Old Fort Inn and Sea View Yacht Club then turns right off the road along the sea wall (path R91). You soon join the Toll Road (no charge for pedestrians) above the beach leading into Springvale Road.

Just inland can be found Flamingo Park, a bird sanctuary laid out on grassy slopes above the old salterns. Tame peacocks, flamingos and macaws, as well as numerous species of ducks and geese, wander around freely, while more exotic species are on view in the Tropical House.

At the Battery Inn the road bends inland to Puckpool Hill but the coast path keeps straight ahead along the pedestrian sea wall (CR90) above Spring Vale Beach; the concrete wall curves round Puckpool Point towards Ryde, now visible in the distance. Beyond the cafe at the edge of Puckpool Park, a delightful fringe of trees reaches down to a fine sandy beach (although here at the eastern end of Ryde Sands the tide comes in extremely quickly, covering some quite large depressions). You pass Appley Tower, a Victorian Gothic folly, and Appley Park woodlands and where the sea wall ends simply continue on past the Inshore Rescue lookout and the boating lake to the oriental-style Pavilion at Eastern Gardens. Bear inland here and walk along The Esplanade to the left of the railway, soon reaching the pier entrance.

In the early 19th century Ryde grew rapidly from farming and fishing hamlets either end of a connecting street into a major bathing resort. It has a wealth of elegant Regency and Victorian buildings, many now converted to hotels and guest houses. It was the construction of the pier, completed in 1824, that triggered this transformation. At last visitors from the mainland could disembark without the discomfort of being bumped over sandbanks and shallows by horse and cart in all weathers, as was previously the case. The pier, one of Britain's longest, runs out for almost $^{1}/_{2}$ mile (800m) and carries the Island Line Railway out to Pier Head station; there it connects with Wightlink's high speed catamaran service to Portsmouth. Near the pier entrance, hovercrafts depart noisily on their super-fast passage to Southsea taking around 9 minutes! The Island Line Railway utilises old London Underground tube trains on its unique service between Ryde and Shanklin, including seasonal connections with the Isle of Wight Steam Railway at Havenstreet. The Nunwell Trail, incidentally, shadows the Island Line for much of its course from Ryde to Sandown.

STAGE 6:

Ryde to Cowes.
8 miles (13km)

In many ways this final stage of the coast path is the least satisfactory from a walker's standpoint. There is a good deal of road walking west of Wootton, particularly to by-pass the extensive grounds of Osborne House, which is a pity because coastal paths do exist there. Perhaps at some future date a more truly coastal routing will be established; at the time of writing the Ramblers Association is tackling this issue. Despite these disadvantages the stage's initial section past Quarr Abbey is delightful and even the road walking that ensues west of Wootton Creek is for the most part on quiet lanes through beautiful, rolling countryside. A recommended alternative over the last couple of miles deviates

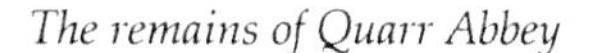
The remains of Quarr Abbey

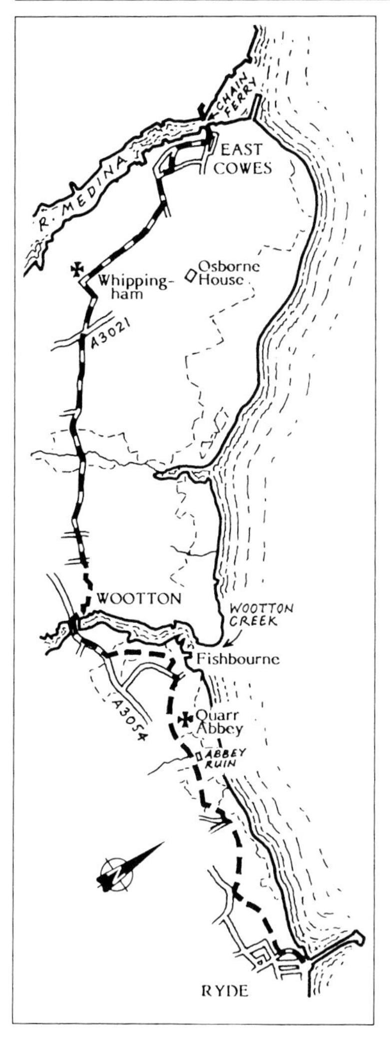

from the official route to visit Whippingham Church. Thereafter it's a mater of taking the Floating Bridge chain ferry from East Cowes to West Cowes, the original setting-off point and where this description of the path ends.

From Ryde Pier bear left then right into St Thomas Street and take the next right turn into Buckingham Road. This leads to Spencer Road where you turn right, following it for about $^1/_2$ mile (800m) where, as a gravel track, it reaches the main A3054 road at a bend by a house. Pass through the gate ahead and bear right onto a shady, tarred path known as Ladies Walk (R48), heading north-west through Ryde Golf Course. The path dips over a stream bridge (beach access to the right) then rises to Binstead's Church of the Holy Cross. Turn left here and almost immediately turn right by the very picturesque Keys Cottage into Church Road.

Parts of Binstead Church date from Norman times when it served the quarrymen excavating stone for Quarr Abbey from local limestone outcrops. The same stone was later used in other notable buildings, including Chichester and Winchester cathedrals.

At the lane corner bear left into a bridleway track through trees and at the entrance to Kingarth Lodge fork left (signed Fishbourne). At Quarr Road turn right. The road soon becomes unsurfaced and continues west past the old ruins of Quarr Abbey.

The original small medieval Cistercian Abbey was founded in 1132 by Baldwin de Redbers, Lord of the Island, and takes its names from the nearby limestone quarries. The valley site was chosen for its easy access to the sea, its fresh water and its oak woodlands. The Island benefited a great deal from the foundation's work in education, poor relief and agriculture but Henry VIII's Dissolution of the Monasteries in 1537 put paid to all that.

Walk through the archway - part of the old Abbey wall - then cross the driveway to the 'new' Quarr Abbey, opened in 1912 as a community of French Benedictine monks. The large, imposing building with its domed tower is built of imported, rose-red Flemish brick and the Church is open to the public.

The onward path leads down to a road (Fishbourne Lane) opposite the Fishbourne Inn (food). Turn left to pass Wightlink's Portsmouth ferry terminal and take a narrow path over on the right by a telephone box (R1). In 100m you turn left onto a shady private lane - Ashlake Copse Road. A little further on be sure to fork right by a pipe down through trees. Continuing due south, the way becomes surfaced at houses and reaches the A3054 at Kite Hill. Turn right and cross Wootton Bridge, branching right to pass The Sloop Inn (well situated for a lunchtime break; with creekside views from the terrace it offers walkers a warm welcome).

Wootton Creek flows through pastoral countryside upstream and there is boating on The Old Mill Pond from Lakeside Leisure Park. Further downstream the waterway, flanked by boatyards and a sailing school, is an immensely popular venue for small craft.

Walk straight up the gravel track from The Sloop and along the tarred path to the right of Unity Hall. At residential New Road ahead, turn right then in about 100m turn left along a track called Red Road beside Wootton Youth Centre. Weaving on a narrow path between gardens, you soon reach some lock-up garages. Swing right and turn left onto a residential estate road. In about

100m turn left off the bend to pass more lock-up garages where steps on the right lead to a path emerging into Church Road. Keep virtually straight over along Footways, at the end turning left into Palmers Road then immediately right along Brocks Copse Road.

Before long the residential outskirts of Wootton are left behind for deep countryside with Solent views. The road drops to cross Palmers Brook then rises to a junction. Keep straight on (north-west) along Alverstone Road, past the tiny Post Office, and at the A3021 turn right.

The official coast path routing now follows the main road all the way to East Cowes. Land to the east surrounding Osborne House is either in private ownership or belongs to the Crown and the public have no right of access.

Designed by Prince Albert in conjunction with his builder, Thomas Cubitt, and financed from the private royal fortune, Osborne House became a cherished country retreat for Queen Victoria and her family: her 'little paradise' as she called it. The grandiose Italianate villa was built in 1845-6 and surrounded by extensive, terraced grounds in which the children learned gardening with their own scaled-down implements. Swiss Cottage chalet, another favourite with the royal children, is reached along a driveway, either on foot or by Victorian horse and carriage.

Osborne House interior, immaculately preserved and sometimes overwhelmingly opulent, allows us a rare glimpse into the private tastes and lifestyle of a 19th century monarch. State and private apartments are on view, many unchanged since Queen Victoria died there on January 22nd, 1901. Her son, Edward VII, less enthusiastic about Osborne House than his parents had been, presented it to the nation in 1902 and it is now managed by English Heritage.

Neighbouring Barton Manor, bought by Queen Victoria as an extension to the Osborne Estate, has become a privately owned vineyard producing award-winning wines; along with its lovely water-gardens, the winery is open to the public during the holiday season.

A worthwhile alternative routing to East Cowes turns left off the A3021 after about 150m onto Beatrice Avenue past a school. Follow the lane round and you will come to the Royal Church of

St Mildred at Whippingham. Also designed by Prince Albert and on many an Island sightseeing tour, Whippingham Church with its five-pinnacled spire evokes Balkan architecture rather than anything English. The church and village of scattered estate houses witnessed numerous royal events during the reign of Queen Victoria.

All that now remains is to walk along the country road past Cowes Power Station over to the left, and to turn left at the junction with the B3321. Passing riverside industry at East Cowes, you turn sharp left along Ferry Road (the town centre is just to the right). Signs direct you to the Floating Bridge chain ferry over the River Medina to West Cowes, while nearby is Red Funnel's Southampton car and passenger ferry terminal.

CHAPTER 4

The Vectis 8 Trail

WALK 20: THE VECTIS 8 TRAIL

Yarmouth - Brook -
Carisbrooke Castle - Brading -
Whitwell - Shorwell - Yarmouth.
71 miles (114km)

The Vectis 8 Trail was originated by the Isle of Wight Area of the Ramblers Association. Planned to give approximately 6 days' walking, the route meanders across the Island and back in a rough figure-of-eight. Because there is a separate coastal path, the Vectis 8 Trail concentrates on the Island's beautiful inland countryside, passing through areas of outstanding landscape quality and providing the best viewpoints.

Dividing a long-distance trail into sections will never satisfy everyone! While the following 6 stages of approximately 12 miles (19km) represent daily hikes of average length, fitter walkers could complete the trail in 4 or 5 days. By the same token, a more leisurely pace or the inclusion of rest days would extend the walk to around 10 days. Being circular, the Vectis 8 Trail can be started at any point along the way if it is more convenient than Yarmouth. Equally, each stage can be considered as a worthwhile walk in its own right.

Because the Vectis 8 Trail inevitably follows rights of way used by other walks in this guidebook (all of which are selected for their fine quality), the description below concerns itself with finding the way. The trail is not waymarked as such and therefore careful navigation is required in places. For simplicity's sake and to keep the route description flowing, individual stiles and gates are only mentioned if they are likely to be missed or are important for other reasons.

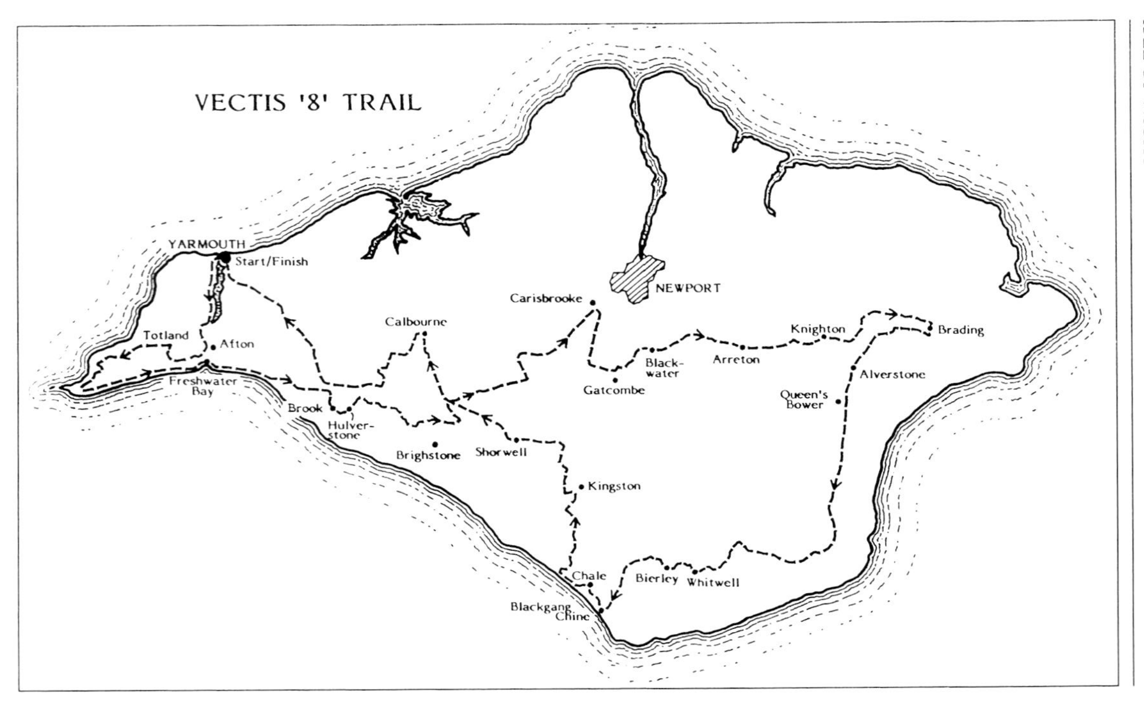
VECTIS '8' TRAIL
YARMOUTH
Start/Finish
Totland
Afton
Freshwater Bay
Brook
Hulver-stone
Calbourne
Brighstone
Shorwell
Carisbrooke
NEWPORT
Gatcombe
Black-water
Arreton
Knighton
Brading
Alverstone
Queen's Bower
Kingston
Chale
Blackgang Chine
Bierley
Whitwell

Background details about the places passed through can be obtained by referring to other walks in this book where they appear (see Index).

STAGE 1:

Yarmouth to Brook.
13 miles (21km)

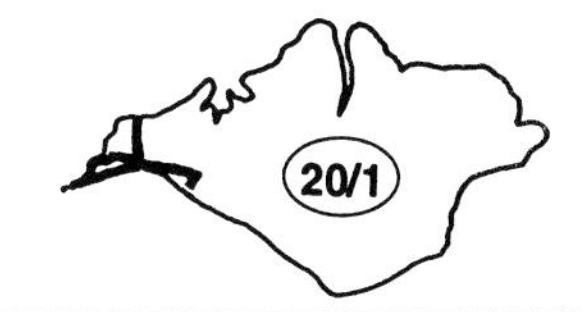

From Yarmouth's ferry terminal walk west beside the A3054 over the Yar Bridge and take the first lane on the left (signed 'Freshwater Way'). Where the lane swings sharp left carry straight on up through **Saltern Wood** and along field edges. At a copse bear left and cross the stile immediately on the right into trees, crossing footbridges and continuing south up the field track. Go over the access driveway to **Kings Manor Farm** and through a handgate on the right, through a tree enclosure and along the field behind the farm where a stile leads out onto a tarred lane. Turn right and maintain the same southerly direction into a pathway beside All Saints Church, emerging at the road by the Red Lion pub.

Bear left along the road and turn off right at a stile into a path through reed beds; if waterlogged, take to the old railway trackbed 50m further on. Either way leads out to Hooke Hill where you turn left down to the main A3055 and left again past a garden centre. Cross over and turn right into **Afton Marsh Nature Reserve** (path not on OS map). With the river on your right at first, cross a footbridge to the other bank and on reaching the Blackbridge Road turn right along to the main road near Freshwater Bay.

Take the hedged path opposite, to the left of thatched **St Agnes Church** and stay on the lower, wider track, passing a National Trust sign for **Tennyson Down.** In about 400m turn right down a narrow path and right again over a stile. Walk north down two fields then bear left towards the gate and signpost in the hedge ahead.

At the road (Moors Hill) turn right and in about 400m at a right-

Tennyson's Monument, looking towards West High Down

hand bend turn off left onto a bridleway track; it veers sharp right by trees but the trail continues straight on from Stonewind Farm towards a copse. Walk through the trees and across a field, turning left along the road at **Totland** and passing the Catholic Church and the youth hostel. Hurst Hill leads onto York Road where you meet the B3322 Alum Bay road.

Cross over into York Lane opposite the church and in 100m turn right, almost immediately turning left along a narrow path to another road. A short distance up to the left, turn right on a fenced path bearing left to the National Trust owned **Headon Warren.** At a grassy clearing follow the track on uphill, forking right beyond a bench and arriving at the fenced-in summit Bronze Age tumulus. Bear left with the fence and continue along the ridgetop path, doubling back just before the old gun emplacement and descending a track to an unmade road. This leads down to the **Alum Bay** access road.

Turn right to the **Needles Pleasure Park** and follow the road round left up past toilets and the coach park. At the top where the lane curves right, go left up steps, signed '**West High Down'.** (Walkers wishing to visit The Needles Headland and Old Battery, carry on westwards along the lane.)

The Vectis Trail now heads east along a grassy track by a fence and in about $^{1}/_{2}$ mile (800m) trends right towards a signpost. Cross the stile and fork right up onto the downs to reach **Tennyson's Monument.** Continue in the same direction downhill to little **Watcombe Bay** where a handgate leads left into a lane bringing you out to the main road at **Freshwater Bay.**

Turn right and walk along the sea wall promenade, climbing wooden steps onto the clifftops at the far end. The coast path rises gradually to meet the A3055 Military Road and runs along a bank beside it on **Afton Down** before crossing a stile on the right and descending steps to grassy slopes. After crossing Compton Chine, turn left at a warning notice towards cottages, cross the coast road and continue to Compton Farm. Follow the sunken, hedged bridleway to the right of the farm and beyond the gate at the top walk along the ridge with a fence on your right. Through the second gate bear left of the summit onto a grassy ledge leading to a gate at the right of a thicket. Turn right at the wood down a track. Past the lane to Dunsbury Farm take the narrow path between fence and trees; lower down it broadens out to become Badger Lane leading to the main village street at **Brook.**

STAGE 2:

Brook to Carisbrooke Castle.
10 miles (16km)

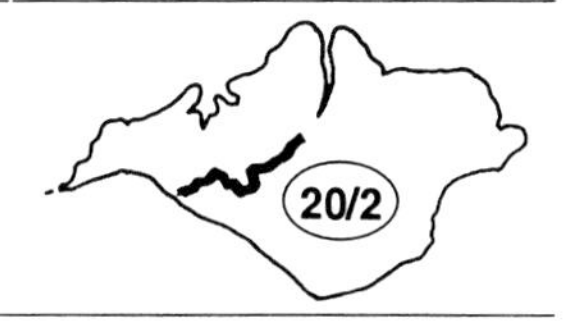

Opposite the entrance to Badger Lane, set off along the bridleway which curves left towards Downton Cottage. Take the narrow path left of the cottage drive and walk up the edge of two fields ahead. At the far corner cross a stile into a private garden, keeping carefully to its left boundary and leaving by a wall step. Turn left and left again along the main B3399 at **Hulverstone.** Opposite the Sun Inn take the stiled path into open fields and walk uphill towards the edge of forestry on Brook Hill. Climb the woodland path and at the main crosstrack ahead turn right, following its twists and turns to reach the famous **Longstone** megalith.

Leave the track which swings right here, instead crossing a stile ahead into a field path past woods on **Castle Hill** to emerge at **Strawberry Lane**. Turn right and in 100m left along a gravel track to Grammar's Common plantation. Turn right on the main track which narrows further on and bears right, dropping to a stile. Cross the sloping field, a fence on your left, and once over the next stile descend steps through undergrowth into a narrow path leading to a track, along which turn left.

Continue up to a stable yard but veer right to join a broad, fenced track swinging left, uphill. At a signpost just before the top, turn right along a path and at the junction ahead go left, through a gate, by-passing a cottage and through the grounds of old Mottistone Mill just north of **Brighstone.**

Turn left along the minor road and in 150m turn right, straight through Coombe Farm and up the bridleway beyond to a T-junction at a fence. Bear left here beside the fence and through a gate, following the clear path as it curves uphill to reach the ancient ridgetop trackway on **Limerstone Down.**

Cross straight over into **Brighstone Forest** and in about 300m turn sharp right on bridleway BS7. The path winds downhill and exits the forest at a gate, continuing down by the forest edge. Where the tree line ends, go through a gate and along the valley of Fern Bottom beneath Cheverton Down. At the far end of the field you join the main track through forestry on Rowborough Down.

Reaching the end of forestry at a gate, the trail continues along a field track. 150m before Rowborough Farm turn left up a steep chalky track passing more forestry on Idlecombe Down. At the top of the climb turn right; beyond old chalk pits the way drops to the B3323 Newport-Shorwell road. Turn left and in a few metres cross over into the bridleway opposite. Soon after passing the small copse ahead, go through a hedge gap on the right and turn left along the track which curves right past Frogland Copse to reach a crosstrack. Turn left for abcut 50m then bear right over a field to a stile. Turn left along the hedged track for 100m then cross a stile on the right into water meadows in the valley of Lukely Brook. The way proceeds north-east, parallel with the brook, hedge on the right, crossing a wooden footbridge to arrive at Millers Lane, Carisbrooke. Turn right and just after the road junction take the path on the left leading up to the car park for **Carisbrooke Castle.**

STAGE 3:

Carisbrooke Castle to Brading.
13 miles (21km)

From the south-west corner of the castle's defensive bank, take the hedged path south-east down and up to Froglands Lane and turn left along to **Whitcombe Cross.** Turn sharp right into bridleway N108 parallel at first to the road and follow it, an ancient 'hollow way', eventually emerging into open countryside again. Continue past the Vayres Farm path, along 3 fields to a crosstrack and turn left. Meeting an acute road bend at **Gatcombe,** carry straight on past Hill Farm, bearing sharp left to a junction with the Newport-Chillerton road. Turn sharp right here and in 150m go left onto a field track which dips through trees beyond a large barn then trends left to cross a stream footbridge. Now fenced, the onward trail heads north to Sandy Lane opposite Paradise Farm's entrance. Turn right along to the main A3020 at **Blackwater.**

Turn left up to the busy junction at Blackwater Corner, crossing carefully to turn right and walk on the verge before taking a track on the left up past the gravel works to the top of St George's Down near Newport Golf Course. Turn right along the ancient road which maintains an easterly course and eventually forks right at a path intersection, dropping to the road at **Arreton Cross.**

Walk along the A3056 verge in the same easterly direction past the White Lion pub and a turning to Arreton Manor, Craft Village and Church. From the pavement, branch left onto bridleway A9 past Arreton Primary School and on along crop fields. The trail crosses a north-south track (Shepherd's Lane) and continues to a country lane south of Mersley Farm. Turn left and in 100m turn right. Beyond a cottage and a small stream, bear right along by a hedge then follow the clear field path to the next lane at **Knighton.** Turn left then in 300m bear right past the waterworks buildings and on to Po House where the way swings sharp right down a rough track. At the bottom veer left up to a sandpit access track, cross over left and continue straightforwardly towards **Kern Farm.** Just before the farmhouse turn right, pass a bungalow and go left to join the rutted track up the flank of Ashey Down to reach the ridgetop road between Brading and Newport.

Cross over into Eaglehead Copse, keeping to the obvious path and emerging into a field. Stay along the left-hand edge and in 200m veer left into another copse, following the onward path for 400m and soon swinging east. Stiles lead clearly over fields and across a tarmac lane near **Nunwell Farm.** Here cross a stile by a large tree and walk in the same direction over fields close to New Farm on your left. Aim for trees in the middle of the next field and continue to West Lane, turning right past the main public entrance to **Nunwell House.** Staying on West Lane will bring you out at the north end of the High Street in **Brading.**

STAGE 4:

Brading to Whitwell.
12 miles (19km)

Start by walking south down the High Street and where the main road curves sharp left, keep straight on up Mall Road. In about 250m, just before a terrace of houses, turn right onto bridleway B39, climbing up the flank of Nunwell Down and joining a wider track into woods on the right.

Stay on this track for about $^{1}/_{2}$ mile (800m) and where the wooded area ends go ahead through a gate into the field, forking right on the lower path which curves round the hillside above Nunwell Farm. On reaching a gate adjacent to some trees, go through and turn right, following the field boundary up to the **Newport-Brading road**.

Turn left and in 100m cross over onto path B43 which drops steadily for about 3/4 mile (1.2km), meets a lane and leads out to the road at **Alverstone** hamlet. Go straight on past The Grange hotel, cross the little river bridge and in 100m turn right towards Queen's Bower. Where the way veers sharp right take the middle (left) path - NC42. In 250m the path bears right, crosses a lane and continues as a track to Skinners Hill at **Queen's Bower**. Turn left and in 75m cross over into **Borthwood Copse**.

At the main woodland track turn right. Bearing slightly left and ignoring branch paths, you will rise to the wood's southern edge. Continue into the field and in 200m swing sharp right round its edge. At a brick and stone house near Bigbury Farm turn left between barns and follow the path to the A3056 Newport road.

Cross over and continue south on the often muddy main path towards **America Wood**, crossing a lane then Scotchell's Brook footbridge in a steep, boggy little valley. Beyond a tea garden the initially narrow path bears right and joins a wider one undulating through **Apsecastle Wood** and over a footbridge. Ignore the right fork just after and near some long, low buildings turn right then in 50m left. The main path crosses a boardwalk and another footbridge to emerge up steps at the A3020 Shanklin to Newport road.

Opposite stands Abbottsford Lodge and the trail continuation is found 20m up the road to the right - a concrete drive crossing the old dismantled railway trackbed at Upper Hyde. Stay on the path heading south and climbing, first along field edges then up through a tree belt and finally more steeply uphill to the gorsey summit of Shanklin Down where it joins a track from the right.

Now heading south-east, the clear ridgetop path undulates along to Luccombe Down with some of the best Island views. In 3/4 mile (1.2km) the trail begins to curve right, eventually joining the access lane past the radar station. 500m further west, fork right off the lane bend onto a track descending from **Wroxall Down.** At a crosstrack go right then left, down over fields and stiles to Pit Farm

Homelands and cross the B3327 Wroxall-Ventnor road.

Walk west past an old bottle bank and down over a stream valley at Rew Lane. Turn left but in only a few paces turn right, up the field path and across the golf course to the crest of **Stenbury Down** where the trail bears right. In 400m take the stile in a field corner on the left and descend with a hedge on your right. Continue losing height down field edges, steeply at one point, to reach a rutted, tree-lined track leading down to the wide crosstrack. Turn right then left past fishing ponds at **Nettlecombe.** The gated path heading south-west crosses the dismantled railway and a footbridge over the infant River Yar to arrive at the southern end of **Whitwell** High Street.

STAGE 5:

Whitwell to Shorwell.
11 miles (18km)

Follow Whitwell High Street north, turning left into Bannock Road. After 150m keep right into Slay Lane, a wide, unmade roadway (NT102), and descend with Stockbridge Manor on your left. Take the footpath straight ahead up by a white fence and cross a stile and field, following the hedge and swinging right at a house to reach the country road at **Bierley**.

Bear right along the road round the curve, and opposite Kilnside take the footpath over on the left, dropping half-right to a stile and footbridge in the bottom corner. Continue north-west through gorse past a small lake down on your right to reach a stile. Curving left with Wydcombe down to the right, follow the path through trees along the bank then cross a stile onto a track. Where this bends sharp left, keep straight ahead uphill on a narrow grassy track and continue to a barn on your right.

Turn left into a sunken path which converges with a stream, passes a small copse and reaches Downcourt Farm. Cross the track and go through the bridleway ahead which bends left behind the farmhouse then heads right, diagonally, up the flanks of St Catherine's Down. Carry on south up to the old Pepper Pot lighthouse and nearby trig pillar, then angle down the hillside to the A3055 Military Road. Cross over and follow the coast path past a car park/ picnic area towards the cliffs. In about 150m at a superb viewpoint, watch for a steep, stepped path on the right which dives down through trees to the top of **Blackgang Chine's** large car park. Walk across it and up to the main road roundabout.

Now turn left along the verge and in about 100m bear left into bridleway C15 which leads down to The Terrace where you rejoin the coast road at **Chale**. Head left along the verge past Chale Church and opposite the entrance to the Wight Mouse Inn take the seaward-bound coast path, first along field edges then along rough clifftop terrain past Walpen Chine.

To by-pass **Whale Chine** further on, the coast path detours inland to the A3055 from a waymark. The Vectis 8 Trail leaves the coast path here, turning back right instead and taking the first lane on the left. Where this curves left, keep straight on uphill along the ridgetop of South Down. At an opening, branch half-left down through undergrowth to Chale Lane, turning right to the T-junction.

Go straight over and through a handgate to Pyle. The way crosses lawns behind Pyle Manor and continues into Windmill Copse. The clear path traverses a marshy area on boardwalks then crosses a paddock to a lane at Gladices. Turn left for about 50m then right beside a ditch and up a tree-lined driveway towards Corve Farm. Bear right between barns then weave to the right through the farm complex, bearing left at the last barn.

In 50m turn left again beside a hedge and ditch, later trending slightly right until after about 600m the way veers sharp right, round the field boundary to a stile through trees. Once over the footbridge you swing left to reach a broad track near **Kingston** hamlet.

Walk west beside Kingston Copse and in 1/2 mile (800m) bear right (north) beneath Gun Hill along another wide track, by-passing Bucks Farm and arriving at the B3399 road. Turn left and in 400m take a bridleway on the right heading towards the TV mast on Chillerton Down. Pass Sheard's Copse and climb to a gate on the skyline ahead. Here the trail bears left on a descending course, passing through two gates, running along by a hedge and finally turning left through a gate into the last field. At the bottom right-hand corner you will reach the B3399 road where, just along the right, stands the centre of **Shorwell** village.

STAGE 6:

Shorwell to Yarmouth.
12 miles (19km)

Turn west at Shorwell's mini-roundabout into Walkers Lane (B3399) and in 300m turn right by the last cottage. In a few paces go through a gate and head diagonally left uphill to the field's top left-hand corner. The way now continues along the ridge, through 3 gates and veering right past windblown trees. At the next gate turn left between fence and hillside and follow the path as it swings right and rises to the top of **Limerstone Down.**

Here turn left along the ancient stony trackway, branching right after 150m into **Brighstone Forest**. In about 500m you pass on the right bridleway BS7, down which the outward leg of the Vectis Trail was routed. Ahead at the main forestry track (also the Tennyson Trail), cross straight over, maintaining this north-north-west direction past a trig pillar in undergrowth over to the right. The track descends to a junction and just to the right will be found the continuation down to a handgate. Walk in the same direction down a pasture field and at the bottom gate turn left along to the road (Lynch Lane). Turn right towards **Calbourne** village and just beyond Westover House's lake turn left by a lodge into Winkle Street, continuing on a streamside path before bearing left over a narrow footbridge and stile into a field. Heading south-west the stiled path crosses 3 fields, aiming slightly right over the fourth to a stile into Withybed Copse. Cross a footbridge and at the wood's edge turn right along a track to Westover Farm. Beyond the farm buildings the way swings left uphill towards forestry on Westover Down.

Enter the forest and turn right along its edge for about 300m before veering left uphill. Go over the first crosstrack and from a track intersection turn half-right up to the next track, a broad one climbing right (south) onto the open summit of **Mottistone Down.**

Follow the well used track westwards past the tumuli and downhill on Pay Down to the B3399 road. Opposite and slightly to the right take the stony lane to a National Trust information board and go through a gate on the left where the chalky ridgeway track bends right and climbs onto **Brook Down**, passing close below the Five Barrows tumuli.

In about 300m, at a corner of woods, fork right off the Tennyson Trail, passing through gates and down a narrow path beside woods. Continue straight downhill to cross the B3401 Newport-Freshwater road and take the grassy, hedged bridleway opposite. Maintaining a northerly direction, this joins a driveway from The Quarries to meet a minor road between Thorley and Shalcombe - **Broad Lane**. Turn left and follow this little used country lane for a mile (1.6km).

Just beyond a fenced pit turn left by a seat and signpost and walk beside a hedged bank over two fields, cross the minor road ahead and the stile opposite. Continue with a hedge on your right and where it ends carry straight on for about 100m. Now bear left towards another hedge, turn right then left into a narrow and often overgrown path near Barnfields Stream which leads out into a field. Walk round the field edge, hedge on your left, and just before the corner of Mill Copse bear left over a stile and follow the path through the woods.

At the far side of the copse a stile leads to a gate where you turn right onto the trackbed of the old Freshwater, Yarmouth and Newport Railway, now a pedestrian and cycle route. Almost immediately fork off left at a bench and follow the tarmac pathway past the old tide mill. Beyond houses this swings left past moorings and reaches the large car park and the main A3054 road opposite Wightlink's ferry terminal at **Yarmouth** - start and finish point for the Vectis 8 Trail.

CHAPTER 5

Short Walks

SHORT WALKS

The following 12 short walks are suitable for families with young children. They will also appeal to those who, for whatever reason, are unable to tackle the longer and rather more demanding routes found elsewhere in this guidebook.

The walks are themed with children in mind and have been selected to provide 'tasters' of some of the Island's finest countryside, coast and features of special interest. Although modest in distance (mostly around 3 miles - 5km), these shorter walks inevitably involve stiles or handgates; there are some hills too and of course footpaths can be muddy at any time of year.

Young children are more vulnerable to cold and fatigue than adults so always pack spare clothing and waterproofs, as well as energy snacks such as chocolate and a drink. If your planned walk is in an exposed location such as coastline or hilltop, try to obtain a weather forecast before setting off. If children become demoralised by bad weather or tiredness, be willing to take a short cut or turn back.

To help readers prepare for the walks, notes about terrain and refreshment points have been included.

WALK 21: CARISBROOKE CASTLE AND THE BOWCOMBE VALLEY

2 miles (3km). Start Grid Ref: 485876

Terrain: field paths and country lanes with gentle gradients except around Castle Hill itself.

Refreshment points: cafe at Carisbrooke Castle.

Standing impregnably upon its chalk spur behind the village, Carisbrooke Castle dates from shortly after the Norman Conquest and was further fortified in the early 12th century by the addition of the massive stone ramparts we see today. Although well able to withstand attack by archery and early handguns, by the 16th century more powerful cannon prompted the building of outer fortifications to protect the increasingly vulnerable medieval walls.

Set at the Island's heart, Carisbrooke Castle was for centuries the traditional home of the Island governor. However, its most famous occupant was Charles I, imprisoned here in 1647-8 before being hanged at London. For exercise the hapless king walked round the same battlements that we enjoy today on a tour of the castle.

Set in 7 acres of grounds and managed by English Heritage, there is much to see, including panoramic views from the ramparts,

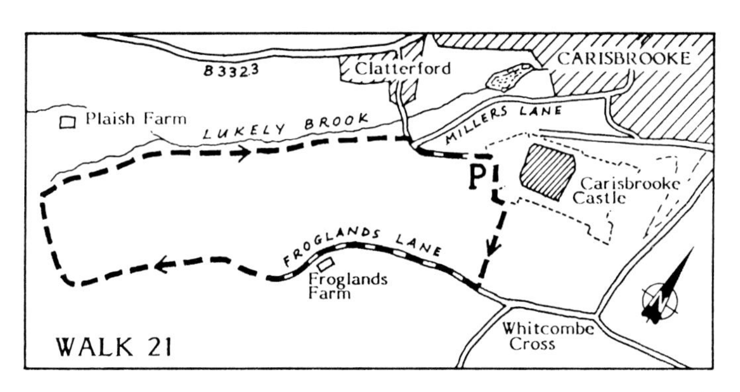

fascinating architectural details, the Isle of Wight Museum housed in the Great Hall, and - a great favourite with children - the courtyard well-house incorporating a donkey-powered treadmill to raise and lower the bucket!

Two or three hours spent exploring the castle is nicely complemented by this short walk in the nearby Bowcombe Valley. Start from the castle car park and go through a handgate in the east corner leading (anticlockwise) into the path round the moat bank beneath the great walls. Almost immediately take a narrow path on the right which dives down the hillside, runs between hedges, then rises to Froglands Lane.

Now turn right and follow this quiet country thoroughfare past Froglands Farm in the pastoral countryside of the Bowcombe Valley. Soon after the farm the lane curves right and narrows to a hedged bridleway along hillside fields. In a few hundred metres the way swings sharp right downhill to the valley bottom. About 100m past a footpath on the left, watch for a path on the right (signed 'Carisbrooke Castle') which heads back towards Carisbrooke by a hedge not far from Plaish Farm. You are accompanied on this delightful return leg of the walk by the tiny Lukely Brook, its banks bright with wildflowers in early summer. In conjunction with timber planks to dam the water, two large grooved stones either side of the stream were once used as a sheepwash.

Having crossed stepping stones you reach the southern end of Millers Lane, just across the valley from the picturesque cottages of Clatterford hamlet. Turn right and immediately after the road junction follow the path on the left climbing up to the start at the castle car park.

WALK 22: EXPLORING AROUND GODSHILL

2½ miles (4km). Start Grid Ref: 529817
Terrain: tracks and field paths, possibly muddy in places. Easy gradients.
Refreshment points: cafes and pubs in Godshill.

Godshill is one of the Island's great tourist honeypots, popular with all ages and justly so. As you would expect, there are gift shops and refreshment places galore but it is the village's attractions that fuel this influx of visitors. The Nostalgic Toy Museum, the Natural History Centre and the Old Smithy are all well worth taking in but for youngsters especially the Model Village takes pride of place. Set out in 1½ acres of the Old Vicarage Gardens, the attraction originally opened in 1952 and has been developing since. Built to 1/10th scale, its miniature houses utilise real thatch and coloured cement which weathers well. The scenes, based on Old Shanklin and Godshill itself, are

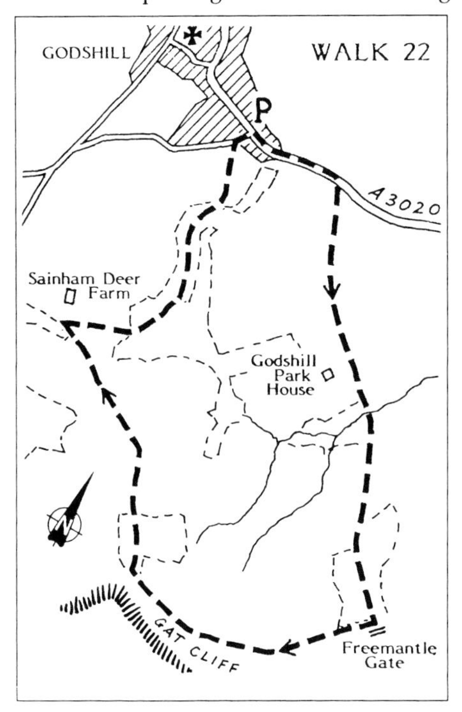

brought to life by hundreds of tiny trees and shrubs, as well as by numerous model people.

This walk south of the village escapes the crowds and provides wonderful Island views. From Godshill's large car park walk east along the Shanklin road (A3020) for about 300m. Just past a farm lane on the left, take a right turn (part of the Stenbury Trail). This is the old coaching drive to Appuldurcombe House, rising gently past Godshill Park House, becoming sandy and entering trees to reach Freemantle Gate. The stately, 3-arched gateway bears the griffin family insignia of the Worsleys of Appuldurcombe, many associations with whom can be found in Godshill.

Don't pass through the gateway but turn right up beside Freemantle Copse. Beyond a handgate the path continues up a field by the old estate wall and follows it along through a muddy hollow. As you walk along, check out the views which extend right across the Island from the distant white cliffs of Tennyson Down to Culver Cliff above Sandown. Over a stile on the left, an offshoot path climbs steeply through the rocky Gat Cliff outcrop to a granite obelisk on Appuldurcombe Down. The Worsley Monument, as it is known, was put up in 1774 by Sir Richard Worsley in memory of his grandfather, Sir Robert.

The path continues along by the estate wall at the top of pasture to a handgate then drops to a path junction in woods. Take the broad right-hand track through deer gates: it leads along then down to Sainham Deer Farm, established in 1987 to breed red deer which can sometimes be seen grazing the hillsides. Here above the farm buildings turn sharp right, following the sign for Beech Copse. Beyond the next gate fork left down the woodland path, over a plank bridge and joining a path from the right through meadow, hedge on your left. Two stiles later you will emerge at the back of The Griffin Inn at Godshill, a stone's throw from the car park.

WALK 23: EXPLORING AROUND NEWTOWN

3 miles (5km). Start Grid Ref: 424905
Terrain: village lanes, field and woodland paths and a narrow timber causeway with handrail.
Refreshment points: none.

Before the ascendancy of Newport and Yarmouth as the Island's principal settlements and the silting up of its river, Newtown was an important harbour capable of docking as many as 50 large ships. Oyster farming and salt production thrived, as did a plethora of dockside trades and services and regular markets. However, such prosperity did not go unnoticed and during the Hundred Years War repeated attacks by the French and Spanish began a process of decline which culminated in the disastrous raid of 1377 when the town was severely ravaged and burned.

It never properly recovered, though as a 'Rotten Borough' it continued to send two MPs to Westminster until the first Reform Act of 1832. Newtown's decline was further hastened by the demise of its salt industry, the inn closed down in 1916 and the imposing Georgian town hall, built by public subscription in 1699, was used as a school, later to become a dwelling then, temporarily, a youth

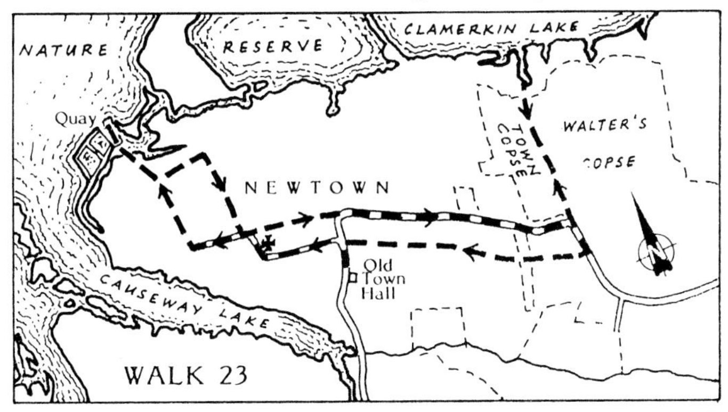

hostel. Now renovated, it is open to the public as a museum.

The Old Town Hall and much of the adjacent river estuary, saltmarshes, fields and woodland have been acquired by the National Trust. The little town itself remains almost a 'time capsule' with many features from the past three centuries of its history still traceable, including the now overgrown grid of old streets and backyards.

Start from the Old Town Hall and turn left opposite a stone house called Noah's Ark along what was originally the High Street. Pass the restored village pump and follow the road as it bends right down to a gate. Carry on along the narrow timber causeway over the tidal marshes to the old Quay. The once-busy salt pans can still be seen but today this is the quietest of spots frequented only by fishermen and the occasional passing dinghy. The surrounding Nature Reserve is a haunt for many bird species including curlews, oyster-catchers and terns. The remains of an old seawall embankment bear witness to many efforts over 300 years to reclaim this main saltmarsh - without success.

Retrace your steps over the causeway but turn left and follow

Newtown's old quay

the path back towards the church. Bear left before reaching it along a grassy way that was once Gold Street. In about 300m keep left into the lane and at a sharp right bend 600m ahead walk left between Town Copse and Walter's Copse to the shore of Clamerkin Lake, an arm of the River Newtown. About 300m further along to the left stands a hide from which wildlife can be observed.

Turn round and walk back through the woods. At the lane carry straight on (south). Soon you will reach a National Trust sign and stile on the right. The path from here back to Newtown leads straightforwardly across narrow fields through a succession of hedge gaps and stiles, parallel to the road. The final stile brings you out a short distance away from the start at the Old Town Hall.

WALK 24: EXPLORING AROUND CALBOURNE

24

3 miles (5km). Start Grid Ref: 414868
Terrain: village lanes, farm tracks and field paths, possibly muddy but mostly flat.
Refreshment points: cafe at Calbourne Mill; pub in Calbourne village.

The Domesday Book census of 1086 records 34 watermills on the Isle of Wight. Water power is not a feature of this gentle countryside so many were modest affairs working only when required. Wheat and barley were widely grown but the Calbourne area specialised in oats.

Calbourne Mill, an excellent base from which to explore on foot, derives its power from the Caul Bourne, emanating from a natural spring in nearby Westover Park. The stream originally powered local fulling, corn and paper mills too. In the late 19th century when traditional stone-grinding was replaced by roller mills producing finer flour, many small country mills ceased operation. However, Calbourne responded to the challenge in 1894 by installing a new roller plant driven by a portable steam engine and later by suction gas. Owners since 1878, the Weeks family have preserved the mill complex and grounds as an example of a bygone agricultural era. In addition to the working mill machinery and a cafe offering home-cooked goodies, there are several collections of domestic and farm memorabilia housed in outbuildings.

Turn left (east) from the car park and walk along beside the B3401 for about 400m. Just beyond Fullingmill Farm buildings, climb some stone steps on the right, cross the stile and follow the field path. Continue straight ahead to another stile, cross the track and maintain the same direction to reach double stiles. Once over, the path becomes feint, bearing half-right across the field to the stream. Cross a stile to the left and you will find a shady waterside path leading out to Calbourne's famous Winkle Street.

Immensely picturesque, this row of ivy-clad, 18th century stone cottages facing the lush Caul Bourne provides the perfect backdrop for a family snapshot!

At the far end of Winkle Street turn left past the church (also mentioned in the Domesday Book) and take the next turning left - School Lane - opposite a tiled well. You bear left past the old School House and a recreation ground and keep straight on over field stiles. Again the path grows sketchy but veers half-left to

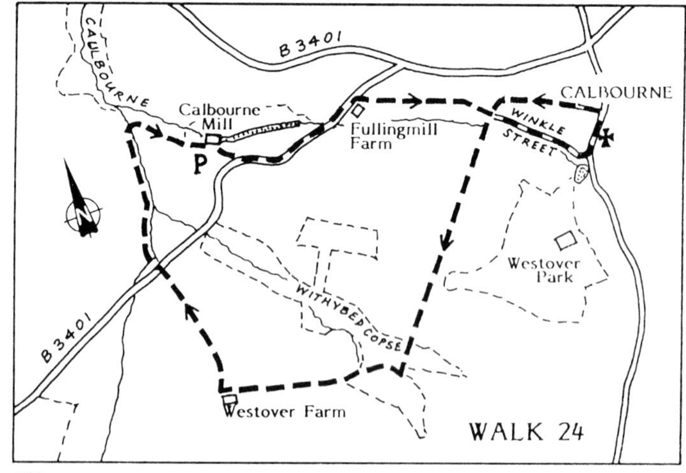

cross the path walked earlier. Go over the Caul Bourne footbridge, whereafter the path bears gradually away from the hedge on a bee-line over fields to Withybed Copse. Over on the left lies Westover Park with its lake and Regency mansion.

At the copse the path drops over a stream and rises to meet a broad chalky track at a stile. Turn right and on reaching Westover Farm in about 500m, turn right again along the farm track to a thatched lodge at the B3401.

Opposite are sometimes overgrown double stiles and the onward path (signed CB11 - Newbridge). Once more there is no definite path on the ground but simply keep along beneath overhead wires past a rusty shed over rough pasture, following the west bank of a tributary stream. Carry on to the confluence of the tributary with the Caul Bourne where you will find a plank bridge. Cross it and turn left to a stile but turn right before it. With the Caul Bourne to the left, the path's final leg rises for about 50m and picks up a clearer trod heading back to the mill.

WALK 25: EXPLORING AROUND BRADING

3 miles (5km).
Start Grid Ref: 606874
Terrain: village lanes, field and woodland paths and tracks. One significant climb.
Refreshment points: cafes and pubs in Brading.

Brading was once a rumbustuous east coast sea port lying at the head of a tidal inlet known as Brading Haven. In 1877, however, an embankment was constructed to carry a road between St Helens and Bembridge, previously separated by the broad estuary of the East Yar river. This immediately cut Brading off from the sea, marooning it a couple of miles inland behind an expanse of wildlife-rich freshwater marsh and meadow.

Today Brading is much visited because within about a ½-mile (800m) radius of the town centre can be found historic Nunwell

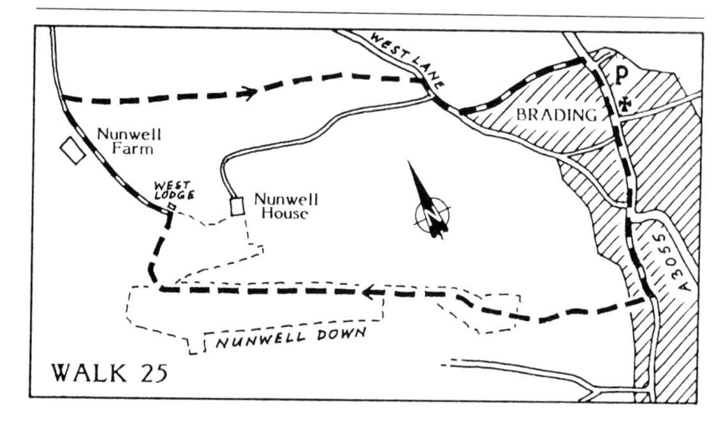

House, a Roman villa, Morton Manor and vineyard, the Lilliput Doll and Toy Museum, Graham Osborn-Smith's famous Wax Museum and Animal World, as well as interesting old buildings in Brading High Street.

Brading has a station on the Island Line railway running between Ryde and Shanklin. Instead of conventional rolling stock, the line uses ex-Piccadilly Line London tube trains equipped with simulated steam whistles!

From the car park at the top of the High Street set off south towards 12th century St Mary's Church with its unusual porch tower. Over on your right stands the Old Town Hall complete with barred gaol, stocks and whipping post. Walk down past the Wax Museum and follow the High Street up past the Bull Ring, used for bull baiting right up until 1820.

Now the walk forks right onto Mall Road and in about 250m turns right into bridleway B39, passing Little Jane cottage which dates from 1547. (Both Morton Manor and the Roman villa are situated further south off Mall Road.) Climb the path, ignoring left and right offshoots, until you join a clear track at the top which bears right into woods. Stay on this track through glorious beechwoods on the steep flanks of Nunwell Down for approximately ½ mile (800m). Next turn right down bridleway N59 to the half-timbered West Lodge and follow the lane left down past Nunwell Farm. In about 150m watch for a stile on the

right (B23) and aim across the field towards a leaning oak tree. Cross a wooden footbridge and stile and continue straight ahead over another two fields past New Farm over to your left. Following a line of trees, you will emerge onto West Lane. Now turn right past the public entrance to Nunwell House.

This was the seat of the Oglander family from Norman times until 1980. A well known Oglander - the royalist and diarist Sir John - sheltered Charles I at Nunwell on the king's last night of freedom in November 1647 before his incarceration in Carisbrooke Castle and subsequent execution the following year. Surrounded by 6 acres of grounds and containing a military museum, Nunwell House is open to the public on certain days during the summer.

Staying on West Lane as it curves left will bring you out at the north end of Brading High Street and the car park is just along to the right.

WALK 26: SHORWELL AND LIMERSTONE DOWN

26

3 miles (5km).
Start Grid Ref: 455829
Terrain: field and downland paths and tracks. Mostly uphill outward and downhill return. Exposed to wind and weather.
Refreshment points: pub in Shorwell.

This walk makes an ascent to the crest of Limerstone Down where a toposcope, or view table, identifies landmarks visible over great distances in clear weather. One consolation for the uphill outward leg is the knowledge that it's all downhill to end with!

Shorwell's picturesque thatched cottages nestle in a fold in the downs above the Island's wilder west coastline. Two manor houses - West Court and the reputedly haunted Elizabethan Wolverton Manor - lie to the south of the village, while on the slopes above St Peter's Church stands many-gabled North Court whose gardens are occasionally opened to the public.

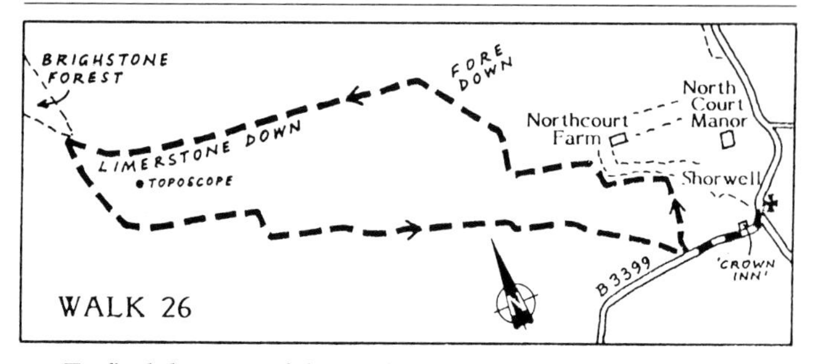

To find the start of the walk, set off west along Walkers Lane down past the Crown Inn and in 250m turn right by the last cottage into footpath S6 (signed 'The Downs and Brighstone Forest'). Go through the gate and, although there are no obvious paths on the ground just here, bear slightly right uphill to a hedge. Follow the hedge to a gate then go down the field towards the edge of a small wood. Ignore a waymarked stile on the right and instead veer left alongside the wood on a feint trod. It curves right downhill into a shallow valley near Northcourt Farm and in 100m bears left towards a gate. Before reaching the gate turn right and tackle the steepest section of the walk up the flank of Fore Down.

Before too long you pass through a gate where the way swings left on somewhat easier ground and reaches open downland. Continue in the same direction (north-west) uphill and you will soon meet a broad stony track running along the crest of Limerstone Down. Turn left and enjoy the wonderful views from this ancient ridgeway. Follow the trackway for about 1/2 mile (800m) then detour over to your left where you will discover the toposcope. Views are extensive indeed, stretching north over The Solent and all along the Island's west coast to St Catherine's Point and the English Channel.

Return to the trackway and stay on it for another 200m or so before turning sharp left at a signpost for Limerstone and Shorwell near a corner of Brighstone Forest. The good path angles steeply at first down the hillside but after about 300m you bear left from a gateway along by small hills on your left. In a further 400m turn right through a gate, passing trees sculpted by the strong winds that often buffet this exposed sector of the Island.

The path now bears left along a modest ridge above Northcourt Farm's shallow valley. Keep walking in the same direction (just south of east) and you will pass a thicket and go through further gates before angling half-right down to the B3399 Walkers Lane at Shorwell and retracing steps to the starting point.

WALK 27: ARRETON AND HASELEY MANORS AND ARRETON DOWN

$3^{1}/_{2}$ miles (5.5km). Start Grid Ref: 534867
Terrain: country roads, field paths and tracks. One significant climb.
Refreshment points: cafes at Arreton and Haseley Manors; pub at Arreton.

Two of Wight's most historic manor houses and a short climb onto the Island's chalk spine for magnificent views combine to provide a varied and stimulating walk. The following route directions begin from the car park at Arreton Craft Village, though you could equally well start at Haseley Manor, the halfway point.

To visit Arreton Manor, walk up past the Craft Village studios which welcome visitors and follow the path (A12) between a large pond and the churchyard, to the right of a tall barn. 12th century St George's Church is worth looking at. Mellow Arreton Manor stands on your left, much of it dating from Elizabethan times. Royalty from Henry VIII to Charles 1 has variously owned and occupied the manor over the years and there are 14th century rooms inside, reached down a spiral stone staircase. Of more contemporary interest are a fascinating Museum of Childhood, a lace collection and the National Wireless Museum.

The walk itself starts off by heading east along the main road (A3056) pavement. In 200m cross over to a footpath sign beside Arreton's Community Centre building and walk south over the fields to a stile above a tributary valley of the East Yar river. Here a footpath diversion directs you half-left downhill to the corner of

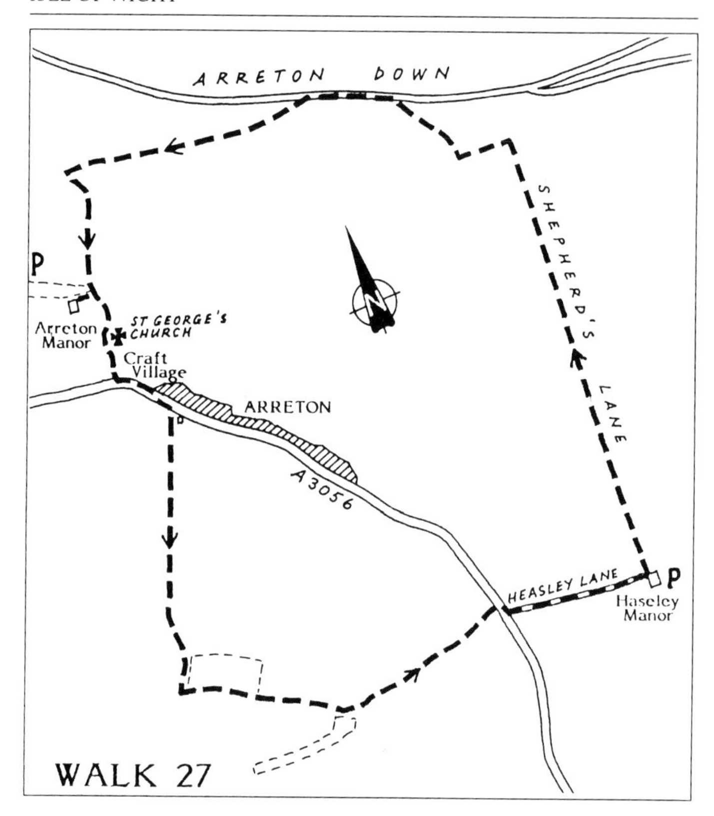

a small wood. Continue up the edge of trees where you will meet a track.

The way now turns left along the wood's southern edge, passes through one gate and at the next bears half-left to cross a side stream. The narrow path leads on between hawthorn trees and dips to cross a plank footbridge over the main stream before climbing left and following the north bank. Cross the stile straight ahead and continue to the A3056 road. Turn right here and almost immediately cross over and walk down Heasley Lane to Haseley Manor.

When the manor's present owner, Raymond Young, purchased

the property in 1976, it lay derelict and open to the elements. Twenty years of dedicated restoration, funded by visitors' entrance fees and sales from the studio pottery begun by Mr Young's late wife, Krystyna, have transformed a near ruin into a truly splendid complex. And experts in the field have confirmed a degree of historical significance that exceeds even Mr Young's original vision.

As well as the studio pottery, there is a gift shop, a small sweet factory, tea rooms and extensive grounds with free-ranging animals and a children's adventure area, all making Haseley Manor an ideal spot at which to break this walk.

From the north-west corner of the manor where Heasley Lane comes in, take the straight track heading north towards the downs (Shepherd's Lane). Ignore turnings off and you will steadily gain height between vast crop fields here in the fertile Arreton valley. Turn left at some old chalk pits then angle right, more steeply uphill, to arrive at the road along the crest of Arreton Down.

Turn left for about 250m, taking in the marvellous views which embrace The Solent and mainland coast, with Ryde to your right and much of southern Wight to your left.

A stile and signpost on the left indicate your descent towards the corner of a wire fence, with Arreton's church and manor visible ahead. On reaching the bottom power line, watch for a stile in the hedge and after crossing it veer sharp left by a handrail down into a field where the clear path aims for the church. Now simply keep left of the tall barn and retrace your outward steps through the Craft Village to the car park.

WALK 28: EXPLORING AROUND ST HELENS

$3^{1/2}$ miles (5.5km).
Start Grid Ref: 637894
Terrain: country lanes, field paths and tracks and a causeway. Gentle gradients.
Refreshment points: cafe at St Helens Duver; pub in St Helens.

St Helens, situated at the head of Bembridge Harbour, once enjoyed considerable importance as a supply point for the naval fleet anchored off Spithead; its spring water was in particular demand. Today it lies on a quieter stretch of the Island's east coast, joined to Bembridge by a road bridge and embankment across the East Yar river. This damming of the tidal flow in 1877 created a vast area of freshwater marsh, reed beds and water meadow but left the old seaport of Brading high and dry.

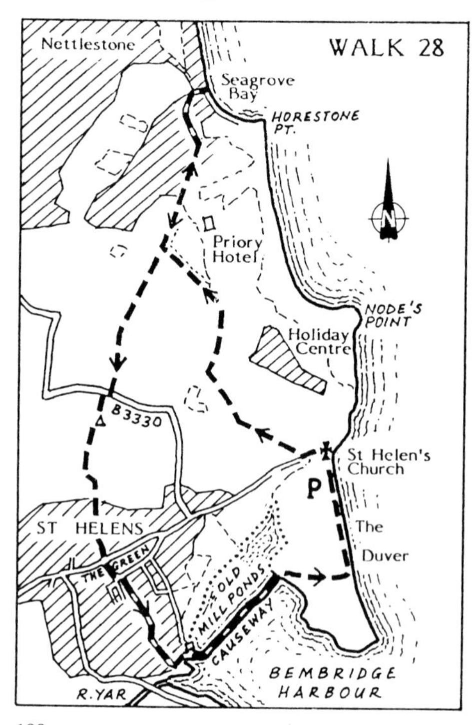

At around 9 acres, St Helen's village green must be one of the country's largest! From its centre, take the road downhill, joining Latimer Road at the bottom. Turn left to some lock-up garages where you will find

a coast path signpost (R108 to Seaview). Walk ahead to the little quayside and bear left behind Mill House to reach the footpath over the Causeway, one of the 18th century dams that impounded tidal water used to power the mill. It's a thrilling stretch of walking, especially if the tide is high and you can gaze across 1/2 mile (800m) of open water to the houses of Bembridge and its harbourside industry.

The Causeway ends at a 30-acre spit of grassland, sandy scrub and marsh called The Duver, home to a rich variety of plant and insect species and owned by the National Trust. The coast path bears slightly left over St Helen's Common but it's well worthwhile wandering across to the seawall for views of shipping and St Helen's Fort. The granite fort, one of four built by Palmerston in the mid-1800s against a feared French invasion, sits defiantly offshore.

Walking along the seawall past the cafe brings you to the ruined tower of 16th century St Helen's Church, now painted white as a navigation daymark. There are low-tide rocks to explore all round nearby Nodes Point. Mainly due to private property, the coast path now meanders away from the actual shoreline for a while.

Walk inland from the church tower for 150m and cross a stile on the right (R85). Continue up the possibly marshy field to its top right-hand corner and up the next field to double telegraph poles and a metal gate leading into a lane. Turn right past Nodes Point Holiday Camp and into the Priory Hotel's driveway. At the next gateposts the way bears left onto bridleway R84 beside Priory Woods then turns right. (A stile on the left here is crossed on the walk's return leg.) The track you are now on comes down to join residential Ferniclose Road and beyond Gully Road on the left you arrive at Seagrove Bay beach. It's a delightful spot at the walk's halfway point, with gently shelving sands, rock pools and safe water for paddling.

Retrace your steps to the track beyond Ferniclose Road and when you reach the stile ahead, cross it into a field path with wide views, a hedge on your left. The walk continues in the same south-westerly direction to the B3330 Eddington Road. Turn right then almost immediately left at a signpost to St Helens. With a short left-hand 'jink' midway, the path leads straightforwardly over a

lane, past a gate and back to The Green, emerging by the pub and bus stop.

WALK 29: YARMOUTH AND FORT VICTORIA

3½ miles (5.5km).
Start Grid Ref: 353896
Terrain: pavement, seawall,
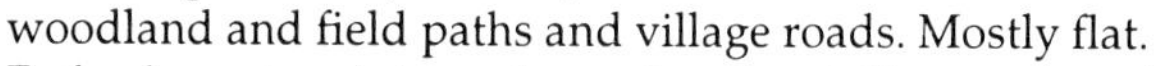
woodland and field paths and village roads. Mostly flat.
Refreshment points: cafes and pubs at Yarmouth; cafe at Fort Victoria.

With its Tudor castle, Victorian pier and old town buildings, Yarmouth is a fascinating place to explore. There are many refreshment places and shops to browse around, overlooked by the tall tower of 17th century St James Church. The town is also a busy foot passenger and vehicle terminal for Wightlink's Lymington ferries and the harbour marina is usually a hive of activity.

Start by heading west past the waterfront and across the Yar swing bridge opened in 1987. There are good views inland along the estuary. Stay on the pavement until the road bends sharp left;

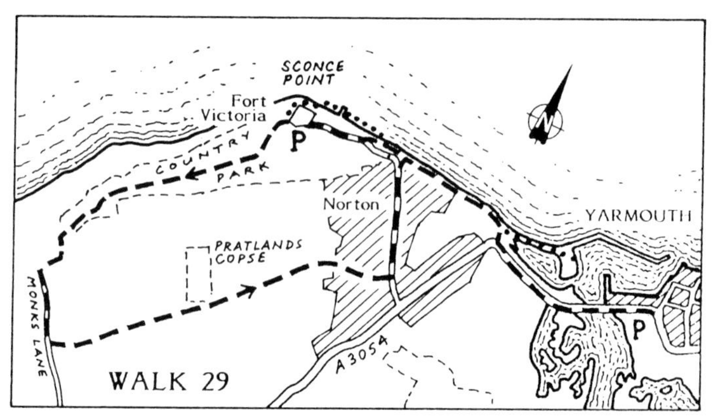

here the coast path which we begin by following turns off right to gain the sea wall. (In summer a pleasant alternative start is to catch the little Sandhard passenger ferry across the harbour and walk along Norton Spit to join the route at the sea wall.)

Further along past villas, wooden steps on the left lead into a narrow path through trees where you pick up the minor road and turn right along it to Fort Victoria. It is also possible if conditions are favourable to reach Fort Victoria by continuing along the shingle foreshore past an old jetty.

The L-shaped single-storey casements of Fort Victoria are the remains of a much bigger complex built between 1852-55 to guard the waters of The Solent which are very narrow here at Sconce Point. Like many similar coastal defences, it never saw action and joined the ranks of 'Palmerston follies', named after the prime minister of the time. The old casements have been developed into a series of tourist attractions, including a Planetarium, a Maritime Heritage exhibition, an excellent Marine Aquarium (very popular with children) and a recommended cafe.

Continue by crossing the lawns between fort and shore, aiming inland to a corner of woods by an old experimental searchlight pit. Here you will find the onward coast path - in fact a nature trail in the fort Victoria Country Park. Threading up through delightful mature woodland, it turns right onto an overgrown cobbled roadway originally built by the army to link Fort Victoria with Fort Albert at Cliff End just along the coast ahead (now a private residence). Walking through the woods, especially where steps are climbed, there are occasional glimpses over The Solent to the Tudor Hurst Castle and adjacent white lighthouse, less than a mile away on the mainland coast.

Eventually the path follows a holiday bungalow estate fence and reaches a road (Monks Lane). Turn left down the lane and in 300m watch for a stile and footpath sign on the left. It leads into a grassy field path through a secluded valley rich in wildflowers during early summer. Beyond Pratlands Copse on the left you reach a stile at a road. Keep right here, following the road as it curves left to a T-junction, then turn left and walk up through the village of Norton. In the trees ahead cross the road and take the coast path down to the foreshore where you will recognise the sea

wall from the outward leg of the walk. All that remains is to retrace your steps over the Yar bridge and back into Yarmouth.

WALK 30: TENNYSON DOWN AND THE NEEDLES

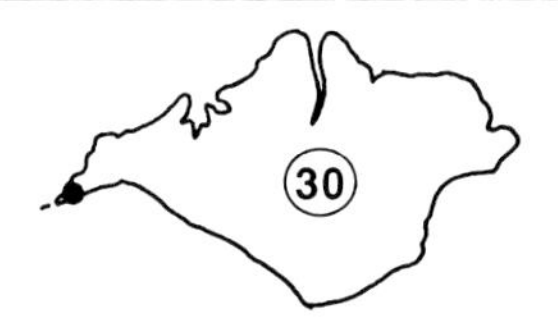

4 miles (6.5km).
Start Grid Ref: 325855
Terrain: downland paths, tracks and lanes with one steep climb. Exposed to wind and weather.
Refreshment points: cafe at Needles Old Battery.

No visit to the Isle of Wight is complete without experiencing the dramatic cliffs and coastal downland in the far west, culminating in the famous Needles chalk stacks with their historic naval defence batteries.

Grey and white limestone forms the Island's spine, running west to east as an often steep-sided ridge and producing high, vertical cliffs at the coast. Before rising sea levels at the end of the last Ice Age 7000 years ago finally broke through it, this great chalk ridge extended westwards to Dorset where similar cliffs and downs are found today.

Walking on the exposed western tip of Wight can be breezy when conditions inland are much calmer. Underfoot, however, the going is usually firm.

A lane leads south off the Freshwater-Alum Bay road at the 'High Down Inn' crossroads; it ends at a car park created in old chalk workings. From the east side of the chalk pit a path climbs

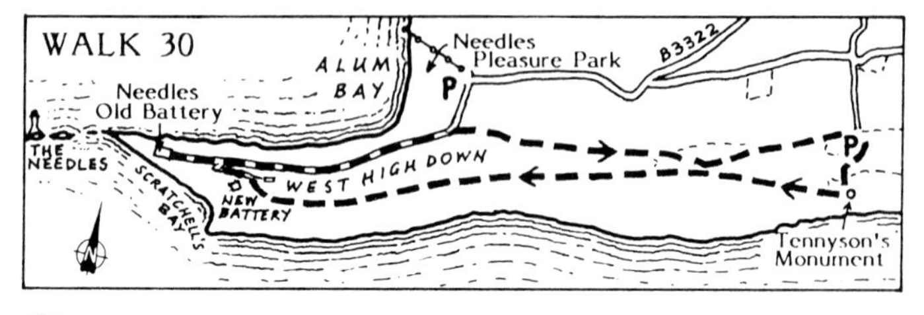

steeply - stepped in places - through low woods up onto Tennyson Down. Ahead looms Tennyson's Monument, a granite cross erected on the downland summit 482ft (147m) above the waves in memory of one of England's most celebrated poets, Alfred, Lord Tennyson. Views are tremendous, embracing the whole of West Wight and extending down the west coast to St Catherine's Point.

The walk now heads resolutely westwards along the coast path which drops gently towards the finger of narrowing downland. Cross a stile by the remains of the Old Nodes Beacon and continue up over West High Down to where the coast path veers right down to a row of Coastguard cottages. Cross a fence stile on the left then take the right-hand path ahead to a road, bearing left to reach the New Needles Battery. Further left still are the concrete remains of an old rocket-testing site, as well as a fenced viewpoint, accessed down steps, over the precipitous cliffs of Scratchell's Bay to The Needles.

Follow the track steeply downhill to the arched drawbridge entrance to the Needles Old Battery. The entire headland was

The ever-popular Needles Pleasure Park above Alum Bay

acquired by the National Trust in 1975 and much restoration work has been carried out by volunteers. The batteries provide us with a fascinating insight into coastal defence systems since Victorian times. A visit is recommended and not to be missed is the 200ft (61m) long tunnel through the chalk to a spectacular 19th century searchlight emplacement intimately overlooking The Needles stacks and out to the mainland coast.

Leave the Needles Old Battery by the tarmac access road whose seaward bank carries a good path for most of the way. Ahead stand the coloured-sand cliffs of Alum Bay, encapsulated in glass shape novelties for holidaymakers to take home. Where the lane bends sharp left at a garden full of gnomes, cross a stile on the right (path T25). This path heads back east below West High Down, eventually rising gently to a junction. Take the left-hand, lower track through scrubby woods which leads directly back to the car park at the start.

WALK 31: BLACKGANG AND ST CATHERINE'S HILL

31

4 miles (6.5km).
Start Grid Ref: 488767
Terrain: clifftop, field and downland paths with one or two steep climbs. Exposed to wind and weather.
Refreshment points: cafe at Blackgang Theme Park; pub at Niton.

The Island's southern tip around St Catherine's Point is characterised by dramatic landslips backed by coastal downland. Its best known attraction is the Blackgang Chine Theme Park from where this walk begins. Summoning visions of smugglers and shipwrecks, Blackgang's name derives from the original 'chine', or coastal ravine, that once extended back inland from the sea to a height of some 500ft (150m). Beds of Gault clay - the so-called 'blue slipper' - have caused massive landslips along this coast and Blackgang Chine itself has long since disappeared into the sea, together with much clifftop land and property. Started by the Dabell family as

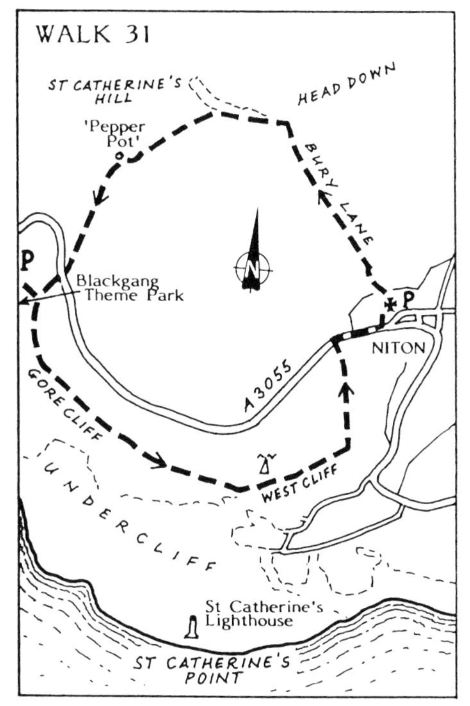

landscaped gardens and a beach path in 1842, Blackgang Chine rapidly became a tourist destination. Today the Theme Park encompasses a whole cowboy town, fairy castle, animatronic dinosaurs, historical exhibitions and wonderful views - a day out for the whole family, particularly if combined with this circular walk.

Set off by climbing the stepped path through woods from the top of the car park onto the coast past at Gore Cliff. Here is perhaps the Island's finest coastal viewpoint - an uninterrupted span of 15 miles (24km) to the distant white cliffs of Tennyson Down and The Needles.

The coast path (anti-clockwise) now heads south-east, soon encountering sheer chalk cliffs above an extensive Undercliff composed of copses, grassy hillocks and tiny fields formed on the

Dramatic landslips in the Blackgang area claim up to 10ft (2m) of clifftop every year

slumped land and rich in wildlife. Outside fields, the onward clifftop path is mostly flat, eventually passing Niton's 'ship-to-shore' radio masts at West Cliff. As you round St Catherine's Point, below you stands the gleaming white St Catherine's lighthouse, built in 1838-40 after the tragic wreck of the fully-rigged *Clarendon* under Blackgang cliffs which resulted in the loss of 24 lives.

After a hedged section of path, stiles lead across a field. Before the way dips downhill, turn left over a stile and walk along by a hedge. Beyond the next stile a descent in a groove leads down to the main A3055 coast road. Turn right along the verge footpath to the car park then walk left up towards Niton's restored 12th century church, bearing right into Pan Lane which is followed uphill towards Head Down. Niton village, clustered around a crossroads in a downland hollow, retains a 'villagey' atmosphere with its thatched roofs, old stone houses and numerous trees.

Where Pan Lane swings right, keep straight on up the hedged path known as Bury Lane - a reference perhaps to Bronze Age

burial 3000 years ago on Head Down. Reaching a crosstrack turn left and stay on it, heading west past a strip of woodland towards the bracken-cloaked ridge of St Catherine's Down. Once beyond a field fence ahead, bear left through a gate and aim over grass for the old octagonal tower on St Catherine's Hill, fence on your left. A steep final slope brings you up to the summit trig pillar at 777ft (237m) above sea level.

Resembling a stone rocket, the adjacent medieval lighthouse, known locally as the Pepper Pot, was built in 1340 by a local landowner as a penance for looting holy wine from a shipwreck in Chale Bay. The tower was too often mist-shrouded to be of significant value to ships and a similar problem afflicted a later 18th century structure nearby known as the Salt Cellar.

To conclude the walk set off downhill from a stile on the right towards the sea. The path is virtually non-existent across the field at first but by trending a little to the right you will arrive at a fence corner then a stile and steps at the bottom leading out onto the main A3055 coast road. Constructed in the 1860s to service coastal fortifications, it is known as the Military Road.

Cross over and take the coast path past a small car park viewpoint. It quickly leads to Windy Corner on Gore Cliff where the stepped path on the right returns you to Blackgang car park.

WALK 32: HAVENSTREET STATION AND FIRESTONE COPSE

4 miles (6.5km). Start Grid Ref: 556897

Terrain: country roads and woodland rides and paths, possibly muddy in places. Mostly flat.

Refreshment places: cafe at Havenstreet Station.

The Isle of Wight is not renowned for large areas of woodland. However, Forestry Commission plantations do total around 1500 hectares, two-thirds of which are broadleaved trees which are gradually replacing conifers. About 8000 tons of timber are harvested

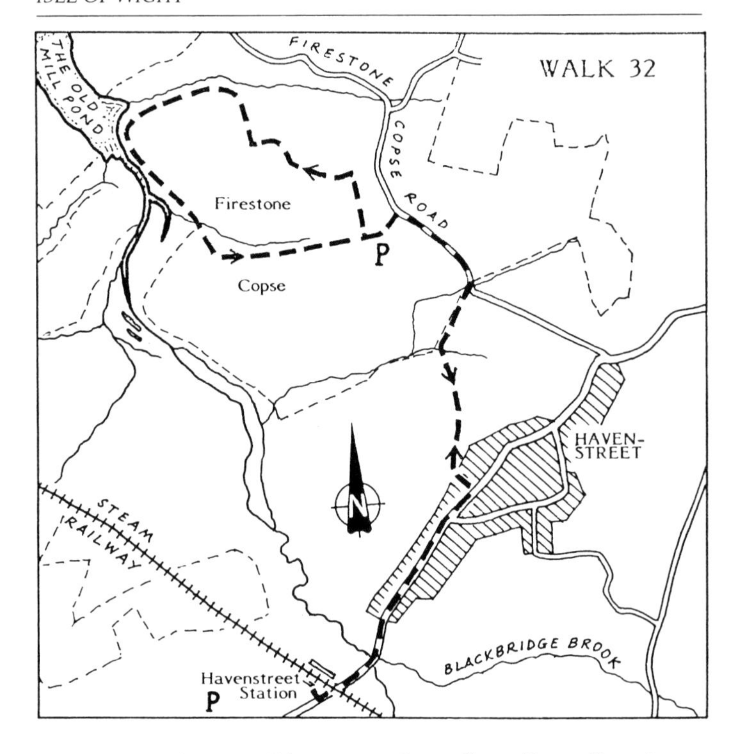

annually but these small forests are also well used by walkers, horse riders and lovers of wildlife.

This walk incorporates a 1¾ mile (2.8km) circuit of Firestone Copse between Newport and Ryde but begins and ends at a more widely publicised attraction - the Isle of Wight Steam Railway whose headquarters are at Havenstreet Station.

Isle of Wight railway companies were never able to afford new rolling stock with the result that many vintage locos and ageing coaches were pressed into service. The old branch lines were closed down in the 1960s by the infamous Dr Beeching but have enjoyed a revival in many parts of Britain, not least here on the Isle of Wight.

The 5-mile (8km) route each way from Wootton to Ryde through beautiful countryside takes about an hour but tickets may be purchased to intermediate stations too. At Havenstreet you can browse around the Museum Gallery and Railway Shop, enjoy a drink or snack at the Refreshment Bar, picnic in the gardens if the weather's fine, or simply wander round, soaking up the atmosphere of a late-19th century/early 20th century working steam railway.

The walk starts from the station car park and heads north-east along the road, over Blackbridge Brook into Havenstreet village. About 100m past the road junction on the right, watch for a narrow path on the left between gardens. Follow this towards Firestone Copse which you enter by first crossing a stile on your left, keeping that direction for some 20m then crossing a stile and footbridge on the right. The path threads along inside the edge of woods and reaches the Firestone Copse Road. Walk left for 300m and left again to the Forestry Commission car park (an alternative starting point, incidentally, for this out-and-back route).

Three forest trails have been laid out by the Forestry Commission. The shortest (400m) is waymarked red; a middle distance trail blue; and the longest (1¾ miles - 2.8km) green. Any of these could be followed but the longest is suggested as the best. Throughout this woodland section of the walk, look out for daffodils and primroses in springtime, butterflies in summer, the red guelder rose berries in autumn and purple dogwood shoots in winter. About 230 flower and 70 mosses and liverwort species have been recorded in the copse.

The 'green' trail leaves on the right from the car park, turning left at the first crosstrack. Stay on this track for about 400m, passing several side paths. Where the track bends sharp left, turn right on a path down to a stream and bear left with it. The waymarked trail, created independently of map-marked paths in places, now curves left and right to reach the edge of forest at a river inlet upstream of The Old Mill Pond, itself part of Wootton Creek which flows north into The Solent. The tidal mill pool attracts herons and, in wintertime, wading birds, while in the fringing woodlands nightjars nest in the rides.

The trail crosses a tributary stream and eventually meets a broad ride curving left. Stay on it, ignoring side turnings, and it will return you to the car park. The walk's return left to Havenstreet Station simply reverses the outward leg.

USEFUL ADDRESSES

Isle of Wight Tourism - Quay House, Town Quay, Newport, I.O.W. PO30 2EF tel: (01983) 524343

Tourist Information Centres
Marina Walk, Cowes, tel: (01983) 291914 (summer)
Church Litten car park, Newport, tel: (01983) 525450 (summer)
Western Gardens, Ryde, tel: (01983) 562905 (all year)
The Esplanade, Sandown, tel: (01983) 403886 (all year)
High Street, Shanklin, tel: (01983) 862942 (all year)
High Street, Ventnor, tel: (01983) 853625 (summer)
The Quay, Yarmouth, tel: (01983) 760015 (summer)

Ferries
Hovertravel, Dept H, Quay Road, Ryde, I.O.W. PO33 2HB, tel: (01983) 811000
Red Funnel Ferries, Reservations Dept, 12 Bugle Street, Southampton, Hants. SO9 4LJ, tel: (01703) 330333
Wightlink Ltd, PO Box 59, Portsmouth, Hants. PO1 2XB, tel: (0870) 582744
Rail enquiries: (01703) 229393

Bus services
Southern Vectis Omnibus Co Ltd, Nelson Road, Newport, I.O.W. PO30 1RD, tel: (01983) 522456

Step by Step Walking Holidays
Hambledon Hotel, Queens Road, Shanklin, I.O.W. PO37 6AW, tel: (01983) 862403

Wight Merit Hotel Group
7 Carter Avenue, Shanklin, I.O.W. PO37 7LQ, tel: (01983) 868868

Orchards Holiday Caravan and Camping Park
Newbridge, Yarmouth, I.O.W. PO41 0TS, tel: (01983) 531331

Field Lane Holiday Park
St Helens, Ryde, I.O.W. PO33 1UX, tel: (01983) 872779

County Surveyor
I.O.W. Council, County Hall, Newport, PO30 1UD, tel: (01983) 823741

The Ramblers Association
1/5 Wandsworth Road, London SW8 2XX, tel: (0171) 5826878
I.O.W. Group - Mr C.R. Johns, 19 Manor Road, Lake, Sandown PO36 9JA, tel: (01983) 406949

Youth Hostels Association
Trevelyan House, 8 St Stephen's Hill, St Albans, Herts. AL1 2DY, tel: (01727) 55215

Long Distance Walkers Association
7 Ford Drive, Yarnfield, Stone, Staffs. ST15 0RP

The National Trust
36 Queen Anne's Gate, London SW1H 9AS, tel: (0171) 222 9251
I.O.W. Office - 35A St James Street, Newport PO30 1LB, tel: (01983) 526445

English Heritage (South-east)
1 High Street, Tonbridge, Kent TN9 1SG, tel: (01732) 778000

Council for the Preservation of Rural England
Warwick House, 25 Buckingham Palace Road, London SW1W 0PP, tel: (0171) 976 6433

The Countryside Commission
John Dower House, Crescent Place, Cheltenham, Glos. GL50 3RA, tel: (01242) 521381

INDEX OF PLACES ON WALKS

LISTING OF CICERONE GUIDES

BACKPACKING AND CHALLENGE WALKING
Backpacker's Britain:
Vol 1 – Northern England
Vol 2 – Wales
Vol 3 – Northern Scotland
Vol 4 – Central & Southern Scottish Highlands
End to End Trail
The National Trails
Three Peaks, Ten Tors

BRITISH CYCLING
Border Country Cycle Routes
Cumbria Cycle Way
Lancashire Cycle Way
Lands End to John O'Groats
Rural Rides:
No 1 – West Surrey
No 2 – East Surrey
South Lakeland Cycle Rides

PEAK DISTRICT AND DERBYSHIRE
High Peak Walks
Historic Walks in Derbyshire
The Star Family Walks – The Peak District & South Yorkshire
White Peak Walks:
The Northern Dales
The Southern Dales

MOUNTAINS OF ENGLAND, WALES & IRELAND
FOR COLLECTORS OF SUMMITS
Mountains of England & Wales:
Vol 1 – Wales
Vol 2 – England
Ridges of England, Wales & Ireland
The Relative Hills of Britain

IRELAND
Irish Coast to Coast Walk
Irish Coastal Walks
Mountains of Ireland

THE ISLE OF MAN
Isle of Man Coastal Path
Walking on the Isle of Man

LAKE DISTRICT AND MORECAMBE BAY
Atlas of the English Lakes
Coniston Copper Mines
Cumbria Coastal Way
Cumbria Way and Allerdale Ramble
Great Mountain Days in the Lake District
Lake District Anglers' Guide
Lake District Winter Climbs
Lakeland Fellranger:
The Central Fells
The Mid-Western Fells
The Near-Eastern Fells
The Southern Fells
Roads and Tracks of the Lake District
Rocky Rambler's Wild Walks
Scrambles in the Lake District:
Vol 1 – Northern Lakes
Vol 2 – Southern Lakes
Short Walks in Lakeland:
Book 1 – South Lakeland
Book 2 – North Lakeland
Book 3 – West Lakeland
Tarns of Lakeland:
Vol 1 – West
Vol 2 – East
Tour of the Lake District
Walks in Silverdale and Arnside

NORTHERN ENGLAND
LONG-DISTANCE TRAILS
Dales Way
Hadrian's Wall Path
Northern Coast to Coast Walk
Pennine Way
Reivers Way
Teesdale Way

NORTH-WEST ENGLAND
OUTSIDE THE LAKE DISTRICT
Family Walks in the Forest of Bowland
Historic Walks in Cheshire
Ribble Way
Walking in the Forest of Bowland and Pendle
Walking in Lancashire
Walks in Lancashire Witch Country
Walks in Ribble Country

PENNINES AND NORTH-EAST ENGLAND
Cleveland Way and Yorkshire Wolds Way
Historic Walks in North Yorkshire
North York Moors
The Canoeist's Guide to the North-East
The Spirit of Hadrian's Wall
Yorkshire Dales – North and East
Yorkshire Dales – South and West
Walking in County Durham
Walking in Northumberland
Walking in the North Pennines
Walking in the South Pennines
Walks in Dales Country
Walks in the Yorkshire Dales
Walks on the North York Moors: Books 1 and 2
Waterfall Walks – Teesdale and High Pennines
Yorkshire Dales Angler's Guide

SCOTLAND
Ben Nevis and Glen Coe
Border Country
Border Pubs and Inns
Central Highlands
Great Glen Way
Isle of Skye
North to the Cape
Lowther Hills
Pentland Hills
Scotland's Far North
Scotland's Far West
Scotland's Mountain Ridges
Scottish Glens:
2 – Atholl Glens
3 – Glens of Rannoch
4 – Glens of Trossach
5 – Glens of Argyll
6 – The Great Glen
Scrambles in Lochaber
Southern Upland Way
Walking in the Cairngorms
Walking in the Hebrides
Walking in the Ochils, Campsie Fells and Lomond Hills
Walking Loch Lomond and the Trossachs
Walking on the Isle of Arran
Walking on the Orkney and Shetland Isles
Walking the Galloway Hills
Walking the Munros:
Vol 1 – Southern, Central and Western
Vol 2 – Northern and Cairngorms
West Highland Way
Winter Climbs – Ben Nevis and Glencoe
Winter Climbs in the Cairngorms

SOUTHERN ENGLAND
Channel Island Walks
Exmoor and the Quantocks
Greater Ridgeway
Lea Valley Walk
London – The Definitive Walking Guide
North Downs Way
South Downs Way
South West Coast Path
Thames Path
Walker's Guide to the Isle of Wight
Walking in Bedfordshire
Walking in Berkshire
Walking in Buckinghamshire
Walking in Kent
Walking in Somerset
Walking in Sussex
Walking in the Isles of Scilly
Walking in the Thames Valley
Walking on Dartmoor

WALES AND THE WELSH BORDERS
Ascent of Snowdon
Glyndwr's Way
Hillwalking in Snowdonia
Hillwalking in Wales:
Vols 1 and 2
Lleyn Peninsula Coastal Path
Offa's Dyke Path
Pembrokeshire Coastal Path
Ridges of Snowdonia
Scrambles in Snowdonia
Shropshire Hills
Spirit Paths of Wales
Walking in Pembrokeshire
Welsh Winter Climbs

For full and up-to-date information on our ever-expanding list of guides, please visit our website:
www.cicerone.co.uk.

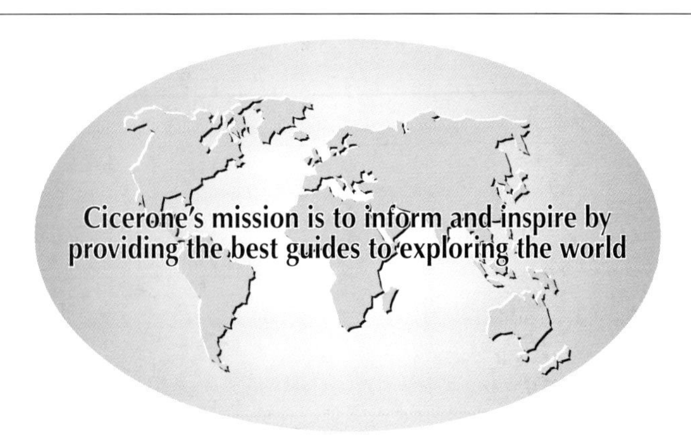

Cicerone Press
2 Police Square Milnthorpe Cumbria LA7 7PY
Tel: 015395 62069 Fax: 015395 63417
info@cicerone.co.uk www.cicerone.co.uk